# HOUND of THE FAR SIDE

**Other Books in The Far Side series**

The Far Side
Beyond The Far Side
In Search of The Far Side
Bride of The Far Side
Valley of The Far Side
It Came from The Far Side
The Far Side Observer
Night of the Crash-Test Dummies
Wildlife Preserves
Wiener Dog Art

**Anthologies**

The Far Side Gallery
The Far Side Gallery 2
The Far Side Gallery 3

The Prehistory of The Far Side:
A 10th Anniversary Exhibit

# HOUND of THE FAR SIDE
## by Gary Larson

Futura

A Futura Book

Copyright © 1984, 1985, 1986, 1987 by Universal Press Syndicate;
Copyright © 1980, 1981, 1982, 1983, 1984 by the Chronicle Publishing Company

This edition published in 1988 by Futura Publications,
a Division of Macdonald & Co (Publishers) Ltd
London & Sydney
Reprinted 1989, 1990 (twice), 1991

ISBN  0  7088  4193  7

Printed and bound in Great Britain by
The Guernsey Press Co Ltd, Guernsey, Channel Islands

Futura Publications
A Division of
Macdonald & Co (Publishers) Ltd
165 Great Dover Street
London SE1 4YA

A member of Maxwell Macmillan Publishing Corporation

# HOUND of THE FAR SIDE

5

"Whoa! *That* was a good one! Try it, Hobbs — just poke his brain right where my finger is."

"We're gettin' old, Jake."

6

"OK, OK, you guys have had your chance — the horses want another shot at it."

Beginning duck

Primitive fandango

Gary Larson
age seven

Aaaaaaaaaaaa!... This isn't the ball!

Dog threat letters

"Uh-oh! ... Stuart blew his air sac!"

Happens every time... I just get in the shower and someone yells "stampede"!

Amoeba porn flicks

"Oh, for heaven's sake! Your father left in such a hurry this morning he's lost another antenna."

"Goldberg, you idiot! Don't play tricks on those things — they can't distinguish between 'laughing with' and 'laughing at'!"

"Hold it right there, Doreen! ... Leave if you must — but the dog *stays!*"

"Gee, that's a wonderful sensation. ... Early in the morning, you just woke up, you're tired, movin' kinda slow, and then that ooooold smell hits your nose ... blood in the water."

"Here comes another big one, Roy, and here — we — goooooowheeeeeeeooo!"

Rock Shop 101

"OK, let's take a look at you."

Early Man

Cow joyrides

"Think about it, Ed. ... The class Insecta contains 26 orders, almost 1,000 families, and over 750,000 described species — but I can't shake the feeling we're all just a bunch of bugs."

Continental drift whiplash

"Well, that does it! Look at our furniture! The Shuelers have visited us for the last time!"

"Donald ... Trade you a thorax and six legs for two of your segments."

"Second floor, please."

"Well, I'll be ... Honey, it's the Worthingtons — our favorite couple of slimebags."

20

In God's den

The secret python burial grounds

"Dang, that gives me the creeps. ... I wish she'd hurry up and scoop that guy out."

"You idiot! We want the scent on the pillow! *On* the pillow!"

"I'm *talking* to you! ... You're so ... so ... so thick-membraned sometimes."

"And here we are last summer off the coast of ... Helen, is this Hawaii or Florida?"

"Wait a minute, Vince! Last summer — remember? Some little kid caught you, handled you, and tossed you back in the swamp ... *That's* where you got 'em."

Unknown to most historians, William Tell had an older and less fortunate son named Warren.

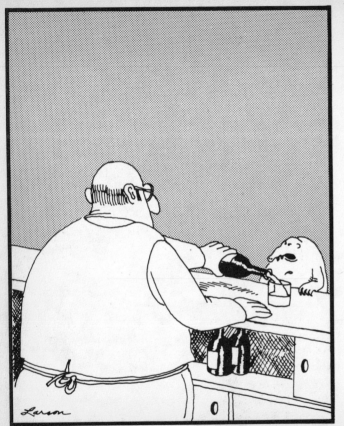

"Sho I sez to her, 'Hey, look! I'm tired of living in this hole, digging dirt, and eating worms!'"

The old "fake harpoon" gag

26

"Well, sorry about this, Mrs. Murdoch, but old Roy and I got to arguin' politics, and dang if he didn't say some things that got my adrenalin flowin'."

Yakity yak yak yak!.. Yakity yak yak yak!..

Going out for the evening, Tarzan and Jane forget to tie up the dog.

"Uh-oh, Norm. Across the street — whale-watchers."

An impressionable moment in the childhood
of Buffalo Bill

"Nik! The fireflies across the street — I think they're
mooning us!"

"No, he's not busy ... In fact, that whole thing is just a myth."

"Margaret! He's doing it! He's doing it!"

32

Elephant campfires

"Now, here's a feature you folks would really enjoy ...
Voila! A tree right off the master bedroom."

33

"Grog ... They play our song."

Same planet, different worlds

"I'm sorry, Mr. Caldwell, but the big guy's on his way out. If you want my opinion, take him home, find a quiet spot out in the yard, and squash him."

"Come on, baby ... One grunt for Daddy ... one grunt for Daddy."

Flora practical jokes

"I don't mean to exacerbate this situation, Roger, but I think I'm quite close to bursting into maniacal laughter and imagining your nose is really a German sausage."

"It's back, Arnie! Get the book! ... We're gonna settle whether it's an alligator or a crocodile once and for all!"

"Larry? Betty? ... Stand up, will ya? ... These are some friends of mine, folks, who flew all the way in from the dump."

"Doesn't have buck teeth, doesn't have buck teeth, doesn't have..."

"Now!"

Clumsy ghosts

"Remember the ... uh ... Remember the ... Remember that place in Texas!"

"You know, I wish you'd get rid of that hideous thing — and I think it's just plain dangerous to have one in the house."

"So tell us, Buffy ... How long have you been a talking dog?"

Before paper and scissors

42

Appliance healers

Another case of too many scientists and not enough hunchbacks

"Gad, that's eerie ... no matter where you stand the nose seems to follow."

"Looks like some drifter comin' into town."

"Maybe we should write that spot down."

Testing whether fish have feelings

"Hey c'mon! Don't put your mouth on it!"

"Yes, yes ... now don't fuss ... I have something for you all."

The primitive game of "Kiss-the-mammoth-and-run"

"Because it's not there."

"Well, that does it for my tomatoes."

Headhunter hall closets

Shark Food-fights

How social animals work together

"And so I ask the jury ... is that the face of a mass murderer?"

"Hey! They're edible! ... This changes everything!"

Braving the Indian "pillow" gauntlet!

THE EYE!
THE EYE!

"I don't know what you're insinuating, Jane, but I haven't seen your Harold all day — besides, surely you know I would only devour my *own* husband!"

56

"Be firm, Arnold ... Let them in once and they'll expect it every time."

"Coincidence, ladies and gentlemen? Coincidence that my client just *happened* to live across from the A-1 Mask Co., just *happened* to walk by their office windows each day, and they, in turn, just *happened* to stumble across this new design?"

"C'mon, c'mon! ... Either it's here or it isn't!"

Brain aerobics

No man is an island.

Left to right: Old Man Winter, River, and Higgins

"Bird calls! Bird calls, you fool! ... Not mountain lions."

Gong birds

"Uh-oh, Stan ... I guess it wasn't a big, blue mule deer."

"Nuclear warheads, huh? ... More like *defused* nuclear warheads, if you ask me!"

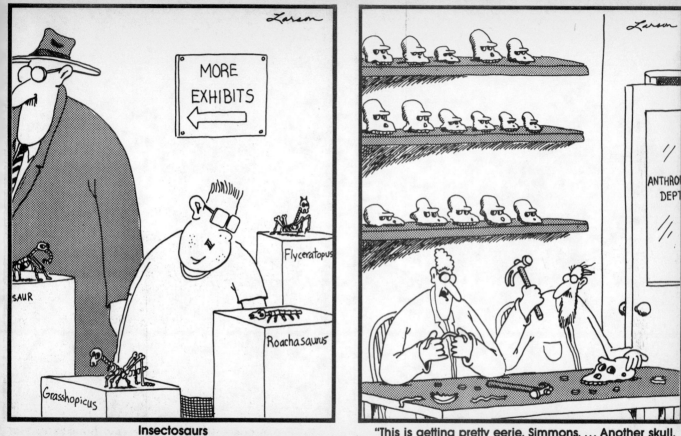

Insectosaurs

"This is getting pretty eerie, Simmons. ... Another skull, another fortune."

"Well, one guess which table wants another round of banana daiquiris."

"Excuse me, sir, but Shinkowsky keeps stepping on my sandal."

Medusa starts her day.

Evening on a beached whale

Primitive mobsters

June 24, 1876: Custer's last group photo

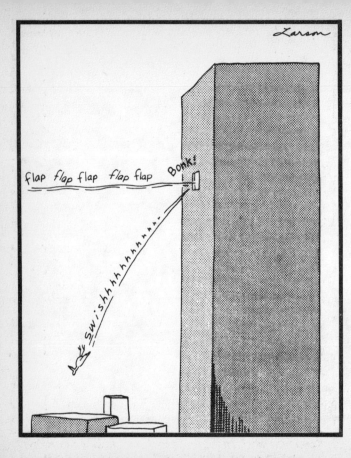

"Ohhhhhhh ... Look at that, Schuster ... Dogs are so cute when they try to comprehend quantum mechanics."

"Wheeeeeeeeeeeeee!"

"You know what I'm sayin'? Me, for example. I couldn't work in some stuffy little office. ... The outdoors just calls to me."

Knowing the lions' preference for red meat, the spamalopes remained calm but wary.

"Oh please, Mom! ... I've already handled him and now the mother won't take him back."

"Oh, lovely — just the hundredth time you've managed to cut everyone's head off."

"OK, let's see ... That's a curse on you, a curse on you, and a curse on you."

Group photo disasters

"One bee! ... One lousy little bee gets inside and you just lose it!"

Alien family dinners

As the first duck kept Margaret's attention, the second
one made its move.

"I wonder if you could help me ... I'm looking for 523 West Cherry and ... Oh! Wow! Deja vu!"

The birth of jazz

**Fly whimsy**

"MY reflection? Look at YOURS, Randy ... You look like some big fat swamp thing."

"Mr. Mathews! Mr. Mathews! I just came back from the restroom and Hodges here took my seat! ... It's my turn for the window seat, Mr. Mathews!"

"Quick, Abdul! Desert! ... One 's' or two?"

The Grim Reaper as a child

Witch doctor waiting rooms

**Places never to set your electric eel**

50,000 B.C.: Gak Eisenberg invents the first and last silent mammoth whistle.

Roberta takes on a dust rhino.

African rakesnake

"Dang, if it doesn't happen every time! ... We just sit down to relax and someone's knockin' at the door."

"You call this a niche?"

Back-hump drivers

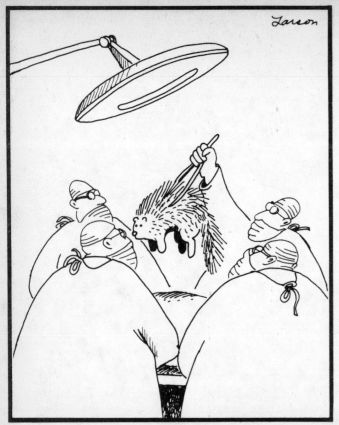

"Well, I guess that explains the abdominal pains."

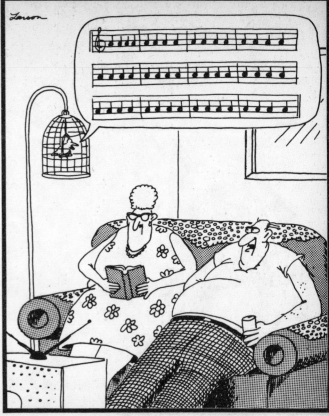

"Hit the bird, Ruth — he's stuck."

"Bummer of a birthmark, Hal."

"OK, folks! ... It's a wrap!"

"Sidney, just take one ... Don't handle every fly."

"I heard that, Simmons! I'm a wimp, am I? ... Well, to heck with you — to heck with *all* of you!"

94

"Hey, Bob wants in — does anyone know how to work this thing?"

"Hold it right there, Frank! ... If you're gonna shake, you do it in another room!"

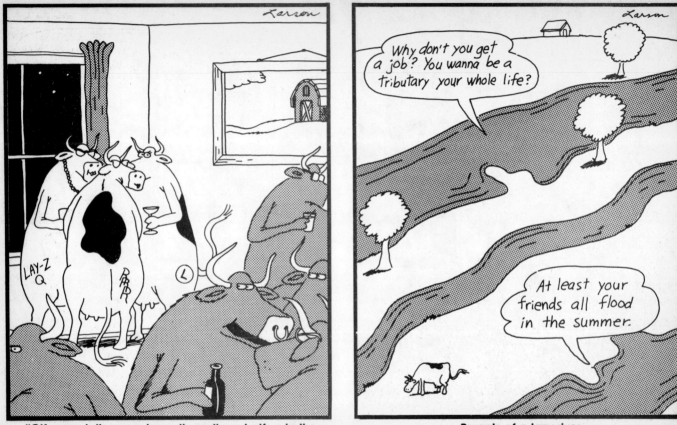

"OK, guys, let's move in on those three heifers in the corner. ... Bob, you take the 'Triple R,' Dale, you take the 'Circle L,' and I'll take the 'Lazy Q.'"

Parents of a lazy river

16th-century Mona wanna-bes

So, if I have four apples and I give two away, how many do I have left?

clump clump
clump clump clump
clump clump clump
clump clump clump
clump clump
clump clump

"Oh, and here's Luanne now. ... Bobby just got sheared today, Luanne."

Neither rain nor snow nor sleet nor hail, they said, could stop the mail. ... But they didn't figure on Rexbo.

"Listen. We may be young, but we're in love, and we're getting married — I'll just work until Jerry pupates."

"Criminy! ... It seems like every summer there's more and more of these things around!"

"In the wild, of course, they'd be natural enemies. They do just fine together if you get 'em as pups."

"Buffalo breath? *Buffalo* breath? ... Shall we discuss your incessant little *grunting* noises?"

The last thing a fly ever sees

"OK, sir, would you like inferno or non-inferno? ... Ha! Just kidding. It's all inferno, of course — I just get a kick out of saying that."

"And that's the hand that fed me."

104

All Futura Books are available at your bookshop or newsagent, or can be ordered from the following address:

   Futura Books,
   Cash Sales Department,
   P.O. Box 11,
   Falmouth,
   Cornwall TR10 9EN.

Alternatively you may fax your order to the above address. Fax No. 0326 76423.

Payments can be made as follows: Cheque, postal order (payable to Macdonald & Co (Publishers) Ltd) or by credit cards, Visa/Access. Do not send cash or currency. UK customers: please send a cheque or postal order (no currency), and allow 80p for postage and packing for the first book plus 20p for each additional book up to a maximum charge of £2.00.

B.F.P.O. customers please allow 80p for the first book plus 20p for each additional book.

Overseas customers including Ireland, please allow £1.50 for postage and packing for the first book, £1.00 for the second book and 30p for each additional book.

NAME (Block Letters) ..........................................................................................................................

ADDRESS ...........................................................................................................................................

...........................................................................................................................................................

☐ I enclose my remittance for_____

☐ I wish to pay by Access/Visa Card

Number ☐☐☐☐☐☐☐☐☐☐☐☐☐☐

Card Expiry Date ☐☐☐☐

Pelican Books
People Power

Tony Gibson's first taste of community action groups was
as a student volunteer during the East London Blitz. In North
China, with the Friends' Service Unit during the last stages of
the civil war, he started experimenting with co-operatives. Later,
as a BBC producer and scriptwriter presenting programmes
on youth groups, social workers and decision-makers, he became
increasingly interested in finding out about action groups and
what makes them self-propelled. He went on to develop the use
of do-it-yourself video in schools and neighbourhoods, and
became concerned about the gap between the fluent verbalizers
and others in the community who also have experience and
commonsense, but find words a barrier. He developed packs of
materials which set out situations visually to help mixed ability
groups in schools work out their own decisions, without
depending on teachers to tell them what to do. Pupils could
show, as well as say, what they meant, and could move the
materials around to explore alternatives. This led to a request
from the Department of the Environment to produce
*Neighbourhood Action Packs* for adult use, and Tony Gibson
is now developing a parallel series of packs for young work
groups with Inter-Action for the EEC.

Tony Gibson

# People Power

Community and Work Groups in Action

**Penguin Books**

Penguin Books Ltd, Harmondsworth,
Middlesex, England
Penguin Books, 625 Madison Avenue,
New York, New York 10022, U.S.A.
Penguin Books Australia Ltd, Ringwood,
Victoria, Australia
Penguin Books Canada Ltd, 2801 John Street,
Markham, Ontario, Canada L3R 1B4
Penguin Books (N.Z.) Ltd, 182–190 Wairau Road,
Auckland 10, New Zealand

First published 1979

Made and printed in Great Britain by
Richard Clay (The Chaucer Press) Ltd
Bungay, Suffolk
Set in Monotype Times

# Contents

# Acknowledgements

The study of self-help groups in industry and in neighbourhood action, from which many of the interviews quoted in Part I of this book have been drawn, was undertaken with help from the Rowntree Trust.

The Neighbourhood FACT BANK is a shortened version of one element in the Neighbourhood Action Packs, which have been devised and developed for the Social Research Division of the Department of the Environment. It is reproduced here with their permission. The BANK was put together with the help of many fieldworkers and groups in different parts of the country, and in particular Julia Atkins, Guy Dauncey, John Huff and Mike Martin in England, and Alex Black and Janet Castro in Scotland.

Jim Radford allowed me to read and quote from his detailed notes and comments on the early stages of the Family Squatting Movement in east London. Rosina Lucas, Gill Tilston and Hazel Blackman have coped with the typing and the collating.

I owe a debt which is less easy to express to some hundreds of people, in schools, factories and in neighbourhood work, who have shown sympathy to these inquiries, and taken trouble to share their experience. I have tried to do justice to them, and interpret their veiwpoints fairly in my selection of the comments they recorded on tape, and the factual information they provided. But any shortcomings are my own.

TONY GIBSON

# Preface

This book is intended to work in two ways:

*Part One* describes action groups that have made their mark in housing, industry, education, neighbourhood improvement: what they were up against, how they coped, what made them self-propelled. It sets out to show why such groups have an importance now out of all proportion to their own immediate achievements.

*Part Two* provides detailed information, – financial, legal, technical, social – in the NEIGHBOURHOOD FACT BANK, for any group to use with the least possible fuss to get itself self-propelled, and to extend its links with the rest of the community.

Both parts relate to what Dr E. F. Schumacher (author of *Small Is Beautiful*) said about 'people's power' in a speech, in 1974.

I know that on a small scale people's power can be mobilized and that, when the scale becomes too large, people's power becomes frustrated and ineffective. What, precisely, is the right scale, I cannot say. We should experiment to find out . . .

The discovery and mobilization of people's power may be nothing less than the condition of survival for the hitherto affluent societies of the West.

# Part One

# Chapter 1
# 'The Teacher, the Landlord and the Boss'

This book is about Action Groups. By 'Action Group' I mean people who come together to get something done properly, where so far things have been done badly or not at all. They could be concerned about housing, jobs, traffic dangers, run-down neighbourhoods, children's play facilities, conditions at work, shoddy goods, vandalism, nature conservation, police behaviour, or a better bus service. They see for themselves what is wrong, and they fail to see why everyone should sit around any longer waiting for something to happen. Exasperation builds up a head of steam which overcomes inertia: they begin to move.

They may start out as a pressure group; drumming up support for a scheme that is being starved of resources; exposing botched services and bad management; bringing public opinion to bear on official negligence or private greed. A pressure group relies on those in charge being capable of doing something positive if enough pressure is applied. But what if the authorities can't or won't respond? They may prove to be blinkered, obstinate, tired out, or hopelessly incompetent. So the pressure group finds itself moving in and taking over. It organizes a sit-in and sets up a workers' cooperative; or it accepts responsibility for running an estate; or it decides something must be done about young vandals and it converts a waste site into an adventure playground.

The odds against success are considerable. The group takes charge of a situation which has been neglected or mismanaged by others, and there has been no time to acquire special knowledge and experience. Too often it's all flash-in-the-pan. A lot of energy goes into creating a stink at the start, everyone works off their indignation, and when it comes to constructing something new there is no staying-power: the whole thing fizzles out. But once in a while a group does survive to make its mark: Meriden revives; a local Mums' group deflects the juggernauts; vandalized flats

13

are reoccupied and transformed; derelict land becomes an inner city farm; a Tenants' Association takes the Council to court and gets its long-delayed repairs effected.

These might seem small-scale local enterprises of no importance to outsiders. But they are happening at a time when what is going on in the rest of society makes them suddenly and crucially relevant.

They are straws in the wind. They show how private enterprises and public institutions can waste the skills, equipment, and buildings they have available; and they reveal the widening gulf between these organizations and the people they exist to serve.

Many of those responsible for running things in our society are frustrated because they can no longer make them run smoothly. Organizations have become too big to manage exclusively from the top. But at the same time they are too impersonal and unwieldy to make effective use of people lower down. Middle management and junior staff are so deeply embedded in departmental routines, so insulated from the outside world, that they see precious little point in what they do. Government departments, education authorities, trades unions, industrial corporations, housing directorates find that policies planned at the top fail to percolate down through the organization. There are resistances – conscious or unconscious – which filter or divert. What trickles out at ground level satisfies no one.

Take three areas that affect us all closely: school, homes, jobs. The numbers of the school drop-outs, the homeless and the jobless are glaring signs that for those people the system isn't working. But it's not working well for anyone. Management seems to have lost its bearings. How many secondary schools are really preparing youngsters to fend for themselves, to make the most of their own physical and emotional development, their free-ranging interest in the outside world, their capacity to learn from their own experience? Often lip-service is paid to these ideas, but the reality is classroom bound, rigidly timetabled to fit examination subjects, cut off from more than token contact with parents and future workmates – a battery-hen system where half the eggs are addled.

The world outside school doesn't seem any better at using what is available. Too many houses and flats stay empty while housing authorities negotiate high interest loans to replace or modernize them. Meanwhile too many building workers wait for

14

jobs; and householders have to put up with damp walls, ill-fitting doors and windows, costly heating and faulty ventilation, because the contractors got their profit from system-building in a hurry. Too many estates are inadequately serviced and maintained because the work force has no incentive to take pride in the job.

In industry, productivity too often fails to keep pace with better pay and improved technology. People on the shop floor can see time, space, equipment, manpower being wasted by inter-departmental rivalries, demarcation disputes, mountains of paper-work delaying decisions and holding up supplies; and by the unobtrusive asset-stripping which goes under cover of 'rationalization'.

People at the top are often just as frustrated. The trouble is that there's a communications gap. Those at the top find it easy to handle words. Words are their tools. They live in a world of committees, conferences, memoranda, Minutes, questionnaires. But when they try to communicate to those lower down, their words slide past. At ground level, the workers on the shop floor and the tenants on the estate find this verbal flow either bogus or meaningless. They suspect that the management doesn't know what it's talking about: whereas they themselves have direct and often bitter experience of learning difficulties, housing problems, industrial inefficiency. They know each other's interests and backgrounds, they understand how people fit in with each other. They can judge needs and weigh up priorities. But when it comes to making the top brass see sense – they can't find the right words.

This is a see-saw situation which nobody wins. Each side thinks in terms of Us and Them: '*They* are incapable of understanding what *We* are driving at or appreciating what we're up against.' The rank-and-file show their bitterness in increasing truancy and aggro in traditional schools; absenteeism and high product-reject rates in traditional factories; vandalism and indifference on traditional housing estates. The professional teachers and managers sit tight and try to make their systems child-, and tenant-, and worker-proof.

The result is a massive loss of confidence all round. This happens at a time in the history of Western society when our belief in our own capacities – or in anyone else's – is seeping away imperceptibly like a man dying from internal haemorrhage. The more we depend on centralized, remote control of the machinery on which society runs, the harder it is to adapt to changing conditions, and the easier for anyone who chooses to chuck a spanner in the works. The symbol of our weakness is the soul-destroying tower block: imposing to look at, extravagant to run, vulnerable whenever the maintenance men choose to strike. No wonder *The Towering Inferno* made a killing at the box office.

When our dinosaur society finds it cannot adapt, it becomes the natural prey of the tyrannosaur – the urban guerrilla force, or the right wing alliance with police and military – which knows exactly where and whom to strike. Which side seizes power may not make much difference. What matters is their use of that power to ignore and eventually to suppress opposition, on the grounds that they alone know what's good for the rest of us.

This feeling of powerlessness against the indifference of the authorities makes people bloody-minded. The Palestinian terrorists began as refugees, left by the rest of the world to rot in the arid camps on Sinai. The same bitterness can be seen among those in featureless suburbs, on barren housing estates, whose schooling has taught them that they are also-rans. Vandalism is one way of making one's mark on society.

There are radical solutions to the injustices which generate terrorism. But so long as responsibility is concentrated at the top, the system is too cumbersome for anyone to get to the roots in time; or having got there to overcome the cynicism and contempt for 'do-gooders' that saps people's initiative and destroys their will to bring about for themselves the changes which are needed.

If this seems doom-laden, blame history, not me. This book is not about the prospects of destruction but the agents of survival; about the kind of action groups which dare to do things for themselves instead of leaving it to someone else to do them; and about the sporting chance that eventually such groups could prove too many, too self-sufficient and too determined for British versions of Amin or Vorster or Brezhnev or the Chilean junta to neutralize or liquidate.

We need to discover what successful action groups have in common, how they survive setbacks and achieve staying power. In the chapters that follow I shall be quoting from the tapes I recorded with a selection of such groups, in industry and in the community, whom I have been visiting at various times over the past seven years. I have concentrated on a few groups whose experience seems to me typical. As groups they became self-propelled. But there was nothing special about the individuals in them. They started out from zero.

> Our people . . . have no experience of managing for themselves. They always had the landlord to tell them all his rules; and at work, the boss. Even at school they always had the teacher telling them what to do.

Wanda Tamakloe, who figures later in this book, is talking about people like herself who have had to put up with their bosses' mismanagement in the shape of indifferent schooling, botched housing, and blind-alley jobs or none at all. People without experience, and with little confidence in themselves individually – but as will appear, they took on the management, and in some cases took it over.

One reason for writing this book is to show that, although it often goes unnoticed, people do have this ability to work things out together and make their joint decisions stick. This ability is disregarded because it is seldom used. Many people don't believe it exists. Most of us have been brought up with the idea that the world consists of leaders, followers, and bystanders. To get a move-on you have to accept a leader: someone who is elected from below, or appointed from above, or who has the means to buy, blarney, or bulldoze a way to the top without waiting to be asked up. Once in position, this exceptional person 'gives a lead' and explains to the rest of us what has to be done. Sometimes there is a 'collective leadership', a handful of activists who put in so much time and energy that the rest leave the decisions to them. The more active they are, the more apathetic and hostile the others become. Most of us know this situation only too well. So any group which claims to involve all its members in reaching and carrying out its decisions must seem out of this world. It's against human nature.

I want to show that this is not true. And the first piece of evidence comes from the classroom – where as everyone keeps telling us, you soon see human nature in the raw. I tape-recorded a series of inquiries and experiments which took me backwards and forwards to over 200 classrooms in junior, middle, and secondary schools, in England and Scotland. The trials that the teachers agreed to undertake involved the widest possible age and ability range; and in most classrooms they extended over many weeks, sometimes for as long as a year. The whole research took me some four years to complete. Then the word got around that the materials the teachers used in the experiments seemed to bring some of the most unpromising youngsters out of their shells – with the result that many more teachers have since tried out the basic materials and techniques on their own initiative. This has meant that over roughly the same seven-year period during which I have been recording the work of adult groups in industry and the community, I have been able to compare them with the tape transcripts and the eye-witness accounts coming in from the class-rooms. What the children have been revealing in the classroom may seem to you, as it does to me, to go some way to explain why action groups don't need people out of the ordinary to make them succeed.

## The 'Living Space' Experiments

The classrooms were all in 'run of the mill' schools, up against the usual pressures and limitations. In most of them the children were well used to 'teacher telling them what to do'. I wanted to find out what would happen when they had more opportunity to make decisions for themselves, working together as a mixture of abilities to sort out their own priorities in their own way, using their teachers but not being dependent on them. If this situation could be created in each classroom, what responses would there be from the 'bright' children accustomed to take the lead, and from others whom their teachers called 'apathetic', 'passengers', 'low-achievers', 'drop-outs'?

I began by visiting a cross-section of teachers, 128 in junior schools, 84 in secondary schools, and getting them to tell me in lengthy interviews about the ways they were accustomed to teach, and the responses they normally got from their children. Two kinds of teaching emerged, overlapping here and there but usually quite easy to tell apart. A minority of teachers described how they tried to create situations which encouraged children to take the initiative in bringing their own ideas and experience to bear, in trying out different ways of sizing up a problem and of working out a solution to it. These teachers had to work hard to keep pace with their children's demands for the knowledge and the basic skills they found they needed in order to reach the objectives the children had set themselves. The remaining teachers, the large majority, were often on excellent terms with their classes; they concentrated their efforts on organizing the flow of information and instruction, seeing that it was absorbed, and then getting their children to regurgitate it in an orderly manner. But they found they had to work hard to keep the class on the move, spur on the stragglers, maintain discipline.

How much of this difference in the children's response was due to the differing personalities of the teachers? Or did some classes happen to contain a higher proportion of lively, self-confident children to whom innovation came naturally?

To test this out I got the help of some teachers and contrived two versions of the same work-scheme, each in the form of a 'learning pack' which a teacher could try out in normal classroom conditions, and without me or anyone else interfering. The theme chosen for each version was 'Living Space': our own surroundings (room, house, street, housing area, town, landscape) and how they might be changed for the better. The two versions roughly corresponded to the two broad teaching approaches that teachers had described to me, and I checked this by getting a selection of teachers in each category to try out the versions that were meant to embody their own teaching approach. Yes, they said, this is what I normally do, and the responses I'm getting from my children and the demands they make on me are what I would normally expect.

The classes involved included every age level from eight to sixteen, and each class was usually a mixture of abilities, sometimes from IQs of 135 to below 70. They were in tough urban districts with a tradition of truancy and aggro as well as in villages and small towns.

The materials in both versions of the learning packs attracted children over the whole age and ability range. There were table-top models of housing layouts, selections of decoration materials, facsimiles of plans and messages, photographs, tape recordings. The teachers found there was plenty of 'meat' in each scheme to suit their own teaching objectives, and out of 183 who were offered one or other version of the packs to try out, only two chose to drop the experiment, as they were encouraged to do if they wished, after the first hour's trial. The rest found the work continuing acceptably for many weeks, and sometimes for a term or more. Many went on to use the materials with other classes as well.

At intervals after each launching period I interviewed the

teacher to hear how things were going, and how the teaching approach in the pack being used compared with his or her own. I had explained that different versions of the same 'Living Space' theme were on trial, but gave no clues as to what these differences were. Apart from the 'control' group which received packs they recognized as embodying their own approach, every teacher received an unfamiliar version, but was free to adapt it gradually to his or her customary approach if this seemed desirable.

Almost at once a contrasting pattern emerged. The teachers who usually encouraged their children to take the initiative found themselves with a pack which required a different approach. They had to give an introductory lesson, illustrated by the materials provided (plus anything else they cared to add) and then issue individual assignments, each supported by additional materials which closely defined the way each child should tackle the work it was set. The attraction of the 'Living Space' theme and the novelty of the materials kept everyone busy at first; but then, most of the teachers reported, interest began to wane. It was only when they changed the approach to something more like their own that interest revived, and they began to get the sort of response from the class that they were used to having.

The other teachers, who normally relied on telling their children what to do, were at first disconcerted when they looked through their versions of 'Living Space'. * Their pack materials were arranged for use by groups, not individuals. Each group of four or five youngsters found itself handling not one set task but a whole complex of problems and opportunities which it took the combined resources of the group to exploit effectively. There were materials which one group could use to design their own room, on a cardboard model, comparing samples of wallpaper, furnishing fabrics, floor coverings, experimenting with the positions of furniture, estimating costs, deciding priorities on a limited budget. For other groups there was a model townscape to be laid out, adapted, argued about; competing claims to be put forward for houses, factories and farms on a strip of countryside;

*This version is described in more detail in *Resources and the Teacher* by Tony Gibson, Pitman Education Library, 1975. The preliminary inquiry with the different accounts teachers gave of their normal teaching methods is given in *Teachers Talking* also by Tony Gibson, Allen Lane The Penguin Press, 1973.

an overcrowded urban housing area to be replanned; 'planning inquiries', 'Press conferences', 'radio interviews' and 'TV reports' to be used in ventilating grievances or promoting alternative schemes.

Most of these teachers said afterwards that they had expected the whole thing to peter out: either in chaotic over-excitement, or in apathy and indifference because it demanded too much. They had been inclined to think that this sort of thing worked, if it worked at all, for 'bright' classes in well-equipped schools with no discipline problems. But not for their children who they knew from long experience needed constant supervision and control – coaxing, prodding, guiding, threatening – before they could be persuaded to get down to anything. However, they resigned themselves to giving their packs an hour's trial, with every intention of dropping the scheme, or adapting it to their normal teaching approach as soon as possible afterwards. So they allowed the groups to form, issued the materials, explained the job cards to those with reading difficulties – and made ready for a salvage operation:

I thought there would be a lot of noise and confusion and not very much done . . . I opened the box and there was very great excitement and noise. I gave out the packets: still great excitement, still great noise, but this died down when they'd opened the contents, read the cards and started to work. It died down of its own accord. I didn't have to quell it, and I thought this was very interesting . . . There was great enthusiasm, very great enthusiasm. I didn't expect the response to be so great. I thought two lessons and they would finish their interest, but it's going on. They're taking it home. I didn't tell them to do this. It was their own free will. The interest is there, very strongly . . . There is quite thoughtful discussion, I can tell this as I go around. 'How shall we do this?' 'What's the best way to do that?' 'What does that mean?' They've organized themselves quite well, they've worked out their plans of campaign and they are solving various difficulties as they come to them. If they feel that their first plan doesn't work, they'll make another one. I think one of the things I've learned is that I've under-estimated their powers of thought and their powers of organizing themselves . . .

This teacher, with 29 years' experience behind her, was one of 92 teachers (73 per cent of the total in this category) who chose not to revert to their customary teaching approach, and who were able to report responses from their children that were above normal expectation.

Teachers with classes of widely different ages and abilities seemed to be receiving the same message:

### 16–17-year-olds (*Sixth Formers*)

... They were working things out for themselves ... questioning themselves in the group ... In this school there is too much talk-and-chalk and instructing the class ... When I was talking about giving this to the Lower Sixth, some teachers were absolutely horrified: 'You'll have a revolution on your hands' and actually ... they were very happy doing it. It just made me stop and think.

### 14–15-year-olds '*below average*'

... Two groups in particular showed tremendous initiative ... I was absolutely amazed at the results they produced ... in another pretty weak group which produced quite reasonable plans there was one boy ... it's about the first time I've ever known him really achieve something.

### 12–13-year-olds '*mixed ability*'

... Response very high indeed ... there was a sense that they were teaching themselves.

### 10–11-year-olds '*mixed ability*'

... It has given me a different side to the children; made me realize that they are more capable of doing things on their own than I thought.

### 10-year-olds '*remedial class*'

... The children are keen and interested. You see them meeting with difficulties, you see the reaction to difficulties, you see the conversation between them as they are working in the group ...

### 8–11-year-olds '*mixed ability*'

... children who achieved very little in their time at school, achieved something in this. It's amazing really ...

These teachers said that 'problems of behaviour' disappeared: groups had surprised their teachers by working on together when the teacher was called away, although there were no team leaders to keep them in order; they seemed able to manage themselves. Although the membership of a group was usually a mixture of attitudes and abilities, they collaborated much more than usual. They were more helpful to each other, more tolerant of criticism. They became unexpectedly self-reliant as time went on. They seemed to be thinking much harder. A group was seldom dominated by one individual; if he or she was uppish at first, this need for self-assertion seemed to lessen as the work itself absorbed and focused everyone's powers. Quite often, everyone. This was the most impressive item of the lot. For teacher after teacher reported the 'amazing' fact that children who were usually written off as 'backward', 'passengers', 'alienated', were becoming involved just as much as those who were academically 'bright' and 'well-motivated'.

In one school, for example, there were several classes taking part in the experiment, each dealing with the same theme, but not necessarily using the same version of the pack. The teacher of one class told me beforehand that she had got 'a proper set of Norfolk dumplings' this term – 'they're lethargic in their play and work and everything else'. Two doors away another class had been given one of the 'control' packs of materials which allowed the teacher to carry on much as he usually did, using his own lively personality to guide and stimulate the class as a whole along the lines he laid down for them. He reported that during the first few weeks he got the usual class response: the 'brighter ones' kept going, but the others gradually lost interest. Then, unexpectedly, there was an upward turn. Various children began to contribute ideas for developing the work, and they persuaded him to let them develop these ideas in little syndicates. The atmosphere improved, everyone was involved and the whole project got a fresh lease of life. Why? At first the teacher couldn't fathom it. But gradually he learned that his own children were picking up their ideas from the 'Norfolk dumplings' in the other class who were head-over-heels involved in the group work set up by the alternative pack. Their enthusiasm had spilled over, at break times and after school hours, to revive the class that had lost its momentum.

These more formal, traditional teachers did not know what to make of it at first. But as the initial excitement died down, and they no longer had to tell the children how to think or what to do, they began to see their own roles changing. They found they could help by sharing and enriching the ideas and the experience that were being generated within the groups. The materials in the pack made it possible for children over the whole age and ability range, from nines and tens to sixteens and seventeens, to deal with situations for which many of them could not always find the right words. But they could handle the problems, none the less.

They could rearrange the materials on the layouts, add to them, use them to try out each other's suggestions, compare alternatives, reconsider solutions. They had another medium besides words in which to explore the possibilities, consider the options, formulate decisions. Ideas could be exchanged in an *alternative currency*, which everyone could lay their hands on. So the decision-making, and the leadership, could be shared. The group could become self-propelled.

The problems these groups of youngsters tackled in their classrooms were only practice runs for the real-life situations they might encounter in adulthood. But they showed that a mixed bunch can get off from a standing start, and generate staying-power and self-reliance which no one believed the majority of its members possessed.

They qualify as action groups because their activities created channels of communication which everyone within the group could use; each group became a network. The groups are significant because, youngsters and adults alike, they represent an awakening of dormant capacities which both the group members and those in authority had overlooked.

. . . I've under-estimated their powers of thought, and their powers of organizing themselves . . .

says the teacher, summing up a situation which holds true of most others in authority, 'the teacher, the landlord, the boss', and social workers, civil servants, politicians, publicists, town planners, too. The situation goes unrecognized unless and until the conditions occur in which a group takes shape, comes alive, and shows its powers by what it does. Perhaps no one in the group is out of the ordinary. But as some of the earliest human societies discovered, a mixture can become a compound, with properties of its own. You can take metals that are soft and malleable, and turn them into bronze tools and weapons that have a cutting edge.

The groups this book is about have begun to isolate the formula and to develop the process. Only just in time.

# Chapter 2
# Plan and Counter-Plan

When at last we got to see the City Engineer he took down the plans and said 'Oh yes. If they put the third stage of the Ring road through here, they would have to pull down various houses.' He got out a map and he just got a pen and scrawled across it to show where the road would go. But I said 'That's my house.' He said 'Oh, but that's progress.' I said 'I don't care a hoot what it is, that's my house.' He was quite determined and said progress is the thing now, they must have the traffic going through the centre of the city and it must be kept moving. I said 'But you are putting motor cars before people; and how on earth are we going to get across our street?' He said 'We'll put subways underneath' and I said 'Why should we go underneath like a lot of moles and all the cars go on top? Why can't the cars go underneath?'

Mrs Betty Dunham has lived all her life in a big Victorian house with a double staircase, overlooking a small garden square in the middle of Carlisle. Her husband was a seafarer; they did not have a great social life; what there was revolved around church work, committee work for the Lifeboat Institution, and the ward Conservative Party.

When she heard a rumour that the Council were building a radial road through the square, she wrote to them and asked if it was true. They wrote back and said there was nothing in it, but if ever it was mooted she would be informed.

The next thing was that she read in the paper that a meeting of the Highways Planning Committee had decided not to go through the square 'at this stage'. The mere fact that 'they were already harbouring the thought of going through after having said they wouldn't, that made me absolutely livid'. She badgered the Civic Centre until she eventually got her interview with the City Engineer, and afterwards had a council of war with her neighbour, Mr Blenkiron, whom she had taken with her. (Mr Blenkiron chaired the Gardens Committee of the little square, which met once a year to keep an eye on the behaviour of residents' pets, and see that the flower beds were in good order.)

Mr Blenkiron agreed that it was time 'to have a little meeting, just of the local people, down in the church hall'. He thought it would be a pity to confine it to the Gardens Committee. So Mrs Dunham mentioned it to Mrs Powell next door, and Mr Powell, who had an allotment, mentioned it to the Chairman of the allotments. Mrs Powell saw a rather good letter in the local paper from a Mr Pitt, who lived nearby, so she rang him; he rang Mr Barnes who was a friend of his. Mrs Dunham also went round to see the Christian Science church, and local nunnery, and chatted up everyone she knew in the neighbourhood and several more that she hadn't even been introduced to.

The meeting at the church hall was packed. Mrs Dunham said her piece about cars being all right if they are kept within reason and a rotten ride being better than a good walk, but that didn't mean the cars should come belting through poisoning everybody with their fumes all the time, and spoiling the houses and taking people away from their environments. Nearly everyone else present had their say too, 'and when we all had had our little say, we decided that we would have an "Action Committee", for want of a better word'.

Mr Blenkiron already had enough on his plate, and some others who were proposed were reluctant to stand, but Mr Barnes had spoken very well, so somebody proposed him and he was made the chairman. Anyone else who wanted to be on the Committee was invited to join it. Before the meeting broke up the Committee had got to know each other and decided on the first steps to be taken.

Jim Barnes said that the first piece of 'municipal education' the group received was when they went to the Civic Centre to obtain a copy of the plans for the Inner Ring road development.

We just got a bland No, and were told that there weren't any plans. Of course we knew there were, but the trick is that if the plans haven't been approved by the Highways and Streets Committee they don't officially exist. Anyway by a bit of subterfuge we did finally get our hands on a copy of what purported to be just a sketch plan. But we knew it was the real one; and the whole bloody thing was so horrendous – they were going to rip the guts out of the town. So the Action Committee decided it was a waste of time to fight just the radial road. We would have to fight the whole scheme.

They leafletted and flyposted the district, and booked the City Hall hoping that with luck they would get fifty people along. It was filled to bursting, with over 600 inside and 200 turned away. The City Preservation Society was formed on the spot, the Committee re-elected, funds raised, and a series of confrontations began to take place, on television, radio, and in the Council's offices, all designed to extract information, street by street and area by area, on what was being planned.

As the probing continued it came out that plans had been discussed between the chief officers of Carlisle City and the firm of Laing. They involved the 'comprehensive redevelopment' – total demolition and rebuilding – of rather more than six acres in the middle of the City. The area is called the Lanes. Some of its buildings date back to the eighteenth century and earlier; they give Carlisle its character and they attract the tourists. It had about 160,000 sq. ft of shopping space which was more than enough (as the Carlisle/West Cumberland Structure Planners later confirmed) since the catchment area of Carlisle was likely, if anything, to get smaller, and any large addition to Carlisle's shopping facilities would take trade away from the smaller shops already there.

Now, in apparent contradiction, the £10 million scheme submitted by Laing provided for 100 per cent increase on the shopping space, in the shape of one enormous concrete store complex, encrusted with offices, restaurant and discotheque, and squatting on a car park. In addition to receiving the profits on the demolition and rebuilding work, Laing would also get a substantial share of the unspecified 'development profit'.

The plans for stage 3 of the Inner Ring road (which had first roused Mrs Dunham) also threatened several working-class areas on the other side of the river. The Action Committee called meetings in these areas, too. The meetings were well attended, and lively. At first 'there was some reluctance to actually go on to the Committee – that scared them – but once they were on, they were full of hell'.

At least half the Committee was made up of people like Eric Scott, a milk roundsman who knew everyone in his manor, kept a fatherly eye on potential young vandals, gave a helping hand to pensioners living on their own, and was not afraid of a dust-up whenever it proved necessary. At first, he said, he was doubtful whether he and his mates could keep their end up with what he called 'the hoity toities' from the garden square: people who were very good at holding coffee mornings to spread the word, and laying down the law to council officials. But he concluded that in his own way he knew just as much what mattered; on his rounds he was in touch with every householder, knew their reactions to every move that was being made, and could spot a lurking surveyor even before he got out his tape measure.

Mr Scott has voted Labour in his time, but says the way the Council are behaving he's inclined to vote Conservative. Jim Barnes, who is a teacher in a school for handicapped children, is a Communist. Mrs Dunham (Conservative) says, 'I don't give a hoot what his politics is. He's an excellent chairman – very fair. I couldn't care less if Stalin was his uncle.'

The mixture of interests and backgrounds on the Committee seems to have helped, like a well-adjusted carburettor, to get the engine pulling well. The meetings themselves have provided a kind of education for everyone. The 'hoity-toities' have grasped some of the facts of life for low-income groups. Their own fluency in sorting out the legal and technical problems has begun to communicate itself to the others. For much of the time everyone has been learning together; as the facts gradually came to light, and the possibilities opened up. There was plenty of talk about. The group fuelled its own development with the information its members were extracting, day-by-day, week-by-week, about the plans that had been kept under covers. Everyone was on the go, getting at the facts, discussing whom to contact next, sharing their findings, hammering out a policy together.

The group involved everyone within reach, by door-to-door contact, then small local meetings, leading to bigger meetings, securing more publicity locally and nationally in the Press and on radio and television, arousing the professional interests of architects and planners, getting their help and advice, and so giving a professional exposure of the situation in local conferences and national journals.

In contrast the Council had been accustomed to rationing the information, to limiting opportunities for outsiders to find out what was going on, to reaching crucial decisions behind closed doors. The publicity obtained by the action group gave it leverage, gradually opening up the situation so that the whole community took an interest. Before long the Committee got the help of a barrister and architect, attended the public inquiry on the road scheme and made such hay of the Council's arguments that decisions were deferred and the authorities were forced to change their ground. The Committee then drew up a statement, outlining the facts, describing the difficulties in extracting them, and making a devastating criticism of the Council's behaviour. It pulled no punches:

Carlisle is rapidly on the way to becoming a planning and architectural sick joke.

. . . the small business plays an integral part in the life of the town . . . growing out of the needs of an area as they arise . . . the local enterprise is a place where neighbours meet, where the owner is known by name. It is a place of social resort and communication . . . an important part of the neighbourhood structure.

It is no part of the function of the local authority to act as midwife to speculators in land and property within the City . . . The elected representatives of the public, and the officers of the Municipal Government, must elaborate and develop a civic philosophy, which includes . . . an active concern for those small commercial units which have served, and do serve the City well.

Whatever their overt attitudes are . . . their covert policy can more and more be seen to be one which favours the large multiples, the chain stores, with national and even international networks of business . . . they are enterprises concerned primarily with commercial considerations to the practical exclusion of all others, opening their doors at 9.00 a.m. and closing them at 5.30 p.m., during which period there is an increasing tendency to feed the customer through a turnstile at one end, and past the cash register at the other.

Publication of the statement put the Committee in very hot water:

The mayor nearly had a fit and a group of the Council officers contacted a London solicitor who wrote to us and said that we were very naughty and that parts of our statement could be construed as nearly libellous. So we wrote back and said we were very sorry and if it was we would apologize, but until such time as he could point out which parts were libellous we would have to continue with it.

No more was heard from the solicitor. But the Council policy, and its alliance with Laing continued. At this point Mrs Dunham had a small brainwave.

I suppose it's my Scottish blood, but I never believe in buying anything unless I ask for another estimate. If you are going to buy a house you would go and look at two or three wouldn't you? So I said 'Why couldn't the Council ask two or three other firms?'

# The Counter-Plan

Come to that, thought the Committee, why leave the initiative to the Council? Why shouldn't the Committee commission its own scheme? They tracked down a local firm, Shield Bros., which had been interested early on, but then discouraged. They discussed and revised the original proposals, recosted them and obtained an offer from the firm to do the job for the building profit alone, and to hand back an estimated £2½ million development profit to the City.

The alternative scheme kept some of the old buildings, provided space for offices and shops in small units, made room for a 500-seat theatre, some craft workshops and a cinema, plus 61 small housing units suitable for elderly single people and young couples. The scheme attracted favourable comment from professionals outside as well as inside Carlisle. This counter-plan was a turning-point for the Action Committee. It meant moving out from sniping positions, and making a direct assault. They were able to offer a constructive, workable alternative. This in turn attracted further publicity and support. It brought in the largest number of Letters to the Editor that the *Cumberland News* had received in living memory (though some which bitterly criticized the activities of the Preservation Society turned out to be forgeries).

At this point a new problem appeared. The Councillors themselves, forced on to the defensive, acquired a greater cohesion. They could reasonably argue that they were elected representatives, and ought not to allow their judgements to be deflected by a self-appointed pressure group. The pressure group did in fact represent strong and widespread feeling but it seemed to be claiming exclusive representation. The crunch came at a meeting of the City Council in April 1975 to consider whether the alternative scheme should be discussed. On the recommendation of the finance subcommittee the Council meeting decided by 23 votes to 19 that it should not be considered further. The argument put forward was that the only basis on which Government approval could be obtained for the redevelopment was that it should be 'comprehensive', meaning total demolition in order to plan all the basic services from scratch. The Preservation Society's suggestion that the Council should check back with the Department of the Environment to see whether this was really so, was also rejected.

The *Architects' Journal*, commenting on 4 June 1975, called this dismissal of the Preservation Society/Shield Brothers scheme 'indefensible'.

Since there is so much at stake for Carlisle (not least the question of whether the Council or the developers should get the development profit) . . . the Department of the Environment should call the schemes in for public inquiry.

Meanwhile the Committee, like a boxer half-way through a gruelling fight, took a deep breath, gave another short jab to the Ring Road scheme, and set about referring the Council's behaviour on the Lanes development to the Ombudsman.

The Ombudsman (or 'Commissioner for Local Administration') exists to investigate complaints about 'maladministration' – such as unjustifiable delay, incompetence, neglect or prejudice – but he can't take sides on matters of policy. He told the Action Committee that he could not fault the Council on its procedures; so there was nothing doing. They asked him what his definition of maladministration was, and he replied that no official definition existed. Stalemate.

Then a reconnaissance party arrived from the Historic Buildings Commission, interviewed Council officials, and members of the Civic Trust and the Action Committee, and backed up the case for conservation on historic grounds. This intervention by 'outsiders' was hotly resented by the Council majority who had by now become convinced that the real issue was their right as elected representatives to act as they thought fit, without interference from anyone else. A Government planning inquiry had upheld their road scheme and they now set about the wholesale demolition of the (not particularly historic) working-class houses in the Charlotte Street area.

The Action Committee returned to the fray with a counter-plan whereby the houses would be rehabilitated for between six and seven thousand pounds apiece, instead of being replaced, far away from the neighbourhood, by houses costing between twelve and fifteen thousand. The plan was dismissed, and in November 1976 the bulldozers went in. But the central area around 'the Lanes' remained intact. A shift in power at the municipal elections had given the Conservatives a knife-edge majority. They decided to refer the whole issue to an independent planning consultant, and meanwhile the agreement with Laing was suspended.

The struggle so far has spanned the period when all over the United Kingdom the idea of 'comprehensive redevelopment' by wholesale demolition of living areas is becoming discredited. There is still a battle to be fought in Carlisle to rescue the Lanes area from gradual decline and to rehabilitate it as a neighbourhood, along the lines originally put forward by the Action Committee. For the moment they can take stock, count their wounds and measure their achievement. No outright victories yet, but a holding action that won time to see the implications of what was being planned, and to judge its true profitability.

It has been a campaign of manoeuvre, exposure, flanking attack and finally pointblank confrontation. What's to be learned from it? One thing emerges: both sides kept each other in the dark. The group met with a bland obstructiveness in its dealings with the Council – and it responded by keeping the Councillors themselves at arm's length, excluding them from membership of its own Committee in case they betrayed its strategy. In this 'Us and Them' situation, Councillors felt the tug of their own group loyalty, not merely the loyalty of the majority party (which happened to be Labour), but a dogged determination to assert their rights as Councillors to decide matters on behalf of their electors. So, on the whole, they held together, and as a group, they resisted.

Could the Action Committee have got further by changing its tactics? Were there lines of communication which could have been opened up to better effect? If there had been more persistent efforts to involve Councillors, and consult them about the alternative development plan, would they have found it easier to compromise?

# Chapter 3
# Committees, Who Wants Committees?

You can't describe the Carlisle campaigning without mentioning committees: the Council subcommittees, where some of the crucial decisions were made behind closed doors; the Action Committee of the Preservation Society which blew the gaff. A good committee can give an action group a cutting edge, with an Agenda which really does focus attention on what needs to be done, and Minutes which actually record decisions on what to do about it. But good committee members need to watch themselves. They soon know more than anyone else about the problems and opportunities before them; it is very easy to become a clique, an In-group of conscientious enthusiasts who may even get a kick out of being the backroom boys who are in the know. It may not take very long for one or two awkward outsiders to wonder just what really does go on, and to suspect committee members of deciding things according to prejudice or graft. If the rest of the membership continue to feel left out there may be 'ill-informed criticism from the floor' at the next A G M, a crop of resignations, and a mood of apathy which the hard-working committee members find difficult to understand.

So how is this vicious circle broken? How do you get the membership involved? Each of the three groups described in this chapter makes good use of the committee, but only because the committee has learned how to know its place.

John Kelly was a young lorry driver who put on a games evening for the elderly once a week. He noticed how difficult it was for elderly people to do their shopping in bed-sitter London; too far to go, too long to wait, too few opportunities to buy items in the small quantities suited to old people's appetites and their pensions. Sarah Anderson was a student who gave spare hours to Task Force, which puts volunteers in touch with useful jobs to do for the community. Between them, they found a job for themselves that nobody else had thought of.

## Pimlico Pensioners' Food Co-op

Late in 1974 they got permission to use a church hall and teamed up with Clive Fowles, a local community care worker. They had the use, once a week for an hour or two, of a delivery van. They got the promise of a £50 'pump-primer' grant through a local Neighbourhood Aid Centre. They leafletted every old age pensioner they could locate in the neighbourhood, announcing the formation of the Pimlico Pensioners' Food Co-operative Club.

Suddenly they were in business. Every Thursday evening the van collects meat from Smithfield, vegetables and fruit from the market, dairy produce and some groceries from wholesalers, and delivers them for temporary storage in a cubby hole under the stairs leading to the church hall basement. Every Friday afternoon schoolboys from a local school, an occasional volunteer from Task Force, the community worker, and several able-bodied pensioners help set up trestle tables, load them with produce, hump the scales, get the kettle boiling for a refreshment service, and man the counters for the 3.00 p.m. deluge.

At least eighty pensioners are queuing up already, out of a membership of some 400. In about an hour everyone has done their shopping. You can buy two or three sausages instead of the eight that go to a pack; you'll probably save two or three pence into the bargain because the counter work is free. Free membership entitles you to a comfortable sit-down and a gossip, a cheap cuppa, and a line in to other social activities which are on offer through the church and the Neighbourhood Aid Centre.

The sequence of operation is clear cut:
    – raise a small loan as a float
    – find out what people want to buy
    – work out what quantities to order
    – decide where to obtain the goods
    – negotiate terms (e.g. obtain a cash-and-carry card)
    – collect from the wholesalers
    – store the food overnight
    – set up the tables

- lay the food out
- list the prices on a blackboard
- weigh out and serve in small quantities
- keep tea on the boil
- stack the tables
- sell off the perishable surplus
- store what's left for sale next week
- tot up the takings
- sweep the floor and lock up
- pay in the cash to renew the float

Operationally, that's fine: once the system starts to turn over; and provided there's the necessary staying-power.

When John and Sarah and Clive talked over the original idea they thought they had better form a committee to sponsor it. The Committee represented various benevolent outsiders and included a local councillor; but according to Sarah it kept on talking about the scheme in general, and nobody had enough time to tackle practical problems, like Which wholesalers? and How much to order? and Who would lend the scales?

Even before the project was launched, John and Sarah and Clive found that they were making the decisions and doing the work; so they stopped depending on the Committee and decided to run things for themselves. They also tried to get help, before the start, by appealing for volunteers among the pensioners. They called a meeting and made a speech. But no one offered.

Once it was launched, however, the popularity of the scheme was overwhelming. The first two Friday afternoons were chaotic. But they became less so, as the pensioners themselves began to take things over. They seemed to do this spontaneously. Individuals would say, How about making some tea for everyone? Shall I help with the vegetables? Do you want the meat cutting up? Without anyone organizing them or putting up rotas they became part of the organization.

Each week the work begins two hours before opening time and finishes soon after 5.00 p.m. The most reliable helpers are the pensioners themselves because if someone feels unwell, or is off to stay with her family, she arranges for a friend to take her place. The idea soon began to spread, and at most sessions visitors were finding out how the thing worked.

John and Sarah have now moved on, but another community worker and a community service volunteer have taken their places. Within six months of starting the scheme its practical value had been recognized by Age Concern who are offering small grants from their funds to help other groups make a start. In addition there is now an advisory service for Bulk Buy Clubs run by the National Consumer Council. In November 1976 a sister scheme to Pimlico opened up in another church hall fifteen minutes away. It looks as though the idea has come to stay.

Pimlico is deceptively simple: a practical proposition that takes shape 'before your very eyes'. It could have been killed by its first committee if it had continued to take time up talking around. Given a cash-and-carry card, the loan of a van, the weekly use of the hall, and the time for talk was almost over: it was simply a matter of alerting people to advantages which they could immediately see for themselves.

The three moving spirits in the scheme, John Kelly, Sarah Anderson and Clive Fowles were practical people who could see exactly what needed to be done. But they couldn't cope alone with the avalanche of success. The scheme could have misfired if it had not been that the requirements spelt themselves out to everyone, almost as people came down the steps and in through the door. Volunteers came forward to brew up the tea, set up additional tables and chairs as the number of produce stalls increased, and stand in for helpers who were ill or delayed.

The preliminary meeting had failed to attract volunteers, because people were strangers, and not used to putting themselves forward; and perhaps also because a meeting at which the convener unfolds a ready-made plan, may not leave quite enough scope for others to contribute. But once the shop was open and the buying and selling began, the scene had changed. Bustling to and fro, everyone felt at home; there was no formality. The mere fact that everyone converged on the place at the same time helped to create a sociable atmosphere, something really worth calling a community enterprise.

## Seeing What Needs Doing

None of the pensioners seemed to think of themselves as a 'committee' or a 'support' group. There was no constitution. The account book was available for anyone to inspect; a friendly accountant typed out a balance sheet when the time came to have an Annual General Meeting. There was leadership – but it was shared. Different people 'assumed responsibility' on the job as needs arose. The routine work got done, decisions were made, moans and suggestions passed on; and if someone was too poorly to come out to do her shopping, her order was brought by a neighbour and the supplies taken back in someone else's shopping bag.

Organization was needed, but it took its shape from the helpers as the situation drew them in: it wasn't imposed from above. Everything was on the level. You couldn't 'manipulate' the situation if you tried. The information that was needed as a basis for decisions was being fed in by all and sundry, all the time.

So the group continued to grow, involving more people and a wider range of services. It acquired schoolboy volunteers to run its carry-home service; it made use of the weekly contact over cups of tea to organize theatre parties and socials. No one needed to feel a passenger: people could see how they fitted in – where to use their gifts for being hospitable, or their abilities to juggle with figures, or their muscle power. There was no scope for ego trips.

The great advantage of such schemes may perhaps conceal a danger. Every week tends to be a sell-out with the perishable surplus sold off cheaply and the decks cleared. This makes running the enterprise quite straightforward; but it may also limit its scope. There's not much occasion for stock-taking, in the sense of seeing where it's all leading. It was a good idea to get things going without fuss, and with the minimum of chat. Things can keep going on the same day-to-day basis. But to make the most of the support that has been generated requires thinking hard about the future. If the project simply marks time, the good job that it is already doing may degenerate into a routine. The younger volunteers find their work a chore, and move on in search of something more demanding.

In October 1976 a new Pimlico Committee came into being, just four workers, one of them a pensioner, all actively involved, all closely in touch with everyone else in the enterprise. Their job was to look ahead and to consider how things could develop. The prospects for groups like Pimlico depend partly on whether they extend their reach: for instance using similar self-help techniques to improve local health facilities, ease the claim procedure for welfare rights, or promote more sheltered housing schemes. It's a question of momentum. It may not be enough simply to keep things ticking over. A going concern has to have somewhere to go.

Pimlico has plenty to do, everyone is on the spot, it is easy for everyone to be involved. But what happens when a group finds itself starved of opportunities to do what needs to be done? This brings us to the differing histories of two groups in Battersea. The first one had its roots in the street-family life that existed between the wars.

## The Tenants of Winstanley

Once upon a time if you stood on the footbridge at Clapham Junction and looked north there was a townscape dominated by a single soaring church steeple. Then the steeple seemed to sink, as the cranes moved in, and the tower blocks grew up and dwarfed it. Finally the houses, the shops, and the community hall at the Plough Road Baths were pulverized, packed into skips, and carted off.

In the old days when the sun shone you could take a chair on to the pavement and gossip with the passers-by; or if you were too old to move, you put a cushion on the bedroom window-sill and leaned out to talk. Sometimes the chatting went on until one o'clock of a warm summer night. At other times there were street parties on trestle tables with garlands stretched between the houses to celebrate a Coronation or a Jubilee. Later, during the war years, neighbours rubbed shoulders with each other once again, in the boot box brick surface shelters that the authorities provided as protection against the bombers.

The air raids cleared a good many sites (and helped St Peter's Church, which survived them, to dominate the view). For the time being there were clusters of prefabricated bungalows, that might well have come from the same mould as the air raid shelters. From above they looked like bush villages in the forest clearings of West Africa. The people who lived in them were still a community, who enjoyed a gossip across the garden fence.

In the early 1960s, when the houses and the garden fences came down and the flats took their place, people who had lived all their lives in the district felt that they had lost their bearings. The first block to go up, thirteen storeys high, was Sporle Court. The

38

designers of the building had failed to conquer the problem of condensation. So most tenants complained that their walls ran with damp, and the bright new wall-papers could be skimmed off with your little finger.

People felt estranged, out of their element. It seemed unnatural to be stuck up so high in the sky, out of sight of your usual neighbours, and for that matter out of reach of your own small children on the ground below. So the local bookmaker's daughter, whose family knew everyone, went round with her husband knocking on all the doors and suggesting a meeting. They thought the little church hall would be big enough, but so many turned up that they had to postpone the meeting and book the Plough Road Baths assembly room (not then demolished) instead.

The meeting was crowded, lively and informal. It was decided to inaugurate the Winstanley Estate Tenants' Association. The first two people proposed for the Chairman's job did not want to stand, but the third accepted, and there was an open invitation to anyone else present who wanted to be on the Committee to consider themselves elected. Twenty-three did. The meeting raised £15 on the spot, and the Association was 'ready for the off'.

Thirteen years later, when neighbouring Associations have mushroomed, then dwindled and disappeared, Winstanley is still going strong. And this is in spite of the fact that the Social Centre, which is marked out boldly on the plans of the estate that decorate each tower block, is still an empty space, walled off by corrugated iron in case anyone should make use of it before the Council get round to starting on the foundations. The old church hall had to be converted to a small youth centre, which manages to do a good job for a fraction of the youngsters who need it. But there's nowhere for the rest of the estate to come together, as people used to do.

Yet the Association thrives. It has an annual turnover of about £1300. This finances outings for the children and for the elderly, Christmas parties, a parcel for every pensioner and a Christmas toy for every child, presents for children who have to be in hospital, a monthly information sheet, edited by a Committee member, which includes news items about past and present residents, job opportunities for retired people, examination successes, household hints and funny stories. Other Associations go in for much the same sort of thing; but they seldom get so far. The secret is that from the very beginning, the Committee members have been determined fighters. They fought the Council over the condensation on the walls; when they got tired of bureaucratic hesitation, the story was given to the national papers, and suddenly the repair squads came running.

Ted Trayfoot, the present Chairman of the Association, is semi-retired. He used to be a very active official of his union, Transport and General, but reckons he was never so busy a trouble-shooter as he is now. He first blew his top about the Council in the early 1960s, just three days after he and his wife moved into their flat in the biggest, and worst designed of the tower blocks. Their bedroom walls were running wet with condensation, and the wind was blowing the rain through the window slits.

My wife and myself were sleeping on a mattress on the floor in the front room to keep dry. When Councillor Sporle came in to see my flat he advised me to go for a rent rebate. I suppose the man was right in a way, but I was so incensed at the time that I said I didn't want a rent rebate. I said 'I want the same sort of place to live in as you have. You sleep every night in your bed and you only pay about £4 a week rent. I pay £7 and sleep on the floor.' I'm afraid this upset him, and he didn't know what to argue. Next day I went to the Council and demanded to be moved. I threw the rent book at them. I said if you want me to live in there, you pay the rent . . . Finally, after twelve weeks, I went to the *Daily Mirror* and asked them if they wanted a good story. I said I am a Trade Unionist. I am a Labour man, I'm not concerned whether it's the Conservative Party, Liberal Party, any Party – they are treating people wrong. So they said 'All right, Mr Trayfoot, I expect you will be hearing from the Council.' Four days later I was offered this flat I now live in.

People soon got the habit of asking Ted Trayfoot to take up their own complaints. His name cropped up at the Council offices so often, he says, that 'they used to speak it with dread'. He gradually learned to concentrate his fire on the appropriate official for each problem.

I can always feel for other people, their predicament, remembering how I was once banging my head against the wall myself, not knowing where to go, not knowing who to see, not understanding the subject.

Now I have a good knowledge. I have learned quite a lot and I know exactly who to have a go at and who not to. I know where my cases are, who the chap in charge is.

I can say to him 'You're not doing your job; you expect me to do mine. Get on with it. Let us see some results.'

Council officials seem to find him fair, if unremitting, and he gets results. This is partly because he has learned the Council organization; partly because he knows the legal limits within which the system has to work, and the legal obligations it can be forced to fulfil; and partly because the Committee has evolved its own methods of sharing responsibilities.

Ted is the contact man for the Council, because in retirement he is free to drop down two or three times a week to the Town Hall. Mr Hill the Treasurer takes a special interest in the elderly, and also keeps an eye on youngsters and tries to get them on to the Committee (a teenager is now the Secretary). His wife is Social Secretary, coaxing raffle prize donations from local shopkeepers, getting up holiday competitions for the children, seeing that funerals, weddings, and children's parties are appropriately supported. There is a Newsletter Editor, and an Assistant Treasurer, and besides a dozen other Committee members there are various helpers who don't want to be on the Committee, or to be named in any way in the newsletter, but who can be relied on for regular jobs; the block representatives who collect subs and sell tickets, the van driver who fetches the food for the socials, the mums who load up their prams and distribute the Christmas parcels for the elderly.

Mrs James, like most of the others, had never been on a Committee in her life before, but after the first couple of meetings she found she could chip in with the rest.

If we don't agree with the Chairman, we soon tell him. He says 'Oh, why not', he likes to know the reasons why, but he doesn't get uppy about it – you know, 'I'm the Chairman' attitude – he never does. He's very good like that, he's just one of the crowd although he's Chairman.

Some of these Tenants' Associations seem to break up because all the work seems to land on one person, whereas it's sort of shared between all of us. If one can't do it, the other one will . . .

I think we've got the members of the Association behind us because if we say we're going to do something we do it . . . whereas perhaps another Committee will go to the Council and take No for an answer, where we'll keep going back until we get Yes for an answer. People that live on the estate feel that they've got a bit more say in their Committee, they've got that bit more say than they would have if you never got anything done.

'Having a say in the Committee' as Mrs James put it, means getting things done. You don't have to make speeches, you don't even have to be on the Committee. The Minutes are the briefest possible statements of what it was decided should be done. The Agenda? – Except for the A G M there hardly ever is one.

To any seasoned committee person this may seem strange. It certainly did to Mick Brown, who moved in to the estate much later than most of the others. A few years ago he felt that things had settled down a little too sedately. He failed to persuade the Committee to take a strong line against rent increases; so he blew some of his own savings on leaflets and personally canvassed every flat on the estate in favour of a rent strike. Eventually he collected enough support to make the strike effective – and to give a healthy shock to the Committee. It reconstituted itself with Mick as its Vice-Chairman.

The first few meetings he attended nearly drove him mad.

> I couldn't grasp what was going on. They'd start off with one subject, they'd skip to the next, somebody would start talking about something else; they'd come back to it. How the Secretary got the Minutes down I never understood, I thought it was a work of art to make anything out of it.

As a bank clerk, and an active Labour party worker in his spare time, he was used to business-like procedures. The meanderings of the Winstanley Committee went against the grain. (I found them pretty strange myself, at first.) But gradually an underlying logic appears. What goes on, within the Committee and outside it, is a powerful exercise in communication.

Each fortnightly meeting of the Committee takes two or three hours, well laced with cups of tea. There is more in this social evening than first meets the eye. The Chairman announces a topic, perhaps introduced by a letter which the Secretary reads out, or by a piece of news brought up by a Committee member. At once the discussion breaks up into several independent conversations. At one end of the room, by the window, sit most of the women. Their conversation is particularly lively, but quite self-contained; nobody else pays much heed to them, or to the other conversations which develop, perhaps between the Chairman and Secretary, or among the remaining males. Then, in his own good time, Ted thumps the table and shouts 'Quiet!'

At this point a general discussion takes place in which only a few are involved while the rest are silent. But it is clear that these few are voicing what their immediate neighbours feel, as well as what they have to say on their own account. If by any chance they haven't caught the sense of the previous mini-discussions, others will chime in, repeating the main theme, with variations.

They will each say what they think is going to happen, what they think should happen and quite frequently what has happened in the past. That does take up quite a lot of time, but then it does give you a bit of background. People say 'Yes that's all right but we tried that in 1968' – they contribute from their experience. They all express their own views and there's no attempt at dominating at all; though we might argue a bit more forcibly about some problems than others.

... It's a question of confidence. Most people have got an opinion on most subjects but they lack the confidence and they feel that if they say anything it's going to sound a bit silly.

But if you can get one person to say something, start the ball rolling, the next person will say 'Well I was going to say something like that' – maybe almost repeating what the first person said – and then he feels he's got going, and he adds another bit of his own. And they each say a bit and you get people feeling well perhaps what I'm going to say isn't going to be silly.

Eventually, the question of confidence doesn't matter any more. Everybody knows each other, they've all had their say before, they know nobody is going to laugh at them. They realize that they are not going to make fools of themselves, or if they do, that somebody else did last week and it doesn't matter.

So you get that sort of general build up ... You'll get 100 per cent of the people speaking. On at least one subject where they think they know a little bit, then they will come in.

In this way, going backwards and forwards over the ground, Committee members sort out the issues involved, consider and reconsider what they think about them, convey their ideas through their unofficial spokesmen, until a point is reached where both issue and the general response have come into focus. When this happens the Secretary puts pencil to paper and writes a sentence or two for the Minutes. (But even these go back into the melting-pot if someone, later in the meeting, has an afterthought and brings the discussion back on its tracks.)

Perhaps this double-digging process explains why so many Committee members keep bothering to turn up. They have converted Mick Brown, despite his background of innumerable political meetings.

The way they turn up is quite incredible. I've never seen such a big group coming so regularly as this crowd. My attitude has changed. I used to think it was just a matter of getting the work done and the Minutes finished, and then out. I see now that was incorrect. I've fallen into their way of thinking: 'Let's do a job, but let's have a bit of fun while we are doing it.'

There's a personal relationship there. There's a feeling of friendship and loyalty to each other. If one wants to drop out of doing something he thinks well that's not fair to the others. That doesn't matter when you don't know people too well, but when you are on a friendly basis with them it's less likely to happen.

Now if we'd done it my way, it might have run smoother, it would certainly be dealt with quicker, but in the end perhaps we'd lose our Committee members. They wouldn't keep coming back.

The meetings of the Committee are only the tip of the iceberg. The issues are talked over in all sorts of other situations, all through the week. The Committee's names are on the newsletter; they are within easy reach, out shopping, waiting for the bus, collecting the kids from school, down at the local. And there are other key contacts, outside the Committee membership, which may be even more important.

In every block there is at least one resident regularly visiting each flat to collect subs, distribute the magazine, and – most important of all – to sell tickets for the twopenny flutter that takes place every week on the 'Useless Eustace' feature in the *Daily Mirror*. The tickets are a certain sell, especially among the pensioners. Some of the volunteer collectors are youngsters, and on their rounds they find themselves mending the odd fuse, or helping to put the curtains up for someone who is too frail to reach. The volunteering ceases abruptly as soon as courting begins; but older people take their share.

The Treasurer's wife, Mrs Hill, is the natural spokeswoman for the little group that sits under the window in Committee meetings. She took on the collecting job for her block until

. . . one day Dolly, who is an old age pensioner, came up here and she said 'You don't get five minutes to yourself, I'll do the block for you.' She starts about 10.00 a.m. She's up here like a lark for her tickets, it makes you laugh. She says 'I've put my little bit of chicken on, and I've got the baked potato on' and sometimes she comes back about 1.30 and says 'I bet it's burnt to a cinder the time I've been on the trot all this morning.'

She'll go round again in the evening, starts about 7.00 p.m. in one

44

flat, has a cup of tea, then goes in another one and has a cup of coffee and she comes up here about 9.00 to 9.30 and says 'I really enjoyed myself tonight', so she has a sherry as well, and she says 'I think it's a lovely job!'

The collectors' network is as sensitive as a spider's web. All the collectors from the other blocks come to Mrs Hill's flat with their takings, at different times in the week. So do tenants from her block, with their own troubles. Rosie's friend next door has died. She is 76, and she worked till she was 72: 'Oh, I wouldn't like to see her go without any flowers.' Mrs Hill gets flowers sent on the Association's behalf. Or there's an emergency: water is coming through the ceiling in someone else's flat, from a cracked pipe embedded deep in concrete. The estate caretaker is notified; and to make quite sure, Mrs Hill tells Ted Trayfoot and Ted goes down to the Council and sees that the right official knows it's urgent. The repair squad works through the night drilling the concrete to get at the pipe; Mrs Hill is up providing everybody with tea.

At another time the sitting-room is packed tight with nineteen tenants from the rest of the block, discussing what to do about another resident who is throwing wild parties, picking up truant school girls, and pissing over the balcony. Mr Hill helps to draft a petition on the spot. The meeting decides that if necessary everyone will turn out and deliver it in person at the Town Hall, then and there. Ted gets on to the Council, and extracts an official to come post-haste to the Hills' flat. He hears the story from everyone all over again; and is persuaded to go straight over to threaten eviction unless the troubles stop.

Mrs James has small children of her own, and often keeps an eye on others when their mums are out. She has moved on now, but when she edited the newsletter her flat was another natural meeting point, mainly for young mothers in the afternoons with children coming back from school. If something urgent cropped up, that needed a second opinion, she could pop across that evening to the Hills.

Most nights there will be several people nattering away just inside the front doorway, while Mr Hill is in the sitting-room trying to relax and watch television. Most of the visitors call in to hand over ticket money (which Mr Hill will bank) but other matters get an airing too. If the discussion sounds like a problem that is getting difficult to solve, he goes outside.

Yes, when the wife hasn't got hold of the gist of it, I shoot out and say, 'Well let me hear what it's all about', to see if I can put it over better.

In the first instance this means explaining the issue to the little group in the hall; or perhaps taking the problem over: seeing the caretaker about it, getting Ted to have another go at the Council. Or it may mean persuading everyone to wait a few days and then come in a body and tell the Committee members. Mrs Hill rings round and asks them to come early to the next Committee meeting so that there can be some chat beforehand. The people with the problem can talk it out freely without feeling that it's all official.

One problem is the pub. Drugs, as well as alcohol, are being pushed. The youngsters are getting hooked: and they're causing trouble to passers-by and waking people up at two o'clock in the morning. The police don't seem to be bothering enough. As a first step it's agreed that anyone on the estate who spots trouble should phone the police at once, the more calls the better. The visiting group disperses, and the Committee begins: and painstakingly chats it all over and sorts it all out. Mick drafts a letter which the Secretary will type and send to the pub's owners. Ted agrees to go along to the police station and have a go at the Superintendent.

At Winstanley there are no great gulfs between those who want action and those with the knowledge to get things done. There are plenty of things that need doing. Here for instance are the MATTERS ARISING that I jotted down during one evening meeting of the Committee:

*Vandalism:* local gang smashing up a parked car.

*Sheds:* some tenants charged rent, but don't use.

*Five-year-old strayed on common*, made drunk on cider by adolescents. Often allowed to roam; needs care and protection order?

*Pollution:* threats to sue two local factories. One has now installed purification system.

*Social Centre:* how to exert more pressure to get one built?

*Squatters:* 'respectable family' deserves to be left in possession – can Council be lenient?

*Tenants' pets:* – dispute between neighbours about cat.

*Rubbish collection:* inadequate storage for bulky refuse.

46

*Senior citizens:* better care for handicapped?

*Parking bollards:* reorganize to use space better.

*Council Lettings Policy:* rent charge on lodgers?

*Traffic hazards* at entrance to estate.

*Nursery schooling:* needs of three-year-olds.

*Redecoration:* is someone doing a fiddle?

*Transfers:* interminable negotiations to get two Councils to do a swap so that an amputee can move in next door and get looked after by her daughter and son-in-law. (Ted reports: 'I badgered the social worker and I barged in to the Council and chucked a few Fs and Bs about; and we've got the transfer through.')

*Estate management:* rumour that Association in next door Borough is to take over management responsibility. Can we do it too?

The talk is not a substitute for action. The Committee is gradually achieving what it sets out to do: the Council's maintenance and repair services are kept up to the mark; the brewers and the police begin to sit up and take notice; old people are cared for; youngsters given some encouragement. And all this happens in spite of not having premises where everyone can meet. It is the lack of anything on which the life of the estate can centre which makes the network of talk so important.

None of the action could take place without the talk. Everywhere there are stepping-stones, which make it easy for people to make a move, make contact, swap experience, join in. Everybody is in the know about what needs doing – the unwritten Agenda. And everyone can take some credit for what gets done (even though the Committee's Minutes don't leave much room to spell out its achievements).

The talk is not a barrier between those who are used to speaking at meetings, and those who are not. There is precious little 'public speaking'; and no procedural dodges to deflect attention or stifle criticism. What stokes the fire and keeps the pot a'boiling, is a public conversation, which scarcely ever stops.

It's a major achievement when an estate like Winstanley succeeds in opening up its communication network and begins to involve the whole community in this way. But the 'public conversation' which is generated should be the beginning, not the end of the story.

In the early days, Winstanley could focus attention on the shoddy workmanship and inadequate planning of the original builders and architects. Achievements in speeding up repairs could be measured. The Association as a whole could share the credit for putting the wind up the Council. The Committee still earns its keep by hammering home each individual complaint, pinpointing the action required and the official responsible, and publicizing the results in its newsletter. As on many other estates this kind of skirmishing is quite valuable in itself, and enough to keep several Committee members busy. But it has not yet mobilized the community as a whole.

There are about 800 flats on the estate, and most of the people living in them know who the Committee members are, and will pass the time of day with them and keep them posted on what needs to be done. The communication network exists; but at the AGM it's unlikely that more than 40 out of the 800 households will have members present.

In any case, if many more came, where would you put them? Nowadays if you want to run a dance, or hold a sizeable party, you may have to book a hall so far away that you need to hire a coach to get the people there. The lack of a meeting-place has become much more serious since the tower blocks went up. Until the 'developers' pulled down the hall at the Plough Road Baths, the women used to organize their own socials once a week, while the Dads looked after the children at home. It made all the difference to the Mums, says Mrs Hill:

'Eight o'clock we started and 10 p.m. we cleared up. It was more of a party really. We used to play bingo; one would make a bread pudding and bring it; somebody else made the tea, and if it was anybody's birthday we had birthday cake; and we'd have a sing song. And the Mums would think the world of all that.

'And once the mothers got out for that couple of hours a week, you'd find they were better to the children. They'd got more time for the children, having had the break. But now they have got no outlet. They are tensed up, the mothers, and they haven't got time for the children. Going round the estate you can see the difference in the kids.'

'And as for the children themselves,' says Mick Brown, 'what is there on an estate like this? – A little play square down there so small that if all the children turn out to play at once you couldn't occupy a tenth of them. So consequently the kids play on the balcony where they are not supposed to play. If you live on the balcony at the lower level

48

where I lived first, you know what hell is then. You can't understand it until you've experienced it.'

At the beginning of 1975 when I first met the Winstanley Committee they were planning a 'mass descent' on the Council to press for action on the promised Social Centre. Six months later the Council's plan for the new Centre to be shared with several other estates was under consideration. It remained under consideration throughout 1976, and by the end of the year the Council felt able to assure everyone that the new Centre on the other side of the main road from Winstanley would probably start building later in 1977 as a joint project with the Inner London Education Authority.

During all this time the waste space on the Winstanley estate remained enclosed and unused within its corrugated iron fence.

> CORRUGATED IRON
> (*said some of the local graffiti*)
> IS THE COUNCIL'S ARMOUR

Periodically someone on the Winstanley Committee would suggest putting up a temporary hut. There were plenty of skilled tradesmen on the estate. There might also be youngsters who would get a kick from helping to build something they could use themselves. But so far the idea has failed to click. After all, it's the Council's responsibility isn't it? Why should we let them off the hook?

## Balham Gets its Social Hall

Over roughly the same period that Winstanley were discussing the problem, another action group, a couple of miles away in Balham, were also negotiating with the Wandsworth Council. They too were fed up with waiting for a Social Centre, but one resident had noticed that a disused church hall was up for sale, and persuaded the others to drum up public support (they leafletted the area and called a public meeting) and to ask the Council to buy it, then and there.

The price was on the high side – £15,000 – because other church halls had been allowed planning permission for conversion to warehouses. But the meeting elected a steering Committee which collected evidence showing the urgent need for a Centre, and vigorously lobbied local councillors, and the Chairmen of the Council's Recreation and Social Services Committees. The Council bought the property. The action group prepared to step out of the limelight and let the authorities get on with the job.

Then came a setback. The Council's officers reported to the Finance Committee that necessary alterations and repairs would cost another £10,000 and mean closing the hall for about a year while the work was done.

At this point the action group could have stayed content, like Winstanley, with 'pressuring the Council' to hurry up. Instead they began to take over.

They did their own calculations and produced an alternative plan with a counter-estimate for £800 to cover the cost of immediate repairs – putting in a portaloo, lights, door locks, and self-closing doors to conform with fire regulations. The Council agreed. Then the community worker obtained £400 for essential furniture and equipment from the Council's Recreation Department. This money was used to buy a water heater, cooker, clock, and cover small running repairs, and pay someone to look after the keys.

Directly after the hall had been bought a public meeting had been called in which all interested groups in the area were represented. About fifty people came including representatives from the Youth Office, the Balham Union of Parents, the Pre-school Playgroups Association, and Senior Citizens. The steering group drew up a constitution and agreed on timetabling for use of the hall.

Local groups were able to use the Centre almost at once. (Part of their activities has been to raise funds for the purchase of more equipment.) Meanwhile the Council went ahead with plans to convert the hall properly. But the plans allowed for most of the new work to be done by extensions across a narrow passage-way outside one wall of the centre. The remaining space indoors could still be used and was soon accommodating a playgroup, a mother-and-child craft workshop, a friendship club for Senior Citizens, a social club, a youth club, a branch of Gingerbread, language classes, and a church group. In less than six months from the first move by the action group the hall was a going concern, growing rapidly.

Responsibility remains largely in the hands of the users'

Advisory Committee which includes a community worker, a councillor, the cleaner/caretaker (as a non-voting member) and representatives from each users' group. This keeps everyone in touch, suggests general policy, authorizes short-term expenditure (which is administered by the community worker) and sees to lettings. Charges were worked out by the Borough Valuer, with local groups being charged 25 per cent of the amount charged to other groups. Bookings and payments are made through the local Library. The Council pays for rates, electricity and gas, and retains ownership of the hall in case the Association folds up or becomes too restrictive in deciding which groups may use it. By the end of the first year the project was already so successful that it was accepted as a model for several small community halls to be built by the Council, each with users' Committees increasing their powers and responsibilities as the scheme develops.

The Balham group surprised themselves, and outdid Winstanley because they found that besides knowing better than anyone else what they wanted done, they were better placed to get ahead and do it.

Winstanley has been able to coast along doing a good job in representing the needs of the community to the authorities, and in making the best of the situation while they waited for the authorities to act. Both groups have had a fund of good will to draw on in the neighbourhood and a reasonable working relationship with officials and with local councillors. They were able to construct a network of interest that involved all sorts of people who normally stay clear of committee-mongering. As committees, they succeeded because they functioned as a heart does – they kept pumping away so that the whole circulatory system benefited.

But what happens when there is no heart left in the system? When local neglect has produced demoralization, and nothing thrives because neither the authority nor the community believes it can. You can't solve this one by setting up a committee. Something has to happen first to get confidence flowing. Which brings us in the next chapter to Gibshill.

# Chapter 4
# Gibshill Puts Down Crime

Gibshill is an overcrowded estate to the east of Greenock, high on a bare hill overlooking the Clyde shipyards, isolated from shops and other services by two low railway bridges, so low that the fire engines have to go the long way round to get to a fire. In 1972 it had nine hundred dwellings, for the most part concentrated in tenement flats, built on meagre Council budgets during the pre-war depression years, and neglected by successive corporations ever since.

This neglect, plus some of the worst unemployment figures in Britain, made people bloody-minded. The record for vandalism was such that one senior police officer used to say that all the vandalism in the United Kingdom started there, and spread as the local authority moved families out to other living areas. There was increasing resistance by Greenock Councillors to the idea of rehousing such families elsewhere. They quoted the 1969 recommendations of the authority's Planning Officer that there should be no major redevelopment of the area since this would 'merely result in the redistribution of the "problems" throughout the town'.

Gradually the area had become a ghetto where it was assumed that 'problem families' and 'delinquent youth' were concentrated. The place lived down to its reputation. There were frequent muggings, burglaries, looting and malicious damage to parked cars. The Gibshill label seemed to attract hostile treatment. Young job applicants reckoned that their chances vanished once the prospective employer saw on the application form where they came from. Relations with the police were bad. Residents were convinced that innocent youngsters were often 'lifted' for offences that others had committed. 'The Panda man' was a bogey to frighten children with. The tenement walls were scrawled with slogans attacking the local police by name.

In the spring of 1972 it would have been difficult to find any area more completely alienated from the rest of the community, more thoroughly stigmatized by the local authorities, or more completely demoralized about its own competence and character.

Four and a half years later, in the autumn of 1976, Gibshill acquired a new reputation. At a time when elsewhere in the country the crime rates for teenagers and young children have been on the increase, a September 1976 police report showed that crimes and offences by Gibshill youngsters had been HALVED. There had been a 47 per cent reduction in the number of children reported, and a 56·6 per cent reduction in referrals, compared with the same nine-month period in 1975. The report said that the credit for this

... continuing and sustained process ... must be given mainly to the Gibshill Community, since it is the people in that community who have brought this situation about, assisted by and supported in their efforts by the Local Authority and the officers of the Strathclyde Police.

How did it happen?

First, there had been a bureaucratic reshuffle. In 1969 the Labour opposition persuaded the Liberal majority on the Greenock Council to encourage changes that brought the heads of the Council departments closer together. Working with the Chief Officer they began to plan a concentrated attack on the needs of each area. The plan remained on the shelf until May 1972, when the second big change occurred: Labour won power in the local elections. The new Council majority was committed to 'major' redevelopment but not at all sure whether any of it should take place in Gibshill. Many Councillors were inclined to argue that the place was such a write-off that any attempt at redevelopment would be good money thrown after bad.

The third new factor was the Tenants' Association. It originated early in 1972 in the spurt of activity generated by the run-up to the local elections. It replaced a long-established local Residents' Association which had very little support, and even less influence in local affairs. The new Association was an almost despairing effort to obtain some say for Gibshill in its own future. Its first big decision was that every available member of the Association should go to the Council chamber for the crucial meeting, in June 1972, on the redevelopment proposals. To everyone's surprise sixty-eight members turned up. They had to listen to 'insults to the Gibshill people spoken by some of the Councillors', but they stuck it out; and their silent presence probably tipped the balance. The decision to redevelop Gibshill, as a priority commitment, went through.

The minority argument (that it would be wasted effort) might well have been justified had it not been for the fourth element in the situation: the youth. The Tenants' Association meetings were well attended by adults, but in its early days many local youngsters showed their feelings about the generation gap by stoning the TA hut as the members came out. Most adults regarded this as typical juvenile behaviour, and left it angrily at that. One member of the Association did not. Danny Keenan was then in his early fifties, an ex-bus driver and shop steward with a heart condition and troubled with asthma. He had no qualifications in youth work, no special experience, and his formal education had been cut short at thirteen and a half, when he had to go out to work to help support his family; but he decided that something should be attempted which would give youngsters a stake of their own.

At this time the only official provision for youth was a club in the church hall, run twice a week on very traditional lines by a policeman paid as a part-time youth leader by the local Education Authority. Attenders tended to be 'goodies' and they and the premises were frequently stoned by the 'baddies' outside (who eventually set fire to the place). With some difficulty Danny Keenan persuaded his Association to allow him the use of their hut for a kids' disco. He managed to borrow a tape-recorder and a radiogram, and to persuade one or two teenagers to help him. In no time at all they had sixty to seventy 10–12-year-olds – ex-baddies as well as ex-goodies – all mixed together and no trouble to speak of.

This was the situation, early in 1973, when the Council took the initiative, in response to the TA's turn-out at the Council meeting, and called a meeting of residents. At this the key officials in the Chief Officer's team unfolded their redevelopment plan for Gibshill. *Their* plan. For though there had been a few minor leaks, there had been no previous consultation. This time 150 residents turned up. They heard out the Council's plans, and then began to comment on them from the floor.

They said that they didn't want the pub that had been planned: it would be better to have licensed club premises, under the tenants' control, free of commercial pressure to push hard drinking. They wanted the chemist's shop kept as a local resource, instead of being absorbed into a shopping complex outside the area because that would be too far away for elderly people. They had more to say on the type of shops that were needed, and on modernizing the houses and flats.

Some senior officials had come reluctantly to the meeting, expecting either an apathetic turn-out, or a barrage of complaints. They began to admit to themselves that the tenants' suggestions were shrewd and relevant. Others who had been more optimistic found their hopes exceeded. Overnight the idea of 'joint consultation' began to make sense. But the structure they set up took some of the steam out of the operation. The inter-departmental Technical Co-ordinating Committee of officials was linked up with 'the Subcommittee' – a liaison group of tenants with a newly appointed neighbourhood worker, and the community development officer. It embarked on a long series of discussions. Meanwhile the plans began to be implemented. There were some minor revisions to meet the tenants' earliest suggestions, but the tenants themselves found it harder and harder to influence official priorities, or to keep track of the costing revisions. The officials blamed inflation: the tenants said 'the monies have been whittled away' because of bad planning. But they couldn't get close enough to prove it.

The work proceeded. Existing houses were modernized, some new houses built, the first phase of the landscaping completed, all more or less according to plan – the officials' plan. Towards the end of 1976 one of the instigators of the whole consultation exercise, Ronald Young, now a Regional Councillor, took stock of what he called 'the planning process':

... in local government terms the progress has been considerable ...
... but ...
... a weakness throughout ... has been the failure of tenants to be supplied with or themselves to collect, basic information to permit them to chase progress – let alone anything more ambitious ...

With one exception, the architects and quantity surveyors particularly could not establish a proper client relationship with the representatives of the neighbourhood ... no real dialogue took place ... the reasonable aspirations of tenants were quickly translated by professionals into expensive schemes which were beyond the willingness (or ability) of the political system to supply.

The programme was tightly controlled by the professionals who in no way changed their traditional operational behaviour and assumptions.

On the official side, then (given the setbacks of the three-day week and the Government cuts), modest progress in meeting deadlines. On the community side, initial enthusiasm that gradually drained away as it became apparent that the officials were going their own way, regardless. With one crucial exception.

The 'exception' can be traced back to the tenants' consultation meeting convened by the Council officials in January 1973. At the back of the hall stood a bunch of the toughest of the older teenagers. When the meeting was formally ended they button-holed the Director of Social Work and asked him 'What's for us?' He handed them straight over to the newly appointed neighbourhood worker, Ralph Ibbott, who put the question back to them: Will you tell us what you want?

Yes, they would, but there must be time and place provided to do it properly. He stepped across the floor, then and there, to the Tenants' Association Chairperson and got her, possibly before she quite realized what was happening, to offer these notorious knife-carrying youngsters the use of the Association's hut in a few days' time. The group turned up on schedule, met Ralph Ibbott and Danny Keenan (whose work with the 10–12-year-olds had first caught their fancy) and told them what was what.

They wanted a coffee bar meeting-place and facilities to organize football and table tennis. And most of all they wanted something done about the behaviour of the police. They backed their criticisms with a long string of detailed allegations.

Adults at the previous meeting had already suggested replacing the panda car patrols by 'beat' policemen, and setting up a police office within the area as a liaison point. Ralph Ibbott and Danny Keenan got hold of the Chief Constable, and the Superintendent in charge of 'community involvement', and persuaded them to meet some of the Tenants' Association members and thrash the whole thing out. As a direct result the panda patrols were reduced in favour of policemen who were allowed to volunteer for the beat, and who began to establish better relations, with adults as well as with youngsters.

The 16–17-year-olds became further involved in the work being done by Danny Keenan (now working full time; with his pay provided by a charitable Trust). Some of those who were out of work joined him in helping to repaint the TA hut. More joined in with him in operating the 10–12s disco (now running four nights a week, with a noticeable drop in police 'liftings' for juvenile offences).

In July 1973 the 17-year-olds helped to organize a very successful holiday trip for thirty-six 10–14s. In August, sixteen of the toughest 15–16-year-olds turned up and explained that they wanted to have a camp for themselves. They went into a huddle then and there and produced their own 'rules for the camp' (unasked and before even the tents had been obtained). They returned from a very successful, and relatively law-abiding camp to become the founder-members of the youth group which now began to form in order to build a youth hut.

The hut project had the advantage of a steady improvement in everyone's morale. Children were getting into trouble less often. The community was beginning to think well of the teenagers. The teenagers began to feel better about themselves. The authorities became much more helpful.

A derelict contractor's hut was obtained via the Police Superintendent. The Council Amenities Committee provided cement, bricks, extra timber, paint, and electric fittings. Brick foundations were laid by six kids from a List D (Approved) school, two of them locals, supervised by their instructor. The contractor working on the estate modernization scheme contributed plumbing materials and allowed two trainee plumbers to work on the scheme in the firm's time. During a strike at the local Chrysler works one of the strikers, who was a skilled joiner, helped supervise the carpentry. Intensive work by the youth group got the hut installation completed and occupied in under three months.

Early in 1974 the 'traditional' youth club, that had been run in the church hall, folded. The new group, now thriving in its own hut, applied to the education department for permission to take over. At first the authority was very doubtful. After all Danny Keenan was not 'qualified' as a youth worker. But negotiations were eventually successful; a new, and greatly expanded club was opened, catering for the whole of the 10–16 age group, with the 17-year-olds helping Danny to run it.

At this point the 'community' strand in the Gibshill story begins to tangle with the 'planning process' mentioned earlier. The professionals, particularly the architects, had their own clear

57

ideas about how Gibshill should look when finished. There would be a splendid new social centre, catering for both adults and youngsters, which would bring the whole life of the community into focus (and look rather well, from a distance – say half-way across the river) as the key feature in the whole design.

The Tenants' Association did not see it that way. They figured, correctly, that the scale first proposed by the planners would price the centre right out of any practical scheme for the immediate future. So their first step was to back those on the District Council who wanted a less expensive scheme (£200,000 instead of £550,000). Their next proposal was even more distasteful to the architects. The TA had recently lost their own premises through a freak electrical fire; they were sharing the teenagers' hut with them. But the Association put its own interest aside. The needs of the youth must come first. They wanted the youth section of the centre separated from the rest of the premises, so that it could (a) have its own open space surrounding it, and (b) be constructed first, without waiting for the remainder of the centre to be completed.

The 'Subcommittee' (the liaison group of tenants set up by the Council's Technical Co-ordinating Committee) was now the arena in which tenants and planners locked horns over the new centre. The tenants won their point and got the youth centre detached, having gained the support of the Social Work Department. But during 1975 as the building work on the youth centre proceeded, they suddenly found themselves with a fresh set of administrators to educate.

The new Region of Strathclyde had lurched on to the scene, sending officials flying in all directions. There was now a new-comer at the head of the Department of Leisure and Recreation whose first step was to announce his plans for the staffing of the new centre with people who should be 'properly qualified'.

The first reaction of the Tenants' Association was to assert their right to share in making these new appointments. It was agreed that they should be represented on the Selection Board. But the more they thought about the situation the less they liked it. Even supposing that Danny Keenan were to apply for one of the jobs, and be selected – what kind of set-up would result? Who really would be running the show? After nine months of negotiations, and with the centre almost completed, the Tenants' Association worked its way through to the final and entirely logical decision, and forced its acceptance, very reluctant, on the authorities: the new youth centre should be run by, as well as for, the community it served. The Council's Leisure and Recreation Committee appointed and paid the caretaker and the cleaners. But the management became the responsibility of the Tenants' Association.

In April 1976 the youth hall opened, with Danny Keenan in charge, helped by a dozen other TA members, plus a loose-knit 'working committee' of upwards of twenty 14–17-year-olds who ran the juniors. The Association arranged to rent the premises from the Council with funds obtained by charging door money (5p to juniors, 10p to seniors). The centre operates seven nights a week, and caters for around 400 youngsters. There is no formal constitution. Membership secures cheaper rates for certain items, but local youngsters who are not members can use the place too, if they behave.

'Behaviour problems' are rare inside the centre, and becoming more rare outside it. The drop in the crime rate reported by the police has been maintained in 1977. By the end of 1976 vandalism had almost ceased; anyone could walk around the area after dark, unmolested; whereas five years earlier you wouldn't park a car at night and expect to see it intact the next morning.

Gibshill has roughly the same number of residents to draw on as the Winstanley Tenants' Association. It lacked Winstanley's strong tradition of mutual help; and it started out with a much worse reputation. But it seems to have caught up; and in some respects come further. It had the advantage of an incoming Labour majority on the Council which had sharpened its principles and clarified some of its objectives while in opposition. The new Council encouraged a few enlightened Council officials to collaborate with each other, and to recognize that the community had something of its own to contribute. But few, apart perhaps from Councillor Ronald Young, had bargained for the strength of purpose the community has shown.

Local people discovered their strength at the Council meeting when sixty-eight TA members by their mere presence seemed to tip the balance in Gibshill's favour. But the really convincing evidence of what could be done was provided by Danny Keenan and his gradually increasing band of teenage collaborators. They convinced first themselves, and then others, by what they did, rather than what they said about it.

When the TA took part in joint consultation meetings with the planners, although their initial advice was good, their influence in the long run was small. When they decided to shift the argument about the social centre to their own ground, their own experience began to count. They could act, and therefore speak, with conviction. They could demonstrate, to themselves as well as to others, not merely what should be done but their own capacity to do it.

The Gibshill story so far is a piece of self-revelation by members of the community, which is slowly being recognized by officialdom. Local people discovered that in certain important respects they knew better, and could do better, than the professionals; and that this was because they cared more.

For many authorities this is still a dubious assumption. They know the sheer size of the problems they are up against. They cannot see how anyone else can expect to achieve more than they are achieving already. For people to take things into their own hands seems impertinent, as well as ill-advised. What's more, as the next chapter shows, it's very probably against the law.

# Chapter 5
# Builders and Wreckers

In the early weeks of 1969 'The Piccadilly Squatters' entered a disused hotel in Drury Lane, barricaded it against forcible ejection, brought in their own food and bedding, and proclaimed a commune. Not long after there was an occupation of Number 144 Piccadilly, followed by the invasion of a disused school in Endell Street, just up the road from Drury Lane.

The world's Press and television displayed them perched on the roof and draped along window ledges; and presented all of us with the perfect opportunity to trot out our prejudices: for and against artists, anarchists, elderly hippies and the irresponsible young. The news stories had enough to stimulate the most jaded reader. There was drug addiction, free sex, swear words and dirt. The whole thing was too much for the authorities. One after the other the communes were forcibly entered by the police, and the communards jailed, fined, or encouraged to melt into the landscape.

Meanwhile squatters of a very different kind anxiously held on to the footholds they were beginning to establish with enormous care and perseverance, in the down-at-heel housing districts of Redbridge and Notting Hill.

The action group that built the Family Squatting Movement of the 1960s and 1970s were radicals with roots. They were not free-booting individualists grabbing themselves a crash pad in a disused building. It is true that they shared the communards' contempt for private or public property owners who left large premises empty because they were too inefficient or too greedy to make them available for people to use. But they set out to create solutions: not merely to air problems. So they were desperately concerned lest the Press and television image of the street communes should camouflage the reality of ordinary families in distress, for whom the housing shortage meant that family squatting was the only reasonable alternative to family break-down.

The people they wanted to help had lost their moorings in a double sense. They were families who had left home in pursuit of a job, or because they could not afford the rents demanded by private landlords or had been displaced to make way for the demolition gangs. For a time they might co-exist with in-laws in cramped accommodation, until family friction edged them out on to the streets. They landed up in hostels, waiting for the local authorities to do their duty as laid down in the 1948 Housing Act, and get them off the housing list and into homes of their own.

## The King Hill Hostel

Efforts had been made, from 1963 onwards, to focus attention on these hostels. In some, the authorities were accustomed to turn out families after three months, and then penalize the family for its homelessness by taking the children into 'care'. In many, husbands and wives were in separate dormitories like the inmates of poorhouses in Dickens' day. In King Hill, West Malling, the Bromley Council maintained a hostel for the homeless in which only mothers and children were allowed to stay; the husbands were allowed to visit at set times during the day, and then had to go away again, as if they were visiting their families in hospital or in jail.

*Cathy Come Home* had exposed the inhumanity of the system on television. Eric Lubbock MP had described the King Hill hostel as a concentration camp. Many others had spoken out passionately, and urged the authorities to step up the pace and get people into homes of their own instead of institutions. But in spite of the talk, the King Hill regime continued.

Then in 1965, Jim Radford, Andy Anderson, and a few others made contact with most of the seventy-five families who were in the hostel, and began a twelve-month campaign to challenge the rule that husbands should not live in. They organized and maintained an occupation of the hostel; the husbands moved in for keeps, and a committee was formed which drew up its own rules for the reasonable conduct of the hostel.

The occupation made news. The group was able to focus public attention on the nonsense made by official policy. Homeless families were being admitted to temporary accommodation in hostels, then thrown out again, the families split up and the children taken into care. The whole sorry business was costing the ratepayers far more than if the Council had done its duty under the 1948 Act and got on with providing homes.

These arguments made little headway with the authorities. What mattered most to them was that the occupation of the hostel was illegal. The law must be asserted by force. Police and bailiffs tried to evict the husbands. There was violence and counter-violence. Husbands who were thrown out were bound over by the Courts not to re-enter. They re-entered. Some were jailed. But the campaign continued, and with it, the publicity, until pressure of public opinion, particularly within the borough, forced the Council to back down and allow families to live in.

By the end of the year the Ministry of Health itself weighed in with two circulars to local authorities recommending the very changes that the 'trouble-makers' had broken the law to effect.

Many people could see the logic of these events:

1. The authorities now recognized that the way the families had been treated – in particular the separation of the husbands from their wives and children – had been wrong from the beginning.

2. Many responsible people had said so long before, but had not been heeded.

3. When the young radicals encouraged the victims of ill treatment to resist, the law was invoked in defence of the system which imposed the ill treatment.

4. When resistance succeeded and the hostel was taken over, the 'victims' and their supporters established a form of self-government. This seemed to be more relaxed, more efficient, and more orderly than the regime it replaced.

5. The media conveyed the 'natural justice' of this illegal behaviour to the public. The public's response forced the authorities to amend.

6. Actions had spoken louder than words.

The message they carried about action groups was spelt out by Jim Radford:

There are many people, perhaps the majority in our society, who are concerned, not only about their own position, but about what is happening to other people. Usually they stop being concerned about other people after a time because they feel so frustrated – there is nothing they can do about it. They feel powerless.

What we have been trying to do is to show people that they are not necessarily powerless if only they get together with other people. They can create power.

On your own you are just an individual, but with a group there are things you can do, there are sanctions you can take.

Radford and the others in the group saw themselves as the spearhead of these 'many people' who were ashamed of the facts that Shelter had recently begun to hammer home: nearly two million people living in places officially described as unfit for human habitation; a million more in near-slums or in grossly overcrowded conditions; upwards of 20,000 lodged in some form of hostel. They wanted to apply 'sanctions' which would go beyond merely exposing the problem; which would begin to solve it. Merely to humanize the hostels was no real answer to the question. Somehow families must get into places they could call home.

The homes were there, half a million of them, empty. In every city there were premises that had been scheduled for demolition, one day, as part of redevelopment plans. But often these plans took years to get off the drawing boards and through the costing systems. Meanwhile it paid no one, apparently, to make these 'short-life properties' available. Indeed, it paid some property owners handsomely to keep accommodation empty, pay no rates, sit tight, and watch the market values go up.

As Nicholas Walter put it in a broadcast:

More and more people are deciding that it is not stealing to squat in an empty house; it is stealing to own an empty house.

From the viewpoint of a homeless family, a 'short-life' house standing empty was a crime against children.

They're only going to stand for two or three years; but two or three years in the life of a child at five or six years of age means a hell of a bloody lot . . .

said Maggie O'Shannon, whose family, in Notting Hill, was one of the first to occupy an empty house and dare the absentee landlord to get them out. But soon a way opened for squatting to become legally defensible. Ron Bailey was a teacher who had also tangled with the law on behalf of hostel families. He once put the case for action in a terse reply to someone who asked him if he was not an interfering trouble maker:

I *am* an interferer, and I am going to make trouble. Isn't it about time that some trouble was made?

Recently he had followed up a hunch by researching law books in the local reference library. The hunch meant trouble for absentee landlords who kept their property empty. In November 1968 he got together a group of fifteen like-minded individuals, Radford among them, and told them of his discovery. The Forcible Entry Acts of 1381 and 1429, introduced during the Hundred Years War in order to protect householders from dispossession by returning soldiery, could be used to protect *any* peaceable occupier from *any* outsider, police and bailiffs included, who sought entry 'with strong hand or multitude of people'.

The group evolved a strategy which has become a model of its kind. First they caught the eye of the media by staging two 'token' occupations. On 1 December, they occupied a block of luxury flats in Wanstead which had been empty for four years while the owner held out for high rents and long leases. Three weeks later, they went into an old vicarage in Capworth Street, E.11, which had stood empty for three years, ever since the vicar had moved into the house next door.

These occupations were strictly temporary, as a means of bringing publicity to bear on the criminal paradox of empty premises and homeless people. They prepared the ground for the real thing. A meeting was announced for Sunday, 9 February 1969 in Manor Park, Newham. The crowd that assembled was led through the streets into the neighbouring borough of Redbridge, where the night before two homeless families had been installed, secretly, in empty houses. The police reacted on the spot and manhandled one family out after smashing in the back door. But when someone told the superintendent about the legal warnings the squatters had posted on their front doors, wiser counsels prevailed. The notices threatened all comers with legal proceedings under the Forcible Entry Acts. The evicted family was smuggled in again on the following night, and allowed to stay.

The only way the authorities could dispossess the families was by taking them to court. On 2 April the Ilford County Court granted the Redbridge Council a possession order against the Beresford family squatting in No. 43 Cleveland Road. The family were required by the Court to leave the premises before 15 April. On the 14th, they dutifully obeyed; but when the Council officials arrived to take possession, they found that another homeless family, the Flemings, had been moved in to No. 43, while the Beresfords had been transferred to another house nearby. As the possession order had to *name* the people concerned, and the names were now no longer the same, it was of no effect.

As Jim Radford put it: 'We comforted the disconcerted officials by telling them not to think of it as losing a home, think of it as gaining a family.'

The group had achieved its first objectives with superb economy. They operated judo-fashion to bring the full force of the law to the support of homeless families. They explained patiently and lucidly what they were doing: instead of making an ass of the law, they were rehabilitating it; restoring its reputation, ensuring that the legal system protected the victim, not the exploiter. In the bright light of well-organized publicity people could see that this action made sense.

Since the law could not be made to serve, the Redbridge Council now resorted to force. With the help of a private enterprise firm of bailiffs a series of assaults was made on homes occupied by squatting families. The families themselves had 'entered peaceably', by means of a back door or window that 'happened to be open' and had then raised barricades to obstruct the bailiffs. The occupants of one house were manhandled and forced out, with serious injury to one helper who had been on guard. But more houses were occupied; and the bailiffs found themselves taken to court in their turn by the squatters, on a charge of unlawful assault.

Television, radio and the Press reported the situation, poker-faced. Their audiences showed the same deep satisfaction that Punch arouses when he hangs the hangman in his own noose. The longer the legal delays, the more time for parents and children who had been homeless or separated to find out what it was like to have a home together; and the better the exposure in the media.

The Council did not help their image by sending demolition gangs to wreck other empty houses, pouring concrete down the lavatories and disconnecting the pipelines. for fear that squatting families might move in and benefit. (Council Minute 2435 noted that the cost to the ratepayers of making twenty-nine houses *uninhabitable* was £2,520.) The Council felt particularly vulnerable to its electors, having already announced its plans to build a £30 million Town Centre. The squatters made the most of the fact that the Town Centre Redevelopment Committee's Chairman happened also to be Chairman of the British Ready Mixed Concrete Association. A local Residents' Association who were already strongly opposed to these 'extravagant' redevelopment plans weighed in on the side of the squatters. Towards the end of the year, the Redbridge Council climbed down, and agreed to make some of its empty houses available to homeless families. They arranged this separately through a Housing Association, because they still refused to recognize the family squatting movement as capable of reasonable behaviour.

The squatting families and their supporters had begun peaceably enough, but the physical assaults by the bailiffs had raised the temperature all round. This was further complicated by the use that other people were making of the legal loopholes that Bailey and Radford and their group had publicized. Like the 'Piccadilly Squatters' these others wanted free living space for themselves, as individuals. Provided they got it, they were not bothered about changing the public's attitude to homeless families or the Government's housing priorities.

There were also some independent groups that were genuinely concerned with squatting homeless families. Some took their cues from Radford and Bailey; others preferred to go it alone, and saw no harm in a bit of aggro in their way.

People were now in two minds about 'the squatters'. How could you tell them apart? Squatting still made a great Punch and Judy show in the media, but public ridicule could just as easily be directed towards the free-loaders in the short-lived squats in Endell Street and Piccadilly. When the police had moved in on them (on the grounds that the premises had been forcibly, not peaceably, entered) public opinion was on the whole behind the authorities. As for the ordinary run-of-the-mill homeless, they lacked news value.

## Mrs Bonedi Moves In

But five months later, in July 1969, the family squatting group had regained the initiative. Jim Radford and some others had shifted their base to Lewisham. They were determined to underline the devastating, painstaking reasonableness of each action they took. The test case was that of Mrs Bonedi:

The procedure in most cases was that we took the family to the Council, to the Housing Department, to the Welfare Department, to the Children's Department, and explained their position, their problem, their need, and asked each department what they could do about it.

We did this with Mrs Bonedi in Lewisham, and of course they said there was nothing that could be done.

This was a woman living in a very damp basement flat, absolutely rotten, every bit of woodwork was rotten, the ceiling was flaking into food. She herself was ill and a doctor and a specialist both told her it was a result of living in this flat; she must get out. Her child was ill, she was separated from two other children solely because of the housing conditions, and the Council couldn't hold out any hope that she would be rehoused within the next five years.

Half a mile down the road there was a street full of perfectly good sound houses, good substantial houses that were going to be empty for at least another year. So we moved her into one of them, and as soon as we had done that, we went to the Council and said: 'Look, we've moved Mrs Bonedi into No. 20 Effingham Road. If you leave her alone she will move out when you want to pull that house down. She'll pay you rent, she'll pay you rates, she is not jumping the housing queue because nobody is queuing up for that house. You weren't going to use it.'

Mrs Bonedi was moved in on 5 June 1969. The following day she was ordered out by the Borough Housing Manager, accompanied by two men in plain clothes whom the squatters' group had observed transfer from a police car further down the road. Radford was there to meet them with a reminder of the legal obstacles to a forcible eviction; but he coupled this with a persuasive outline of a possible agreement that the squatters were ready to negotiate with the Council.

The Housing Manager seemed to think that something could be achieved by discussion. He consulted with the Deputy Town Clerk, the Chief Welfare Officer, the Housing and Estates Manager and the Council's solicitor.

Radford's proposition was that if the Council would list houses that remained empty, and give provisional dates when they would be required for demolition, the squatters in their turn would provide volunteer teams to make each house reasonable for temporary habitation; they would move in families ready to pay rents, and they would undertake that each family would move out again when the demolition date fell due. The Council could have it both ways. Empty premises could be used and rehabilitated without incurring heavy expenditure. At the same time development plans would not be held up when the time came for the sites to be cleared and rebuilding to commence.

The Council at first refused to believe that the squatters could be relied on. But an ally appeared from an unexpected quarter. Councillor Herbert Eames had good reason professionally to condemn the squatters' behaviour. He was a practising solicitor, as well as being at that time the Conservative Chairman of the Lewisham Housing Committee. His first impressions, he told me long afterwards, were very dubious:

We regarded them all as anarchists and I don't suppose I had a very clear picture of what an anarchist was, but I felt quite sure that an anarchist was a thing that I didn't like, and I was therefore suspicious of anything that I didn't know or understand.

On the other hand, there were two strong arguments in favour of negotiation: the bad publicity Redbridge Council had earned for itself; and the paradox of empty houses and homeless people. Councillor Eames set about persuading first his own Conservative members, and then the Labour opposition (which had also opposed negotiations with the squatters), that it was worth having a try.

Councillor Eames:

The lesson I have learned I think in the last eighteen months is that in fact they are people who have got a very real concern; in this particular instance, for people who are living in appalling housing conditions, and I have learned too that they do respect reasonable rules and regulations . . .
They have played perfectly fair with us, and I think we have been probably as surprised that we have been able to do business with them, as they are surprised that they have been able to do business with us.

Under the agreement the Council notified the squatters as houses became available; then the squatters made them habitable and moved the families in until the buildings were due for demolition. When the time came to move out, the squatters kept their word. But only just. One house which had been occupied by a homeless one-parent family became a base for a group of individuals who had been involved in the battles of Redbridge, and acquired something of a siege mentality. Radford exhausted his patience trying to persuade them to budge, and only succeeded when he convinced them that unless they went quietly, the rest of the family squatting group was prepared to put them out by main force.

The agreement held. In little over a year a hundred homeless families were installed in houses made available by the Council. The law had been broken, but, said Eames:

What we had to say to ourselves was 'Is it going to serve any useful purpose if you regard the law too rigidly?' Fair enough, you had to admit that it was from an initial illegal act that the present situation has arisen. But which would have been better – to have said 'No, we are not going to let you stay here; we are not going to let you use any of our short-term accommodation' – or to house 100 families?

The long campaign of the family squatters had won them a victory, without the need to impose a defeat. Officials and Councillors had not lost face; so they could get used to the new scheme without feeling sore and wanting to wreck it.

Wreckers, however, were already present among the squatters themselves. The essence of the agreement reached with the Lewisham Council was that the Family Squatting Association should take over short-life premises in poor condition, and by its own voluntary efforts make a good job of them for temporary use. Each homeless family as it was moved in would take its turn in helping the others to convert the next batch of short-life premises so that more families could be housed. In consideration of the money saved in this way, the Council agreed to charge rates, but no rent. Rates were to be paid through the Association. It worked out how much was needed in order to cover the cost of repair materials, and added this, by general agreement, to the rates due from each family. At around £4 a week in all, the 'rent' was still, as everyone admitted, a bargain.

But now that the two years' struggle was over, the momentum slackened. Some of the families began to default on their payments.

# Wanda Tamakloe

At about this time Mrs Wanda Tamakloe comes into the picture. In 1970 she had been living in one room with her four children, having separated from her West African husband. She was sleeping on the floor because the bed supplied by the landlord was so filthy that she told him to take it away. The Council welfare official who visited her mentioned, unofficially, that it might be worthwhile contacting the Squatting Association. Jim Radford and Christine Bolam found her a house in Forest Hill, and other members of the Association helped her to move in.

For a while, she said, she was so happy to have a proper home to live in that she didn't really want to take any interest in anything else. She paid her rent regularly to the Association, and then one day was persuaded to attend a monthly meeting. She wasn't used to meetings; she felt very shy and sat right at the back.

The meeting was not going at all well. For much of the time it was in uproar. Part of the reason was that Jim Radford and some of the others who had led the squatting campaign had decided that it was time to step aside from the leadership, to move out of the limelight and let those who were directly involved take over.

This was not a decision to quit, or to dodge responsibility. Radford still attended the meetings, but he was determined not to be the person who laid down the law, and resolved the issue:

Given a little power, responsibility or status, we all begin to assume that we know best: and to seek, or hang on to, control.

We must all recognize the need to protect people from 'us' as well as 'them'.

His decision created a power vacuum that one of the defaulting members was trying to fill. This character was demonstrating his own powers of leadership in organizing those who did not want to pay up and in deriding those who did.

A good deal of mud was flying. An attempt was made to attack Jim Radford by preventing his 16-year-old son, who was one of the volunteer helpers, from being a member. Having herself been helped when she settled in Forest Hill, this upset Mrs Tamakloe. She got up at the back of the room, shaking with nerves, and said 'If he's old enough to help, he's old enough to be a member.' And then sat down again abruptly. Everyone turned round to look at her.

When the time came to elect the new Committee, her name was proposed, and as she told me afterwards, 'The West Indians at the meeting said "We could do with a good-looking woman" and gave me all their votes.' So did most of the others.

There were several other new members on the Committee. The old hands had given up the leadership. The new Committee was inexperienced, and a bit apprehensive. But it was quite clear about one thing: there had to be a show-down. It had been elected to make sure that the Association lived up to its reputation, kept its word and paid its way, whatever the consequences.

Being a Committee member, for someone who was not used even to attending meetings, was a mind-blowing experience. Mrs Tamakloe thought to herself 'It's useful to look after yourself – to keep the house clean and get the food cooked, and see to the children. But anyone can do that. Now this is a new job, I must learn it.'

The learning came easily, because the others were learning too.

At first I was frightened – as soon as more than two people arrived I'd shut up and say nothing at all. So first for me was to listen. Then very gradually I had to speak – shaking all the time. After half a year I felt better: I could really stand my ground. I don't mind any more if I make a mistake in my language. If I get in a muddle I start all over again. It's quite nice when people laugh – it makes things easier . . .

She found herself learning to swim at the deep end. The group was afraid that somebody might make a power bid. It was decided that the Chairmanship should be taken in turns by every Committee member.

Every week there was a different Committee Chairman. To start off with, that's not so good for the Committee, having someone who is not sure what to do; but it gives every Committee member some self-confidence.

The first time it was my turn I was very nervous. My voice kept on going away. I felt very hot. The words on the Agenda kept floating away. It was difficult for me to read them.

Later on, I took the Chair at the General Meeting. The same thing happened at first. I was a very bad scholar at school, and I never before had experience on committees and at meetings, or in making speeches. But now I can talk to several hundreds and it doesn't worry me.

During this period when everyone was inexperienced, half

afraid to talk, the Association began to recover its nerve. This happened because one after another the Committee members got used to taking the lead: not just in the sense of taking turns at being Chairman, but being able to face facts, reach decisions and make them stick.

The facts were intimidating. Several of the members who still refused to pay up were seasoned campaigners in the squatting movement. Their leader was an effective speaker at meetings, and he also had a gift for person-to-person contact. He could persuade people that their rights were at stake. Once again it was Us and Them; only this time the villains were their own Committee. Outside the Association, there were some local householders still suspicious of the newcomers; hard-bitten officials; Labour and Conservative councillors who still doubted the wisdom of the Council's squatting agreement. Beyond these there were the media, on the watch for colourful copy.

The Committee evolved its own method of operation. It underlined its democratic authority by sharing out the work between all its members. It was no longer a question of Chairman's action or Secretary's action. 'It's all of us you're up against,' they said. Individual members were delegated to visit each family that refused to pay its rent. If the report came back to the Committee that they still refused without good reason, invitations were sent to the defaulters to attend the next general meeting and explain themselves. If this failed, their names were publicized. If they still held out the Association passed a resolution: 'Pay up or we'll move you out again.' The rents were paid in.

All this took time, but the achievement built up everyone's confidence, and restored the Association's reputation with the outside world. It might still have drifted into a comfortable state of inactivity if it had not been for the steady trickle of empty short-life properties which still came its way under the agreement with the Lewisham Council. Each new property was a reminder that this was a self-help group, not a parasite on someone else's bounty. Each place needed renovation, and there were always new families waiting for a proper home. So there was still plenty of work that everyone, not just the Committee members, could do.

In two years average attendance at the monthly general meetings rose from thirty to seventy. People now had to shout a great deal, not quarrelling with each other, but because there was so much general talk going on (quite apart from the chatter of the children who were allowed to come along too).

In earlier days, when morale was at its worst, the working parties had been haphazardly organized. Often volunteers turned up to find that materials were short, tools were missing, there was no one on hand with the right kind of skill for the trickier jobs. Enthusiasm waned.

Now as the Association pulled itself together, and found itself capable of coping with problems on its own, it was decided to appoint Mrs Tamakloe as its paid co-ordinator, to help organize materials, and see that the work of the volunteers was not wasted.

She made it her business to keep up personal contacts, outside the regular meetings. She noticed practical problems that families were up against – maintenance and repair jobs that an ordinary tenant would go to the Council for. She borrowed a duplicator and began turning out do-it-yourself advice on re-glazing windows, unblocking sinks, and curing rising damp. Meanwhile, she went on reminding all the members of the Association that they were in this together; to remember what it was like to be homeless, even though they were now successfully housed.

Between them they turned the weekend working parties into something worth celebrating. On a Sunday night when the work was done, and the new family moved in, the beer came out in crates, and the sausages were cooked over the rubbish fire in the back yard.

Eventually the paid staff rose to four, with two handymen (for the tricky work) and a 'field worker'.

All four of us are paid the same. I even gave up my children's allowance (£1 a week paid by the Association) because I didn't want there to be any difference between us.

When we do a job I talk it over with the others. We each put in our ideas. Each one says what he would like to do. So you get better work, because it is work they choose for themselves; and they feel happier when they are deciding.

Some jobs only one particular person can do; but he knows it, so there is no argument. Maybe sometimes I get left with the sticky job that no one else wants; but later they maybe come round and help me with that work too. We have more togetherness in this way.

We get out a great deal. We get volunteers to sit in the office so that we can get out more and meet more people. When you come to the doorstep it is necessary to have the feeling that you are going to meet friends. In a day of visits I get twenty to twenty-five cups of tea; so I am getting a bit tubby. Sometimes you must eat a whole meal, even though you have just had your own. You mustn't refuse; they want to please you. You're one of them.

This was the point in our conversation that Mrs Tamakloe said what I quoted in the first chapter:

When our people first come into the Association they have no experience of managing for themselves. They always had the landlord to tell them all his rules; and at work, the boss. Even at school they always had the teacher telling them what to do . . .

You can see now, perhaps, what turns it into a different story:

. . . But they joined the Association – and *there is no boss*. They find themselves telling us, the paid workers, what to do: and that is quite a difference! They learn that very quickly! So then you have to tell them 'you're not the only one'. If they shout too much – maybe to get repair work when others are before them in the queue – usually the older members tell them to shut up.

They are shy at first, in the meetings. They sit in a corner like I used to do; but after five or six meetings they liven up. If they are still not talking, I deliberately say something they wouldn't agree to – and then they'll chip in. If necessary I aggravate people a bit – make them angry and make them think. If you've got a reaction, you are half way already. You can always laugh about it afterwards.

In the early days I used to think and talk squatting all day; and have nightmares about it at night. Now I still talk and think about it all the time, but I sleep easy.

How do you describe Wanda's job? 'There is no boss,' she says. Leadership spans the whole Committee: it does not have to be concentrated in one person alone. Could you call her the Manager? Not quite right, but getting warmer. Successful groups open up possibilities for everyone to have some share in the management. Her real function is to share the management out so that power goes to nobody's head. She helps to construct a framework which allows the whole membership to make the most of everyone's resources, and to grow up together. She's a builder; and a cultivator.

What is the structure which enables such groups to grow? In

the first place, it has to provide a network of communication which makes sense to everyone. A great deal of sociable talk goes on, just as in Winstanley or Gibshill. The 'public conversation' about the work in hand continues all the time – in Wanda's or her team's house-to-house visits, in the weekend work parties, in the general buzz that provides a backing to the vocalist at the monthly meetings. The group communicates by what it does: it can see what it is doing, and take satisfaction from having done it together.

In earlier days, when fluent speakers held the floor, people like Wanda have felt at a loss for words, and appeared at a disadvantage. To the outsider, they seem 'inarticulate'. By this is meant that they cannot, at first, command the jargon, or assemble their ideas in a conventional pattern. This is a misleading impression.

A group becomes 'articulate' when it has been enabled to put its ideas into effect. It can do this once it has evolved its own structure: its own ways of linking up together; or activating those who might otherwise become passengers; of using dominant personalities (like Ted Trayfoot) instead of being used by them; of coming to joint decisions, and undertaking a combined operation. In this sense it is articulated as limbs are articulated: joined to each other so that they can exert leverage between them, and the body can do things. The words come, once people grasp the fact that it is they themselves who speak with authority. Their authority, their right to say what is and what should be, rests on what they are doing and have done. They speak from experience.

This authority, and the power that it exerts, may seem to challenge other kinds of 'authority', local government for instance. To their credit the Greater London Council and sixteen London boroughs followed Lewisham's example and made agreements with family squatting associations. They recognized that the squatters could become allies. Others saw them as a threat. In July 1975 the London *Evening News* disguised one of its reporters in 'tatty denims and beads' for a week's 'investigation' of selected squatting communities. Two full-page articles, headlined LIFE IN A LAYABOUT'S PARADISE and DROP-OUT'S MANSION, made perfunctory references in small print to 'many (who) are homeless families desperate for a roof over their heads', and then went to town describing in lurid detail 'the hippie squatters – layabouts, drug addicts, alcoholics, people on the run . . . and foreigners who can hardly believe their luck at getting a free stay in Britain'.

## Wreckers

The squatters whose life styles provided this kind of copy continued to be given the lion's share of the publicity, partly because like the 'Piccadilly squatters' they looked different from other people; partly because behind the scenes a powerful lobby was at work to get the laws on Trespass tightened up so that both domestic squatting and factory sit-ins could be penalized; and partly because there was evidence, produced by the GLC, that a few squatters here and there were capable of smashing up property for kicks.

There was also the behaviour – in the best Redbridge tradition – of what a *Sunday Times* leader (12 December 1976) called

THE COUNCIL VANDALS

The follies of local government have never been more exposed than in the saga of St Agnes Place, Lambeth. On Friday the Borough Council evicted a tenant of 30 years' standing – and then sent in workmen to wreck the houses so that no one else could live in them.

Altogether they will destroy 49 solid houses in which, for sums similar to the cost of demolition, they could rehouse some of the Borough's 17,000 homeless families. The planners' idea is to create open space in a congested borough, but they have not the money to turn St Agnes Place into parkland. They should have preserved the houses until they had: municipal vandalism is a sickening sight.

Such bloody-mindedness has to be understood before it can be cured. Local authorities have demolished old property and are finding now that there is not enough money to put up new buildings. The arguments in favour of rehabilitation that the family squatters put forward are becoming more and more relevant. Relevant but often unacceptable, for two reasons:

1. The behaviour of what the *Guardian* called 'the destructive minority' of squatters, and what Jim Radford called 'the wreckers', who are not prepared to weigh their own needs against those of others with an even greater claim. The 200 strong squatting community who defied the GLC in Elgin Avenue, Paddington, were themselves attacked by a hostile crowd of local people who accused them of jumping the housing queue.

2. Some officials and some elected members feel threatened because, thanks to the media, the best publicized squatters nowadays are those who no longer believe in the competence of local government, and who want to discredit it completely.

If local government is incompetent its failures should be exposed. But it also has resources of professional skill and experience which should be exploited.

The family squatting groups which have endured in spite of the 'wreckers' on both sides have shown that a combined operation with the professionals is workable and gets results. The power they generated is a political power – a renewal of people's confidence in their own ability to act together. The squatters went further than mere protest. They broke the news to the apathetic, the fearful, the criminally indifferent, that what should be done – could be done. Defeat was not inevitable:

We weren't looking for battles, we were looking for victories. We wanted agreement, we weren't people who were interested in forcing confrontations and conflict with the local authority. We were people who were interested in getting these houses brought into use, getting these families housed, and also politically very much interested in encouraging people to take decisions themselves, and begin to control their own affairs instead of going cap in hand from one official to another, saying 'Please sir, can you help me?' We wanted people to say 'This is the way in which I can help myself', and to be reasonable about it.

Squatters continue to make news, and the news provides leverage. Whether the leverage serves the interest of the homeless or of the absentee landlords depends partly on the squatters' motives, and partly on their skill in putting across what they do and why they do it. The possibilities they have tapped extend far beyond the housing field, as I hope to show in the chapters that follow. They publicized what needed to be done – by doing it. They were prepared to 'make trouble' in order to make sense.

# Chapter 6
# Shop Floor Level

All the groups described so far have been concerned with homes and neighbourhoods. Housing has been a live political issue since before World War II, and the politicians' failure to make good use of the resources available, coupled with the short-sighted greed of some 'comprehensive developers', has driven people to take the initiative themselves.

Jobs, just as much as homes, are everybody's concern, but while shortcomings were cushioned by the easy winnings of the boom years no one bothered much. Now that full employment has vanished and competition is keener, everybody is beginning to look critically at the use industry makes of its manpower and equipment. The Ryder Report on British Leyland described the demoralization and inefficiency which resulted when a top-heavy private enterprise dissipated its profits in dividends to shareholders and under-used the 'ideas, energy and enthusiasm' of its own workers.

Elsewhere in industry, as firms closed down, groups of employees moved in and attempted to take over. Here and there a factory under threat of closure was handed over with Government support. Before they fully realized what hit them, groups found themselves in charge, and expected to salvage the wreck.

On such terms, and in the short run, the odds are against success. But even at its worst the situation holds promise. Once an action group takes root, as Gibshill and Lewisham have shown, it can survive many setbacks. With luck it may be able to hold on, build up resources and acquire experience and, in the long run, win through.

The most promising thing is that in the quest for increased productivity, industry is being forced to change its life style: and the changes favour the formation of groups. There has been a change in production techniques from the robot routines which made Henry Ford a multi-millionaire. He reduced the job cycle – the time it took a worker to repeat a routine task – to seconds, which worked very well, for Ford, so long as the operatives knew no better. In later years when production line workers became restive their employers tried out the 'flower box approach' – background Muzak, attractive rest rooms, better working conditions, fatter wage packets. But these did not make good the damage done to the quality of the work and the staying-power of the workers by the old repetitive, undemanding routines. Industrial psychologists warned that shortened job cycles meant that 'work is drained of mental effort'. This was why vehicles left assembly lines riddled with faults, production was interrupted by absenteeism and go-slows, and employees seldom stayed long in a job if there was a chance to move on elsewhere.

Ironically it was two of Ford's competitors, Saab and Volvo, who broke with tradition by lengthening the job cycle. This made workers' jobs more demanding; and therefore, they found, more attractive. 'Job satisfaction' increased, and with the support of the Unions the idea was taken a stage further. Responsibility was handed over to groups of workers, planning their own operations, making their own quality control, being paid as a team. At the time that the Ryder Report was analysing the failure of traditional work patterns in British Leyland, and the 'frustrations caused by management decisions imposed remotely from above', Volvo's President was reporting that fewer workers wanted to leave their jobs, there was less absenteeism, fewer rejects and a higher quality of work: The reason?

People want to feel that they belong to a group, they must be able to communicate freely, feel identification with the product they produce and have some evidence of appreciation for the work carried out.

Volvo decided to spend 10 per cent above normal capital costs on its latest car factory, at Kalmar, in order 'to create the atmosphere of a small family workshop, combined with the large scale organization of a car factory'. Looked at from the employer's angle, investment in group work pays dividends.

Other employers in other industries have cautiously taken up the idea. How does it look to the shop floor groups who take part? As a start, consider one of the groups that I recorded in an electronics factory. The management had offered the workers in one shop the chance to form their own teams and organize their own production. Eighteen months later, with the idea spreading, the first group, five members strong, took stock.

They had been assigned one complete piece of equipment to assemble as a team, working out their own monthly production run, eventually designing their own jigs and blocks to streamline the work. They drew their own materials direct, without having to go first to a supervisor. They pooled their supply of personal hand tools. Each month they studied the reports of the Quality Check department, and if an item of equipment had been rejected they decided among themselves who or what was to blame, and how to get things right. They could discuss openly 'Was it just that we had an off day, or wasn't that particular person instructed properly?' They knew each other well enough to know who took the credit or the blame. The three who already knew their way around helped on the fourth who was only partly skilled.

When they wanted to expand, the four invited as a fifth member someone with very little relevant experience, and set about building him up until he could pull his weight. He had already been warned three times by his manager 'either take your finger out, or get out'. He says himself that the 'pressures' on him had got him down, so that by the time the team approached him he had half a mind to quit of his own accord. The manager told him 'Quite honestly it won't be me kicking your backside, you'll have four of them doing it.' But inside the team it wasn't like that at all. He drew his own materials and could follow his own pace.

No one says 'Where are you going?' 'What did you walk away from your bench for?' . . . It's easier in your mind, it's much easier.

Part of this freedom seemed to come from the way the group learned to size each other up, and to mesh in with each other; to get used to the mixture of contrasting personalities.

Oh well, they are all characters. I watch how I approach them. I won't say nothing to Vic until at least he's had a cup of coffee. And Dave, I approach him a bit tactful. I wouldn't go up to him and say 'Here I'm in trouble, come and sort this out.' I try to con him. 'Here Dave,' I says, 'didn't you used to do so and so?' 'Oh' he says, 'I'll come and show you.' And he'll come over. But if you say to him 'Oh, can you spare a minute?' he'll say 'No, I'm busy. Go and see someone else.' Oh yes, you have to con them like. I think by now they know that I am conning them some of the time, it's just a way to get them in like, you know.

Nobody wrote down, as part of the job specification, how each member of the team should learn to get round a person, or how best to keep off someone else's wick. Elsewhere on the shop floor it's true that individual workers get wise to the ways of the chargehand or the supervisor, and learn how to handle him so as to get through the day's work with the least trouble. But here the interaction between members of the group seems to be generating something much stronger: a change of attitude to the work and to each other.

You haven't got enough hours in the day, they're so busy showing you and you're so busy trying to get it right. Because you know that if you don't get your part right, the chap who's going to pick it up after you, he doesn't get it right either.

In the old days there's some things I've done, and I've thought 'Well, a pin sticking out, it's just a little bit, it won't make much difference.' At the time, putting it in, it doesn't; but when the next man has it, it turns round and catches at the side. So now I see why they want it flush. You take a bit more care.

Before, I used to get something and say 'Oh well, near enough.' But now I don't. I'd rather take the whole thing down again and put it right. Because I know the trouble we're going to have.

To begin with, the pioneer groups are a bit suspect to the other workers on the shop floor. Is it all a con by the management? Are the team members sucking up to the boss? Or making themselves out to be better than the rest of us? Top management also has misgivings and may begin to clamp down again. There are too many awkward questions: Will they get out of hand? What do we do with redundant supervisors? Will our methods of training have to be revised again?

There's the danger that having proved themselves on a job which makes the most of their abilities, a group gets landed for its next assignment with routine work which the management hasn't got around to redesigning. But the clock isn't easily put back. The mere presence of a group that has shown its mettle begins to have its effect on its surroundings. In spite of the misgivings, the idea seems to be catching on. Others want to get in on the act. Why?

When you're under a supervisor, you are just there to do your job, nothing more. You are more like a zombie, I feel. The work is put in front of you, it's just done and it's passed on . . . but if you are in a team you've got a joint concern . . . it's a form of partnership.

'Partnership': that's a slippery word much favoured by those who want to arrange a deal between capital and labour, splitting the profits and leaving the owner to manage all the assets as he chooses. But when this girl talks of 'partnership' she is not thinking about how to share the winnings. The group probably earns a bit more because the production figures are better; but partnership here means a share not so much in the takings as in the undertaking, the collective effort. The 'joint concern' she's talking about is the group itself; not a deal between employees and employers, but a collective enterprise whose members are on an equal footing.

If this is so, then we're not far off the point at which a group takes over something more than the responsibility for organizing its own bit of piece work assembly . . . when the group takes over the management.

It's clear that already this particular group has successfully taken over one key element in the manager's job. The fifth member of the group had been virtually written off by the official management. The group took him on, and learned to manage him as he learned to manage them. They could do this partly because, working closely together, they got the chance to understand each other properly; and partly because of their interdependence. Vic and Dave had more technical experience than the others: they were in one sense 'authorities' on how to cope with certain problems; but there was no hierarchy, no assertion of authority at someone else's expense. The group did not bear down on its members: it buoyed them up.

Of course such groups are very small, and management often prefers to think big. But the habit is on the way out; partly because giant firms are proving unmanageable, and partly because most people work in much smaller units. The most recent figures issued by the Department of Employment show that 71·9 per cent of all those employed in the United Kingdom are in firms of less than 500 employees. Most Managing Directors have no more people to be responsible for than has a primary school Head Teacher. Many have a great deal less.

Management certainly has to make decisions on market opportunities, cash flow, advances in technology. But managers are not necessarily specialists in these areas. It makes sense to get expert guidance from sales directors, accountants, research workers and technicians. Management itself consists in weighing up the advice the experts give, and relating it to people. From the gate man to the backroom boffin, people with a range of essential skills make up a living body. Management has to cultivate this organism so that it grows and adapts to the changes which the market, or the economy, or the technology impose.

On this scale, management cannot afford to operate by remote control. It has to see and be seen. But the more the manager mixes in with everybody else, the harder it is to keep up the traditional separation between those who make management decisions and those who carry them out. At close quarters both sides get wiser to each other's strengths and limitations. It becomes obvious that management decisions will be the better for some pooling of workers' ideas and experience beforehand. But how is this to be done? Traditionally, the choice has been what employers usually offer – 'consultation', and what workers have begun to demand – 'control'. Recently a third possibility has begun to take shape. A handful of firms have been trying to make two ideas complement each other. They have been quietly developing the concept of common ownership – not just a share-out of the takings, but a shared responsibility for what the company does. Control, based on the fact that the workers own the Company's assets; consultation through a series of committees extending up from the shop floor to Board level. They are also gradually discovering what else is needed to make the process of consultation and control effective.

The pioneer in common ownership is the firm of Scott Bader. Until 1951 it was a family business, and then its owner, Ernest Bader, decided he had made enough to be going on with. He began slowly handing over the assets and the control of his thriving plastics factory at Wollaston to the employees. He phased the handover so that at first he and then his son retained enough power to lay down the lines which the early development of the new firm should follow. Over the years a constitution has been developed. Beside the Company Board which is much the same as in most firms, there is now a Community Council and a Commonwealth Board of Management, each elected by people working in the firm. There are Trustees – some from outside, some elected from within – with no financial interest, who have the right to step in if ever the firm goes into the red. It has not done so yet. It was doing quite nicely, twenty-two years ago, with a turnover of £300,000. It's doing rather better nowadays, with a turnover of £2½ million.

In 1973 an independent study compared Scott Bader with the other giant chemical combines, such as ICI, privately owned and controlled, in the same field. With only 420 on its staff, it had, per employee, the highest return on capital, the highest sales, the highest average salary and the second highest profit of any firm, and this was for the lowest capital employed. In 1978 staff numbers were almost exactly the same, and staff turnover remains low. Not surprisingly customers at home and abroad, besides being eager to do business, want to find out how on earth the company manages to make its profits with so little fuss or conflict.

When I recorded the interviews for this section, the only major dispute anyone could remember had happened six months earlier. The Works Director had decided that the first shift after the Christmas holiday should start at 10.00 p.m. on New Year's Day. This particular shift wanted the start to be postponed until 6.00 a.m. the next morning (then it would be another shift's turn). So they challenged the ruling, and took it all the way up the line to the Chief Executive. The decision was still '10.00 p.m.', so it went to the Community Council as a dispute.

The Council heard out the shift representative and the Works Director, and spent hours discussing all the implications (many of the Council had never worked shift work). In the end they upheld the Director's ruling. The shift duly started at 10.00 p.m. and there were no absentees. The main comment by the factory at large, particularly the shift workers, was 'Why the hell did it take so long to reach that decision?' And there was one exchange during the marathon Community Council meeting: the Works Director said 'Of course, if your decision is opposite to mine, I will accept it.' And someone else said 'You bet your sweet life you will, you've got no choice.'

Once upon a time, the Community Council tended to be written off as a talking shop, spending most of its time on trivialities. But less so recently. This may be because, as one Councillor explained, the sixteen members met together in a two-day session to hammer out what the Council's role should be.

It was incredible, we had sixteen people there who initially appeared to have differing views. In the opening session, we went round in a half-circle and all had our little say. Then we tended to split up into groups, just at random, and then each group would say something, and we would shoot one group's ideas down, and they would shoot ours down. But eventually we realized that we were really all saying the same thing. And we were able to build up on this, and everybody put their own little bit into it. Eventually we had a collective agreement as to what we were there to do.

I think right from the early days the new Councillors were able to contribute much more than probably I did when I was first brought on the Council; because then we didn't have the benefits of this training session. You were a bit scared to open your mouth, because you were not tuned in. You didn't know what button to press for that bloke, and what is important to the other bloke. But this session helped the new people to feel that they were involved in the policy from the start, they got to know everybody and everybody knew them.

Previously there had been a lot of occasions when the Council had taken something up, and taken it so far; and then because it needed a nasty decision making, it tended to get dropped. We would put it on 'continuing Minutes', and bring it up every week for the next fifteen years.

We haven't done that. We have said 'We've got this problem and we're expected to do something about it', and gone through and sorted it right out.

The everyday decision-making still rests with the 'gaffer' at each level in the plant. Provided his decisions are good, nobody else need bother his head. If something goes wrong, then the rank-and-file are involved through their Councillors who act for them. And since the Constitution says that Councillors and Commonwealth Directors have to stand down every so often, sooner or later almost anyone can have a say in policy-making . . . if they choose.

Just how much do they choose to do? The Community Council has the last word if a dispute arises. It approves the Board of Directors (and elects two of them) and vets their salaries – currently no more than four times the rate after tax of the lowest paid in the factory. Management are in touch with workers at every level: formally at meetings of chargehands and workers, Plant Committees, Factory Committees; casually on the shop floor or in the canteen (there is no separate canteen for Directors).

Elections for the Board of Management which decides on admissions to Commonwealth membership, and acts as a public conscience of the company are keenly contested: something like an 85 per cent poll. But the membership of the Commonwealth, through which members have a hand in running the concern, is seldom more than two-thirds of those eligible. (Membership is not compulsory, but anyone can join after a short probationary period.) The remaining one-third never get around to joining. They are still consulted just as much as anyone else, but they don't seem inclined to get further involved.

The hierarchy remains. From chargehands via Plant Managers to the Directors, people are singled out to make decisions on everyone else's behalf, subject of course to the general approval. It's a good firm to work for; few want to leave it; most wish it well. The opportunity for consultation and control are there; but there's no great appetite for them. Like flour and water they are necessary ingredients in the mixture. But they don't make the dough rise.

The problem can be seen in close-up in a smaller firm, Landsman, which began making mobile industrial units, site offices and display units in the 1950s. In 1964 its original owner, David Spreckley, who had built up the firm from scratch to a staff of twenty-five making a modest, steady profit, decided to follow the Scott Bader example and gradually hand over to the workers. In the next ten years the turnover increased from £20,000 to a quarter of a million, which even allowing for inflation was good going. Between 1967 and 1975 (when I first made contact), while the national average wage increase was 72·9 per cent, Landsman's was 107·3 per cent. The staff had grown to 36, and 90 per cent turned up to elect their Works Committee and the Directors. Attitudes were changing, but slowly. It took several years before the workers really believed that the shares that were being handed to them were worth anything. It still hadn't dawned on some that David Spreckley no longer owned the firm. 'Yes', one said to me:

We're all in it together. The boss who owns it, we can talk straight to him whereas in other firms you never get talked to like this. We discuss things openly from the top to the bottom more than other firms might. We haven't got any big sticks on either side as far as I can see.

Spreckley pulled no punches about the function of the management.

One of the golden rules is: management must manage. So just as you don't interfere with a carpenter and tell him how to use his chisel and you don't interfere with a driver and tell him when to change gear going up hill, then you don't tell the manager how to make his day-to-day decisions as a manager. You can sack him if he doesn't do the job.

There was plenty of consultation. From the beginning Spreckley made it his business to keep everything in the open, to 'pour out information all the time', and to attend every Works Council meeting for the first fifteen or twenty minutes to report progress, and to answer questions. Then he left them to it. Afterwards he would learn, through their Minutes, what conclusions they had reached. Upwards of 60 per cent of their recommendations might get accepted. But the actual decisions continued to be made by the management: Foreman, Works Manager, Managing Director.

Control? Well, the Works Committee was elected by the workers, and its Chairman automatically became a Director. No one quite knew whether the Board of Directors could be unseated. So far, no one had wanted to find out.

Later, in 1975, David Spreckley decided to hand over the Managing Directorship to a newcomer, and to 'step sideways', continuing to work on design and to keep a general eye on the factory, but only working for the firm part-time. It seemed a good moment to go back and take stock. Every one of the shop-floor workers, from the Foreman down, talked freely to me about his work, his mates, the management, and his idea about what made the firm tick.

Nearly everyone went out of his way to say that on the whole he liked the set-up, and found the work worthwhile, even if the pay wasn't all that much to write home about. Part of the evidence for this was the fact that people stayed with the firm, or in some cases left and then came back again. The length of time already served averaged five years and no one talked about leaving.

'When I came here two and a half years ago I thought the chaps looked happier working than in other firms I'd been in. A slightly different atmosphere. That's still basically my opinion today.'

'Of course you can't compare this small factory with big industry. Here there is no dead wood, no dead wood at all. There's nobody walking round looking busy with a bit of paper in his hand all day, as there was in bigger places where I worked.'

'You can say anything. Anything you think is wrong, or you think they're not doing right, you can bring it up at the meetings and it's thrashed out. If it's a genuine grievance that they think they can put right, they do it. And if there's other ideas that would turn out the work quicker, then the idea is brought up at the meeting, discussed, and if it's a good idea they take it up and use it . . . It does get acted on, definitely. They've got a notice board and they put up all how the firm's doing, and you can get an overall picture of it.

'You base it on that, and if we're not doing too good at the moment and you want a new power hacksaw, then you don't stand much chance of getting it at the moment; but if we're doing pretty good and there's cash floating around, then they will take up the ideas and do them.'

Although people usually said they were reasonably happy, this certainly did not mean that they were contented with the way things were run. For some, the Works Committee Secretary, for instance, people showed a baffling reluctance to use the power that was on offer. It was still true, he reckoned, that 'you work harder than you would in industry outside' – because everyone's in it together and shares in the firm's success. But when it comes to deciding what should be done, by discussions at the AGM, and through representation on the Works Committee – 'the truth of the matter is that 75 per cent at least of the chaps are not really interested in the meetings. It's a good firm to work for, but they don't want to get too involved.'

Others spelt out the problem differently. It wasn't necessarily lack of interest, they said. The difficulty was to find a way of showing management what could be done in practical ways to improve production. You might be able to work out a better method for yourself alone or as a member of a two-man team. You could natter about it in twos and threes on the shop floor or at the tea break. But to bring it up at the AGM, or through the Works Committee, that's something else.

Somehow it's not put properly. You're not all there, on the job, saying this is what we're doing, this is how we'll make the frames up, this is how we'll sheet them out in metal, any suggestions for improving this? There's a thousand and one things if only you had the chance to put it forward.

On paper, and in fact, the chance existed. But people found it hard to do much about it.

It's basically because people are frightened to say things; although they would like things changed they are not able to speak up. I don't know what people are frightened of, it's difficult to say. You are frightened probably that it's going to go against the grain, management-wise. Myself, I'm a person that thinks a lot but is not able to say things. I'm able to say what I think now probably because I don't know you; you are a total stranger. But I find that when I'm in a crowd of people I'm not able to say really what I think.

Another worker said he didn't mind talking things out together, but he wanted to tie in the discussion with the work itself:

The lads in there all work differently, you see. Now you could do the work differently to me, and I might be quicker than you or your way might be quicker than mine. If we got together and discussed these ways of doing the job, then you could do my way, I could do yours; we could find out which was the quickest. I'm against all these meetings where everybody's got their grievance and they all try to get them in at once and nothing's smoothed out. But the work itself – several of us have thought about this. When the lads are together working, it comes up in conversation: it's being thought out, not just by me, not just the odd one; but it's being thought out right there – on the shop floor.

Once you moved away from the working and talking on the shop floor, he said, the situation changed. The traditional barriers began to go up:

Whatever's done has to be done sort of – formally. Although it's a co-ownership firm the final decision always seems to rest with David and the Directors.

You have an AGM, but I think the blokes are afraid to stand up and say things. You know it's like a group of ordinary working blokes who'll have a chat, and even when they're sort of directors the governor is still the governor.

The most hopeful sign was that very few were content to leave things as they were.

I made a survey on the factory floor and this is the general feeling: that there's this kind of barrier between the men on the floor and the management . . . But everyone is getting a lot more confident, especially the people that have been on the Works Committee. I think being on the Works Committee brings a lot of people out. I was very quiet, I still am; but I can speak to people more now, and I can speak to David more now. I can speak to him now as a person, not as a boss, this is the difference.

When I went back again a year and a half later, some of the barriers were just beginning to come down. The new Chairman of the Works Committee (who had been its Secretary in 1975) had got management along to two 'open meetings' on the shop floor, without formality and with no holds barred. He was now plugging away at the idea of 'an extended tea-break meeting', within reach of the hardware, at which it would be possible

to go through the job from beginning to end, and to really *use* all the years and years of experience that the chaps have got behind them.

Management had got as far as putting in a suggestion box for ideas on productivity. One shop floor worker was even invited for a stint in the drawing office to go through the designs and work out improvements. He found himself spelling out to them the kind of working drawings that people on the shop floor were used to reading through 'as easily as the management reads a balance sheet or a sales graph'. He came back again to the words he had hammered home when he first talked to me eighteen months earlier:

I think a very big thing is communication. It's more important than anything else, communication from Them to Us and from Us to Them. I'm not trying to belittle myself but we're working men and they are business men. They talk a different language: and when we go home, what we do and what they do – they're in an entirely different world. They've got to find a level that we can go up to and they can come down to, an in-between level. I think finding that level is important: and sticking to it.

To operate on that level requires something else besides conscientious committee-mongering. The Landsman worker with 'a thousand and one things to put forward' is not a particularly talkative character. He gets on with the job in hand. On the job it's possible to see where things are unsatisfactory, and to consider ways of improving them, without wasting words. A group clustered round the hardware can literally view the problem from all angles. Discussion can range as widely as on any more formal committee; but there is something visible and tangible to latch on to, which is within everyone's reach. Just as happened in Pimlico and Gibshill and Lewisham, when people on the shop floor get the chance to *show* what they mean, as well as talk about it, they begin to reveal capacities which traditional management did not believe they possessed. They can teach managers part of their job. Come to that, they can make many of the decisions about their own work which management was accustomed to do.

They certainly can do these things; whether they will depends on something else again. It is not enough to establish a 'level of communication'. You can create a common language and still find the doers holding back from deciding what should be done. The mere exchange of views and information may add up to 'participation'; it doesn't amount to commitment. Commitment is an alloy precipitated by shared experience. Its strength rests partly on the fact that everyone recognizes the force of the decisions reached because they had a hand in hammering them out together.

This notion sounds absurd to many professionals because it seems to discount their special knowledge and skill and put them on a par with the man who sweeps up the swarf from the shop floor. It makes sense, however, once you start thinking of the process through which experience and objectives are shared. A firm, like a community, starts off as a mixture of diverse talents and backgrounds. So long as it remains inert the ingredients stay separate. The moment the process of inter-action begins, the situation changes. The mixture becomes a compound with new properties – and a new structure.

It can be a process as traumatic as childbirth . . .

# Chapter 7
# A Share In the Management

We became something different. A separate entity, acting completely on our own without somebody to tell us what to do or how to act. Maybe we didn't have enough time to learn in the early stages . . .

Nancy McGrath had worked her way up to being in charge of fifty-nine women making uppers for leather shoes in a small satellite factory in the town of Fakenham in Norfolk, when in 1972 the Directors of the parent company in Norwich decided that the Fakenham enterprise was uneconomic, and announced that it would close down.

There were two Unions involved and after intensive negotiation they reported back to the assembled women that the firm would not change its mind. There was nothing else to do, they said, but shut the door and get out.

Since jobs for women in Fakenham were scarce, this advice was not well received. The meeting more or less blew up, with Nancy McGrath as the detonator. She and two others said they were going to occupy the premises and bed down on the shop floor. Seventeen more said they would join in, but next day second thoughts, coupled with the advice of husbands not to get mixed up in such unconventional activity, reduced the total work force to ten. The sitters-in remained undaunted.

We settled down to listen to the pigeons in the joists in the loft. We saw those pigeons through from being tiny babies until they flew out of the window and went. I don't know if I could ever go through with it again, looking up at this horrible decrepit, dusty, grubby place and visualizing my lovely warm bed . . . I used to get cold feet a little bit.

The slump in the shoe trade continued. As a branch of the Norwich firm Fakenham had been required to specialize. On their own, they lacked the skills and the equipment to go into full-scale shoe production.

93

We used to sit very late at night trying to decide what we could do next day: what we could make from the remnants of material that we had and how best to sell them. One of the first decisions was to make twelve little shoulder bags. We only had scraps of material, none very big, so we made patchworks with them, cut them up in various little patterns, diamonds, squares, strips, what have you. We made twelve bags which we sold for £12 and that was a fortune to us because it bought us £12 worth of material to use. We made mini skirts after that and we sold some of those from a stall the Council let us have in the market . . . We got a greater stock of leather in, and then Eileen suddenly said 'I know what we can do, we can make coats without sleeves and I know where they would sell'; so we made maxi-coats. And we made a man's jacket and showed a specimen at the college, and they came back with five orders.

To begin with, each member of the group knew only what she was accustomed to do. She had to be convinced that she could make a go of anything else. This conviction was partly built up by each day's experience of improvising answers to crises. And partly it was a matter of generating an atmosphere in which people knew each other well enough to say what needed to be said.

*Nora Brown:*

I think it is knowing who you work with; you know what you can say to certain people and what you can't say to other people . . . we have to be outspoken and frank with people more.

We all know what we can do to an extent, so we see someone doing something and say 'Oh you do that nice, you do that better than I could do.'

If you get a job you haven't done before, you think to yourself 'What sort of job am I going to make of this?'

At the end of it perhaps you don't think you've done a very good job. You ask other people their opinion. I'd rather hear their opinion even if they say it isn't very good. So I give it to someone who can do it better, or go to Nancy and say 'Do you think so-and-so would make a better job of it?' and if she says 'Yes', I'll take on another job. Or if she says 'Well, try and see if you can get it better' I sit down and try again.

In the old days, the whole of the administrative and sales structure of the firm was centred in Norwich. Until they took over control the Fakenham ladies simply fulfilled production requirements which were decided, budgeted, and marketed by 'the office' at headquarters.

The only office in the Fakenham factory was the cubicle in which Nancy McGrath filed delivery notes and answered the phone, in between going her rounds to check on quality and deal with technical problems as they arose. She had made a habit of sharing in the routine work herself whenever she could, so that she was able to take over someone else's work if they had to be away coping with family illness.

She continued much as before, although the phone rang much more often – initially with queries from Press and broadcasting and from sympathizers in the industry; later with inquiries about orders and prices.

Costing was a headache. At first they turned to outsiders to work things out; then they decided to set up their own system, and be self-sufficient. A sympathetic Business Studies department in a nearby College gave one of the ladies a crash course.

*Nancy:*

It's one of the greatest stumbling blocks that I've had, trying to get people to realize that they are capable of doing things they have never done before. 'I can't do it, Nancy, I'm not good enough at figures', she'd say. It terrified her, and yet she can add up figures – like that – in her head.

As orders increased, and the enterprise began to look viable they got a £2,500 loan from the Scott Bader Commonwealth. With this they settled up with the former owners for the twenty industrial sewing machines they had taken over at the sit-in; and they bought enough new materials to branch out further. By April 1974 the firm was making headway. Scott Bader withdrew its two representatives on the Board of Directors that had been set up when it became a limited liability company, and let them get on with it.

Just as they were beginning to consolidate their achievement, the British economy took a sharp turn for the worse; the demand for good shoes and fancy leather work declined still further: orders dwindled. At the beginning of 1975 a financial adviser from outside the firm suggested that it was time to wind everything up. The Fakenham ladies thanked him for his advice and bowed him out.

They decided that rather than halve the work force they would take a wage cut, from £23 to £10. Several could have made more by going straight on to the dole. They continued to turn up for work, whether or not it was there; and when orders came in with a rush as happened sometimes, they worked longer hours to increase productivity without claiming overtime money or adopting piece rates.

*Susan Yallop:*

... We're women, perhaps we're daft enough; perhaps a man would not stand for it.

When conditions improved slightly, they reconsidered the situation and upped their pay.

*Molly Goff:*

... You have to make your own decisions, don't you? In a firm where everything is done for you, you have to take orders from Them all the time; but here we all decide and argue, we have it all out, don't we? I feel more decisive since I've been here, a lot more ... my husband always used to stand up and fight my battles for me, he don't any more.

He doesn't need to: decision-making does wonders for one's self-confidence.

*Susan Yallop:*

... to be quite honest I don't like starting a new job, I'm very shy I suppose. I didn't speak to anyone for at least two months when I came here ... I must admit I've changed since. I'm not as shy as I used to be. I speak my mind now. I'd let anybody walk over me once, but not any more. I stand up for myself a bit more now you see ... even my husband knows the difference, since I've been here.

Everyone has become used to talking things out on the spot. Ideas for products were hatched out in small groups of two and three who happened to be working near each other.

Grievances could be voiced just as easily, though to begin with the very shy ones would leave it to someone more outspoken to tell Nancy, or to voice it at a meeting. The meetings happened as the need arose, without formality.

*Nancy:*

We had an awful lot of meetings, far too many in fact. But when I think back on it I call it group therapy because that's what it used to work out like. Anybody who had a grievance just shouted it out ... People got feelings out of themselves, feelings which in the normal course of events they couldn't have expressed. They'd hurl accusations at each other ...

*Susan Dagless:*

We've all walked out in a huff once or twice . . . When we used to have to work nights, you know, we were that tired for the next morning. You were worn out and you knew you'd got to start all over again and go through again until 8 or 10 p.m. I think your temper just got a bit frayed some days.

*Nancy:*

. . . People would get very mad and very angry. But out of such things, you start to think: 'Was there any truth in what she said, and was I really being a so-and-so, and what am I going to do about it?'

Maybe we just decided that time that we needed chips and chicken, and somebody would go down and buy several lots, and we'd sit and eat and have a cup of tea and a smoke and we'd feel better after that. And somewhere through that conversation we would decide on things.

If the history of the Fakenham ladies is stormy at times, this is because the group has ventured across the division between management and workers and has been forced to reach joint decisions – to develop skills they did not possess before, to evolve new routines, to lay themselves off or to cut back their own earnings, in order to weather the economic blizzard.

None of these decisions was reached easily. The whole enterprise started from scratch. They had to improvise an administration and a marketing policy as they went along. They could never afford to sit back on their assets and wait to see what the market would do. They had to put up with the consequences of bad decisions and make new ones under tension, in the face of more frustration when customers or suppliers let them down.

*Nancy:*

Pat and I had a row one day. I said can you hurry it up or something. There was pressure to get some work out. I probably picked the wrong time and she stormed out swearing. I said 'Well if you go this time Pat I'm not coming after you . . .'

*Q:*

What made you come back?

*Pat:*

Well, I got another job, but I kept wondering about what they were doing here. You keep wondering how they are getting on, you're sort of part of it. You get so involved you have to come back to help.

*Susan:*

After four years you just tend to worry about the place, I don't know why but you do.

After four years, Fakenham Enterprises was still in vigorous operation, with a staff of twenty; making shoes, handbags, rally jackets, anything involving craftsmanship in leather that could bring in orders. But at the beginning of 1976, as the economic ice age began to hasten the death of older establishments, and to nip many smaller enterprises in the bud, no one had any illusions about what lay ahead.

*Nancy:*

The situation for the present is to keep the contracts coming in; and try and develop our own little items in a small way . . . I don't think we could say with any degree of certainty that we'll be here a year from now because the market could suddenly float out of the window.


## Survival Policies

During the year two of their three best customers went into liquidation, and the third firm was crippled by a fire. Despite this 'series of traumatic experiences' as Nancy puts it, they kept in production. By the beginning of 1977 their full-time strength was down to eight. They still hung on. They negotiated a support grant under the Manpower Services Commission's job creation scheme, recruited their own company secretary, general manager, and sales representative, took back most of the staff they had lost, and some others as well. Having survived their first five years they still believed they had a future.

*Q:*

What is your survival policy?

*Molly:*

Determination. Determination and sacrifice, unless you've got those qualities it's no use working here in the first place.

*Q:*

Where does that come from?

*Susan:*

Well, it comes from everybody, don't it?

*Molly:*

It has to. Everybody feels that now we've got this far – and many people outside, they say 'You still keep going?' hoping that you've gone down – and I think you get so determined you think 'I'll show them' and you take on more.

In the end they were defeated by some of their customers' bad debts. They could not keep enough in the kitty to pay the rent and the rates on their premises while they waited for the money to come back on the sales of their products. So the landlord (who also had to make ends meet) turned them out and let the premises to someone else. In August 1977 their remaining stocks of materials were auctioned off to raise £300 owing in rates to the North Norfolk Council.

The Fakenham ladies had the worst of luck in their outside circumstances – inflation, recession, a base far off the beaten track, no satisfactory distribution system. They kept their enterprise alive and kicking five years after it had been written off, because as a group they were totally committed – in the sense of not giving up and not letting each other down. They were swimming against the economic tide, and they had to go all out, all the time, in order to move at all. No one could take a breathing space and make long-term plans. No one; Nancy least of all. Her personality had triggered off the sit-in; her previous experience as Forewoman kept the shop floor work running. But beyond that, when it came to the kind of strategic decisions that managers are expected to make, it was the feeling of the meeting – the gut feeling – which finally determined what should be done. We're all in it together: sink or swim.

## Management Under Pressure

Now compare the 'management styles' that were evolving in a very different kind of firm. You could hardly find a sharper contrast, on the surface, than between the bare boards and rough ways of the Fakenham workshop, and the highly polished, meticulously clean, beautifully appointed premises of Michael Jones, Jewellers, of Northampton. Until 1969 it had been a small, well-established, up-market family firm. Then its owners decided to follow the example of Landsman and Scott Bader and go over to common ownership. Between 1970, when the change took effect, and 1976, the firm more than doubled in size. In 1976, when these interviews were recorded, they had just launched a second shop, in the big new Civic Shopping Centre. It was to begin as a 'daughter' unit, and as it gradually became autonomous would become a 'sister'.

What emerged from many hours of recording was the different ways in the same firm, that a manager could interpret the role of 'big brother'. Any manager, anywhere, is expected to have a bird's-eye view of what goes on, and to keep a close watch on the firm's, or the department's, productivity, and the way each individual contributes to it. The brisk expansion of the company had attracted a young staff, full of zest, capable of learning fast, with a lively interest in the general idea of common ownership. At its head was the Managing Director and a few highly skilled and experienced colleagues, all young as such firms go.

Early in 1976 they were facing the fact that the recent VAT increase from 10 per cent to 25 per cent had begun to knock sales. If the firm was to prosper it would have to watch every penny, and might have to cut back on staff.

## The Sales Team

Each departmental manager was on his mettle, most of all probably the manager of the 'daughter' shop, who had been twelve years with the firm and was now shaping up a team of people who were mostly in their late teens and early twenties. His problem, he told me, was to get across to them his concern about sales, profitability, systems of organizing the shop. He felt that he was talking too much at their weekly meeting, but he couldn't, somehow, get them to contribute their own ideas or show any interest in his. Everyone there seemed

shy ... They were afraid they might sound silly ... They possibly think of the management – this would be myself – as something different. This probably tends to put them off their stroke, and they think twice about saying what they wanted to say.

What they had wanted to get across to him, it emerged, was:
(a) that one of their number was not really pulling his weight;
(b) that the emphasis upon individual, competitive, sales performance – coupled with the fact that another member of the

team had talked back once too often to the Managing Director and got the sack – was making the atmosphere in the department counter-productive.

They told me how they had gone about the problem (a):

So it got to the stage where this person carried on doing it, having a week off here, there and everywhere, saying they were ill; and we started to talk between ourselves.

Apart from the manager and the person who was concerned, the rest of the community was very close knit, we felt that because it was a community everybody has got to help everyone else and do a fair share. We all had the same view and we all wanted something to be done about it but we didn't want it doing the wrong way, because we all liked the person concerned, it was just what they were doing that really aggravated us. So we decided that one of us should tell the manager, and he was very surprised, he hadn't seen through it . . . The result was that he gave the person a very strict warning if they didn't improve within three weeks they would probably get the push. Well, they're still here and they have improved a lot.

Problem (b) was still being worked on. Someone should speak out, and bring things into the open. But who, and how, was still being argued about:

'Well I think it is going to gradually get to this point where everyone is having a good old moan about it. And then there will probably be a lot of discussion, in the shop, tittle-tattling round to one another when there is a few minutes, and in the lunch break up here. Then probably we will decide something ought to be said. Then probably someone will be asked to go and say it.'

'I felt here that I have cared more because I have felt more of a group. At the other shop there were so many of us I tended to sit back and let everybody else do the talking. I am one of those people who tend to shy away from arguments or strong discussions . . . But I think we must sit down and examine all the points that we have noticed and thrash them out between us, in the whole group together. I think it is the only way to do it. It is something that affects us all and therefore we should all talk about it together. I am seriously thinking of saying something like that myself, taking the lead and seeing what happens. I think the stage has come now when it is going to do more damage to keep quiet than to speak up . . . I think this year it will start getting better because I think things will start to be said soon, and it will really come out into the open.'

So gradually and sometimes painfully, this particular department was working its way towards a management style of its own, and a 'level of communication' at which the manager's own special knowledge and experience could be accepted, and used.

Now compare this with another, much smaller, department in the same firm where the manager has had the advantage of playing himself in, over the years, with more time to evolve his own particular management style.


## The Repair Team

Philip started out in the watch repair workshop as one of three apprentices. Each had to fill in a Day Sheet to record his output and profitability. There was an industrial target to meet throughout the year, and a quality check through individual feed-back of customers' returns. He found all this

far too competitive, and a bit sneaky all the time because you get some jobs paying more, nice quick easy watches to do; whereas there are some rather tricky ones that still pay the same money. So there was a bit of a do each day, trying to grab the best work.

After he qualified, the others in the department transferred and he spent two years handling all the watch repairs on his own, happily working out his own systems of tackling the work, and competing with no one apart from himself and his previous year's figures.

Then as the company began to expand, more apprentices were taken on, with Philip as their manager. He was able to build gradually, beginning with the first recruit.

I decided when Des came that it would be just silly starting off this competitive thing again. It wouldn't make him any better, it would make him worse; it wouldn't make him willing to do things like sweep the floor for instance, which has to be done. We all have to do bits like this, but when you are losing money because you could be doing a watch job, you don't want to do these messy jobs. So we decided that we would work as a team, that we would help each other. I got Des to do work for me that he could do, like stripping down watches and I would do the hard bit and he would be learning as well. In the next three years we had an apprentice each year because the work was going up. We were getting more work in and we planned on expansion in the firm so we would be needing watch makers in other shops in five years' time, that was the general idea. When we had got three of us we began working even more as a team; and four even more of a team than we were with three. We were doing each other's jobs, helping each other out . . .

I have a monthly meeting with our Managing Director and we have a budget and we have to pay our way. You have to allow for renting and lighting, it is all down in a book here. So we have to be economically viable for a start. We have targets that have got to be done. We all know, even down to Nicholas here: he knows what we have got to do. He knows the nuts and bolts of the workshop economy so to speak, just as Des and I do. We work together on this particular thing as well.

*Nick:*

It took a couple of months for me to realize how everything worked. We booked our money out and we were allowed so much that we should make. You realize that if you don't get the jobs done, booked out, you don't make the money. If you are not doing the job then there is something wrong.

*Philip:*

As a week goes past we post up our output, that is how much money we have booked out; and every fourth week, we add it all up: how many jobs we had coming in to us to be done and how many returns we get and what the percentage is and how much money we had spent on material to our suppliers. Then at the monthly meeting we discuss it. We have other figures here to see what we were doing last year for comparison, and how far up on target or below target. We have no individual figures, they are team figures and if the team figures are right that is what we are on about.

We all have ideas of how we can perhaps get things better, right down to the youngest apprentice, because he can offer really constructive ideas on how we can run the thing. Sometimes he will make some bad ones, but we don't mind that as long as he comes up with one good one occasionally, which does tend to happen.

As a team we can be constructive because we can come up with an idea and think of how we are going to do it and it instantly appears to everybody and we throw it around, and come across decisions as a team.

## Pub Think Tank

The ideas crop up all the time, but the decisions are reached in the monthly meeting. A rather special kind of meeting.

*Philip:*

We like to get out of the building, free from interruptions. Basically, as craftsmen, we are not very . . . articulate is probably the right word. A salesman would think with his head and it would come out through his mouth; we tend to think with our head and it comes out through our hands, if you see what I mean. So we sometimes find it difficult to get out what we feel.

So at this meeting, at my house, we have a meal, which gets us nice and relaxed and then we start talking about the business of how we can get things better and reporting on how we are doing. Then after we have done that, we wouldn't go away, like after a conventional meeting and think 'Oh damn we didn't bring this up, we didn't bring that up.' We go down the pub then and have a game of skittles or something, but we are still talking, and we are all still there and we can say 'That was a load of rubbish really because it won't work' and then we amend it. It is probably not a very conventional way of doing things, but it is the way we found tends to work. We write the Minutes before we go down the pub, roughly. Des is the scribe, and he will amend them if we come up with another idea.

*Des:*

Yes, I make a note at the time, and then do them again.

Back on the job the pressure of work is as great as in the rest of the company. Disagreements arise, but when they do –

*Des:*

We work on it sensibly.

*Q:*

How?

*Des:*

Well, I will give you a particular instance. Three of us have the whole month off in May to do our exams and obviously we have to make sure that the work flow is there. So we decided to come in on the two Saturdays beforehand (one of which we owed the firm anyway). I am a football fan, and it just so happened that the football cup final fell on the Saturday before and I came in and said to Philip 'Look, it is cup final May the first, will it be all right if I have the Saturday off?' and he said 'If the work is OK but if there is a lot of work you can't really have it.' I said 'Well, it is my day off and I would really like to have it' and we had a bit of a bust up over it because he wanted me to come in and I was saying I would rather not.

In the end we both sort of forgot about it for half an hour or so. Then I said to Philip 'Well, will it be all right if I come in early, work through my dinner hour and leave half past two?' and he said 'Well, you can do that if you like or you can come in early one or two mornings in the week' and I said that was fine. Whereas in other parts of the firm they would argue about it, I wanted to try and find a reasonable solution, not just go away and think 'Oh, he's stupid.' We'd had a heated discussion at 9 o'clock, and by 10.30 tea break we were happy and talking about motorcars and motorbikes again.

It is because we know we have got to work together we don't upset each other, and if we do we tend to laugh and joke about it afterwards. If I tell Nick off or Philip tells Nick off we will laugh about it afterwards. It is that atmosphere.

In other places you can imagine them being the sort of people that when they leave here they don't forget about their work, they go home and talk to their wives about it or their husbands; whereas when every one of us leaves here we have forgotten about work. We think any problems we will sort out here, and if it is not worth sorting out here it is not worth worrying about. It works.

Although Philip is in charge, there are no separate levels in here. If the three of us are working and it has got to 10.30 and Philip is just doing a bit of writing, we will say 'Are you going to make the tea?' and he will say 'Yes, I'll go and make the tea'; and he doesn't think it is lowering himself; whereas in the shop if you had got a manager and one or two of the staff, the youngest one would do it; up here we don't, it makes no difference. I scrub the floors once a week because we feel that we should do it ourselves in here. I don't really feel that I have been lowered that I should do it; and I am the second oldest here.

I think team work works but it can only work in this sort of atmosphere. So therefore in here we are more common-ownership-minded for the reason that we understand why it is good for us. We work in this atmosphere because we learn more from each other. I can learn from someone younger than me by the way they do things whereas in another firm I wouldn't; they would have to learn from me and they would only have to learn what I taught them.

The watch repair group that Philip runs knows exactly what it is doing in terms of productivity, and profit, and work design; and it learns from all its members' experience. But it is not a collective in which everyone has an equal voice. Nothing it does discounts the superior skill and judgement of its manager. He still has the last word. He is still answerable for his department to the rest of the company. Philip may not be on 'a separate level', but he is still in charge.

I chose these three examples of 'shared' management – Fakenham, the jewellers' shop, and the watch repairs team –

because the problem each came up against is the problem that most groups encounter sooner or later: how do you make effective use of the different levels of skill and experience that the group possesses? Must you arrange them as a hierarchy, with the decision-making reserved for the person on the top step, and people lower down taking much less interest because there's so little of what is going on that they can see?

The Fakenham ladies were all on the ground floor together, but they recognized that Nancy McGrath had more experience – on most issues – than anyone else. In the last two examples both departmental managers were expected to tackle the more difficult jobs – the awkward customers, the trickier watch repairs – as the need arose. This experience is the manager's chief qualification to take decisions and to give the lead. But the experience is not all on one side. The manager knows his trade, and has a working knowledge of the capacities and the performance of each individual member of his staff; but the rest of the group also have their collective experience of the manager, shared and compared at the tea break or in the loo. And they have other knowledge besides, to which the manager may not have easy access: the tastes of the customers, the best ways particular members of a team can partner each other. On the other side there is information which comes down to the manager from head office, which must be considered in any decisions that are taken. Does it stop with him, or does he pass it on so that everyone is in the picture? How does he reach and implement decisions? Does he say 'Take it from me, I know' or 'Here's what I know, what can you add to it? And what do we make of it between us?'

# Chapter 8
# From Rehab. to New Build

The full Committee of the Pooles Park Neighbourhood Co-operative just fits into the front room of a terraced house in Islington. It is a multi-racial group and at the first meeting I attended there were a skip-lorry driver, a welder, a post office sorter, a storesman, a housemother, a young teacher, a children's careworker, an office worker and a small builder. Like the Winstanley Committee, a mixture of people left high and dry in a 'stress' area, they are tackling similar problems – sorting out quarrels, raising funds, running socials, caring for people in trouble, keeping an eye on the youngsters. But when it comes to matters like overdue repairs or building delays there's a difference. At Winstanley, Chairman Ted Trayfoot buttonholes a Council official and persuades him to prod the defaulting firm, but at Pooles Park they see things through from start to finish. The defaulter is summoned before the Committee and dealt with face to face.

The meeting started as soon as everyone had snatched supper after getting home from work; it finished only just in time to get to the pub. A packed Agenda bristled with issues to be decided – not one was dodged or deferred. They began by interviewing the head of a small firm of architects. Several such firms were already working for the Co-operative, rehabilitating different properties leased from the Greater London Council. Now they were selecting others to help cope with the flow of new work. For nearly an hour they went over the firm's track record, explained the kind of work they wanted done, the way the firm would take its orders from the Committee and the deadlines it would have to meet. The interview ended with Committee members fixing up to visit some of the firm's ex-customers to check for themselves the standard of the work done and to hear what the customers thought about the way it had been tackled.

Next item: to interview the representative of one of the firms already under contract to the Co-op. He was told crisply that three house conversions were behind agreed deadlines. Would he kindly tell his boss that if the work was not completed by the end of the month the contract would not be renewed. Next item: to report that £11,000 had been received that morning from the Council, and to approve various payments as planned. Next item: allocation of flats now ready for occupation. Next item: development proposals as previously circulated . . . And so on.

## Community Management

How do you classify this organization? A production unit, marketing new homes for old? A voluntary welfare group, improving the neighbourhood? It is both these things. Action groups like this mean business, and the business they are in is community management. They have leverage and bargaining power because they have found out how to blend their local knowledge and experience with the skills of the professionals. A group which shows its mettle soon attracts professionals, particularly younger ones, either as employees or on loan from bodies like Shelter and Inter-Action, which themselves attract people who enjoy helping good ideas to take root and flourish. The Pooles Park Committee has a young architectural adviser on loan from a Housing Association, and three young staff (one full-time, two part-time) to deal with the paper work and keep in daily touch with tenants and contractors. Their experts are on tap, but not on top.

Pooles Park, like the other housing co-operatives springing up in the inner cities, is a natural development from the Us and Them confrontations that the family squatting movement brought about in the sixties. Among the professionals on the opposite side there were some, like Councillor Eames in Lewisham, who could be won at least half-way over. This seemed to be because their first loyalty was to the work needing to be done rather than to the institution supposed to be doing it. If an action group showed its own professionalism by doing some of that work better, or sooner, it could make terms for a takeover. What happened in Lewisham was that the Council split off a fragment of its own management responsibilities and handed it across, with

108

the necessary technical back-up, for the group to tackle in its own way. It ceded a small piece of territory and withdrew. It is stretching the words to call this a 'combined operation' – the management was divided not shared – but it helped breach barriers which fenced officials in. As the idea caught on, housing officials began to realize that 'They' – tenants and squatters – were capable of more than just moaning about the housing shortage; they could actually take the initiative in creating homes; so perhaps it is up to Us, as part of our jobs, to back Them up.

Slowly a new political idea is taking shape. Once if you wanted to get something done 'in the public domain', where central or local government was responsible, the only answer was to coax or bludgeon the authorities into using their powers and their resources to do it their way. Now, it seems, there is an alternative. You can switch the points. The action group takes the initiative, decides the priorities, and then draws on the same powers and some of the same resources, to get things done pretty much in its own way. Technically it is acting on behalf of the authorities, but it uses its local knowledge and local talent to dovetail the job to local needs and preferences.

Some of these powers were already there for the taking in the 1969 Housing Act. Then, late in 1974 the Government set up the Campbell Working Party on Housing Co-operatives. In 1975 its key recommendations were embodied in the new Housing Act. Schedule 1:9 of the Act made it possible for a housing authority to transfer responsibility, powers, and revenue to a recognized tenants' group. Soon afterwards the Department of the Environment began to encourage local housing authorities and New Town corporations to 'sound out tenants' about the possibility of transferring the housing management functions of the local authority to tenants who set up their own co-operatives. Circular 8/76 suggested a transfer of power, step by step, without either party being obliged to go any further than it wished to go:

(*a*) responsibility for upkeep of common areas, community centre, etc; enforcement of tenancy conditions which affect relations between members – e.g. concerning pets and car parking;

(*b*) caretaking/warden service; minor repairs and maintenance; rent collection;

(c) tenant allocations;

(d) fixing tenancy conditions;

(e) large-scale maintenance work;

(f) fixing rent levels;

(g) improvement and conversion of dwellings and the development and improvement of amenities.

At first the group could function as a 'management co-operative', with the Council still owning the property, but handing over the money the group needed to improve the estate and see to routine maintenance and repairs. But the deal need not be limited to this. If both parties agree, the tenants could negotiate a long lease, or even acquire the whole property.

In November 1976 one small but important step was taken towards the transfer of power within industry. The Industrial Common Ownership Act eased the way for a private firm to convert itself into a co-operative enterprise (ownership, membership and voting rights limited to workers actually employed), or for a common-ownership group to set up for itself. The new company could borrow money and with luck get grants for development. This Act put industrial co-operatives on the map at a time when politicians were waking up, left, right and centre, to the importance of 'small firms' and the eleven million workers they employed. Since then, rocketing unemployment figures have forced more and more government money into small-scale job-creation projects. Increasing anxiety about the stagnation of inner city areas has produced the Inner Urban Areas Act, designed to build up resources of each neighbourhood including the development of many small industrial units, in 'stress areas'. Quite suddenly the arguments for devolution – local initiative, local responsibility – have become politically powerful.

It is easy to talk about handing over responsibility. To whom? To many people, or to just a few? In industry, for instance, the argument gets bogged down over the question of representation. The Bullock Committee was set up by Government to consider 'a radical extension of industrial democracy in the control of companies by means of representation on boards of directors'. Early in 1977 it recommended that workers should elect their own worker-directors to each company Board. There they would share in the decision-making with others who represented the

110

company's owners (the shareholders) and some independent outsiders thrown in to leaven the lump. The fierce arguments that followed were mostly about the election of worker-directors: What say should the Unions have? Should the workers' representatives be only a minority on the Board? No one said much about the relationship between the Board – whoever was elected to it – and the rest of the firm. Simply to concentrate responsibility within the Boardroom – or even within the Works Council – leaves Us and Them as far apart as ever. The few who make the decisions are isolated; the many who merely hear about what's done on their behalf feel left out.

It is just as easy for a housing management co-operative to take the same wrong turn. It accepts a bunch of responsibilities from the Council and is then persuaded to hand them over, still on the key-ring, to a 'management agency', such as a Housing Association, which charges a modest fee and takes over 'the day-to-day responsibilities'. On paper there is an imposing system of democratic control: the tenants elect their own Management Committee which banks the money handed over by the Council, and signs the cheques. In theory the Committee controls everything; in practice there's nothing left for anyone to do; no pooling of the community's skills and experience and local knowledge. Before long the management agency is behaving like local authority bureaucrats, the Committee is being written off as a Council talking-shop, and the rank-and-file are being told, kindly but firmly, 'The experts know best: it doesn't do to interfere: leave it with Us.'

Some Committees go the opposite way, with even worse results. They take all the responsibility to themselves, closeted for long hours in private session. The rest of the group wait with dwindling enthusiasm for months, even a year, while the Committee discusses the Constitution article by article with the Registrar of Friendly Societies, negotiates a water-tight Management Agreement with the Council or with a local Housing Association, and then proceeds to draw up the rules for the Tenancy Agreement. But by this stage they may find the tenants ill-disposed to agree on anything very much, because they no longer really care.

In contrast, a group like Pooles Park succeeds because the whole membership shares in the management. The Pooles Park Committee meets every other week, in order to carry out what the whole group decides at its General Meeting; and the General

Meeting takes place not once a year, but in each alternate week. Such meetings need not be talking-shops, any more than those which Wanda Tamakloe described. The work that everyone is busily chatting about is not monopolized by a Committee of 'Them'. (Indeed some groups deliberately make the whole membership 'the Committee' in order to avoid such barriers.) There may be a few officers to keep Minutes, do the accounting, make official contacts; but they have the sense to see that the group's strength depends on delegating jobs, with the job-satisfaction that goes with them. At first this may involve no more than running playgroups, arranging sports fixtures, improving garden space, fund-raising, adapting premises for a social centre; but through these activities the group gets to know itself, and things happen. As one member of a South London co-operative said:

> For the first time we're on an estate where we really know each other. My wife is normally so shy, she'd go to a holiday camp and the first thing she'd say to anyone is 'Good-bye' when we leave. On the last estate during two or three years we got on greeting terms with two or three families at most. Here we know everyone, almost from the beginning. We're talking together, and getting things done.

The things that get done are not merely social frills. A group which starts out to work among the whole membership soon recognizes its priorities. It goes to the roots of vandalism and sets up facilities which adventurous teenagers can manage themselves and which give them the opportunity to share responsibility for younger ones (as happened at Gibshill). If there's nowhere to meet the action group scours the district in search of premises and badgers the Council for a Compulsory Purchase Order. If the houses or the flats it has taken over are shoddily built and need repair, it hammers the architect and the building contractor. An outside body, such as the Council Housing Department or the Housing Association, which parries with 'Leave it with us' may find it has a fight on its hands, and could end up with its management contract revised under threat of a rent strike.

On the shop floor, just as on a housing estate, the nearer the decision-making is to ground level, the more likely it is that people will commit themselves and keep up the momentum. A Lancashire factory had an energetic personnel officer who talked sense and was understood equally well by the Managing Director of the Group and by the workers on the production line. Neither side thought of her as 'one of Them': she saw herself as an interpreter. She tossed around the idea of work-sharing and decision-making, got a shop floor group together, and bulldozed the management into giving them a chance to prove themselves. Soon there were several groups, and the idea spread to some of the feeder factories in the area. When the first group had trouble with their raw materials they phoned their opposite number in the feeder factory, by-passing both managements, and sorted out the problem between them. It happened so quickly and so naturally that the personnel officer had a job to smooth down ruffled feathers. The top management became anxious, and after a diplomatic pause began to play down the whole idea. But the groups continued to thrive, though they had little cash incentive to work in this fashion. They had got the habit of taking the initiative and meeting problems half-way.

A conventional employer might find in such circumstances that he had got more than he bargained for; there have been other firms where having basked in the favourable publicity attracted by 'worker participation', the owners have attempted, as unobtrusively as possible, to wind things down. But the experience cannot be erased. The workers within the firm may lack the muscle to hold their employer to the new pattern. But some may bide their time until they are good and ready and the market is right; then withdraw their labour and their technical know-how to set up on their own. Yesterday such a move would have seemed futile; today it is risky. Tomorrow the bigger firms may find themselves so enmeshed in their own mass-production schedules that they cannot budge without the help of small specialist suppliers and service agencies, nimble and incisive, able to cut through the tangle and deliver the goods on time.

The mouse-and-the-lion argument in favour of small units has been persuasive ever since Aesop invented it. Yes, they can adapt quickly, they get people involved, they operate close to the ground and know how to make the most of the terrain. But, regretfully, No, a take-over group of workers or tenants is unlikely to survive if it has only its own resources to rely on. Sooner or later it must secure professional support. Pooles Park need their architectural adviser to help them pin down their contractors. The Fakenham ladies needed professional help to set up their cost-accounting system; and eventually they foundered for want of an experienced sales manager. Even more important are the professionals working inside the big organizations, private firms and official bodies, which groups must deal with. They possess the technical information, they control the resources, and they operate the procedures on which groups may have at first to depend. Coming to terms with these professionals needs very careful consideration; not least because their attitudes vary. Some, like Councillor Eames, can be won over by a group's 'professional' competence. Some are friendly already. A hard-core remainder have to be eased out of their isolation and taught a different approach.

The 'friendly professionals' on the staffs of the big organizations include lawyers, architects, accountants, health inspectors, research workers, technologists, surveyors. They may strongly resent the way their talents are wasted in their bread-and-butter jobs. They may have inside knowledge of the delays and obstructions which occur. They may know the way round the obstacles, and yet be unable to persuade their own colleagues and superiors to get a move on. But if some group outside knows what it is after, and shows that it means business, it may be able to tap the knowledge and experience of these friendly professionals and learn from them, off the record, how to make the system produce results.

## Threats

This information and advice is valuable, but limited. Professionals can explain how to use grants procedures, what legal rights to quote, how to cut costs, when to apply leverage with the help of the media. But it takes a very senior professional to do as Councillor Eames did, and to permit outsiders to invade and occupy what had previously been official territory. When this happens it may seem to challenge, even threaten, those who are accustomed to running things. The threat is most devastating when the group is already operating on the inside. When it takes over part of the foreman's job on the shop floor, or part of the housing manager's job on the estate, it is showing them up by 'showing them how'; and this is shocking and hurtful. The idea of production workers reorganizing their supply lines, or of a

114

Tenants' Association taking over from the Council, is rather like claiming that children can teach their teachers. It seems to discredit the knowledge and technical skills that have been so painfully acquired. Who do these kids – or workers – or tenants think they are? What right have they to muscle in on the jobs the professionals are qualified to do?

This threat is reinforced by the behaviour of some groups, operating on the outside, who have lost all confidence in the authorities and believe the first priority is to expose the system and discredit those who run it. They have seen enough mismanagement, in industry, housing, education, local government, to conclude that these institutions are dangerously unsound. Any argument or activity which helps to shore up the existing structures is suspect. There is no point in prolonging the life of the powers-that-be by giving them any credit for what they do, even when it is worth doing, and done well. It's time to junk the lot, and clear the site, just as any comprehensive redeveloper would do. This argument bites deepest in those whom society seems to be rejecting. To someone with capacities that school ignored, who has skills but no job or a job and no prospects, who has a family and no home, who is handicapped and inadequately cared for – the arguments for a clean start are charged with emotion as well as reason. 'Scrap the lot!' means getting your own back. You can vent your anger by joining the demolition squad.

The behaviour of what I call the hard-core professionals – those whose first loyalty is to the institutions they serve rather than to the work they do – goes a long way to confirming the activists' worst suspicions. They clam up. They can do this the more easily because their institutions have grown so big. Supermarkets, giant comprehensives, polytechnics, social services departments, planning ministries, nationalized corporations, international syndicates enable management to keep its distance from those whom its policies affect. Loyalties within the institution help to protect it from outsiders wanting to know too much. This is not necessarily a conscious process. In any large organization most of the senior staff may be thoroughly honest and quite able. But if they are ambitious they are soon aware that knowledge is power: and it is most powerful when it is private knowledge, withheld from those who might steal a march, or ask awkward questions, or have other ideas. 'Discretion' and 'confiden-

tiality' harden into official secrecy. One seasoned professional*
says:

From my personal observation and experience, secrecy ... has a
pervasive and damaging effect on the efficiency with which the British
official machine conducts its affairs ... secrecy weakens and dilutes the
responsibility of people; ... its effects in this respect extend to organizations also, which cover their tracks far too easily.

Secrecy protects professionals who are corrupt, or power-
hungry, or inefficient. But the majority of those who shelter
behind it are neither dolts nor villains. They simply want to get
on with their jobs in their own fashion, without being got at. Any
abuse which comes their way makes them even more determined
to show everyone how public-spirited and far-sighted they have
been. So they hug their knowledge to themselves until they can
put together a really impressive answer; tower blocks to meet the
housing shortage, centralized caretaking to combat vandalism,
inner city ringways to make the traffic flow, civic centres to
consolidate public services, British Leyland to streamline the car
industry. These answers may be quite rational, and yet monu-
mentally out of touch with the ways families live and communities thrive.

When the first tower crane was on test in the Building Research Station outside Watford, and the first tower blocks were
on the architects' drawing boards, Michael Young and Peter
Willmott were in Bethnal Green, quietly piecing together the
mosaic of community experience round which they wrote their
book on *Family and Kinship in East London*. In 1977, with
vandalized, half-empty tower blocks littering the landscape,
Young remembered that back in the 1950s 'every man, woman
and child' they met in Bethnal Green was against the idea. But
there was no official listening post at which the planners could
learn how people felt, or what they really wanted; and even if
there had been, the officials' ears were not attuned to what
people had to say.

I have argued earlier that action groups need professionals.
But the hard-core professionals who make policy need action
groups even more. Groups on the shop floor and outside in the

* Professor David Henderson in his broadcast series on Concorde and the
AGR, reprinted in the *Listener* 17.xi.77.

community have a freedom of movement which is denied to officials. They can sense what is being felt even before it is said. They can observe, in close-up, how official policies are being applied, where they fit badly, why they fail. They know what people want, and what they might be willing to do in order to help get it. They can tackle each situation 'one-off', without having to impose a standardized solution. This is expert knowledge which the professionals badly need. But the normal channels fail to let the message through. Parents could tell teachers a lot about children – if they had more than a five-minute interview in which to do it. Workers could enlighten managers, tenants could teach housing officials – if a means of expression existed so that each side could grasp what the other was trying to say. At a public inquiry, or on a joint consultative committee, the whole thing becomes a slanging match: the official party camouflaging its intentions with courteous discretion, the enraged heckler in the back row shouting 'Why don't you get off your backsides and fucking well do something?'

In the spring of 1976 the residents of Dalmarnock decided they had had enough of this communications failure. Dalmarnock was one of the ten most deprived areas in Western Scotland. The threat of a motorway coupled with the territorial wrangling of local government departments had created a 'planning blight' which left the area looking as though it had just been tidied up after an obliteration attack by the Luftwaffe. The Dalmarnock Action Group organized their own neighbourhood survey of housing, health, schooling, crime, public utilities, industry, welfare, shops and leisure facilities. Their Report showed how demoralization had set in as physical conditions and public services deteriorated. They hammered home in capital letters what angered them most of all:

IT IS ALL TOO EASY FOR ELECTED MEMBERS AND OFFICIALS . . . TO COME UP WITH IDEAS FOR IMPROVEMENT WHICH ARE WHOLLY INAPPROPRIATE TO THE NEEDS OF THE PEOPLE WHO HAVE TO LIVE WITH THE RESULTS OF THEIR EFFORTS . . . When we were speaking to people in Dalmarnock about the area it became clear that many things that the former Glasgow Corporation had done in the area – in an attempt to improve conditions – had not been sensitive to the real needs of the community . . . We are trying to say what we want – WHAT OUR PRIORITIES ARE – not what the Region or District Council thinks we OUGHT to have.

During the autumn and winter of 1976 the authorities attempted to get 'joint consultation' in the area by convening public meetings at which they outlined what might be done. The 'platform' put its case, and the public put their grievances, but no one got further. Early in 1977 the Dalmarnock Action Group, with some friendly professionals in local government and some community workers, agreed to try a different approach.

## The Dalmarnock 'try-out'

Two of us contrived a crude scale model of Dalmarnock – half a mile square shown as a 6 ft by 8 ft three-D layout. It covered five tables in a church hall in the middle of the area it represented. One evening, when the model was complete, four separate groups of residents (Mums, elderly, youth and Action Committee members) came in to use the model in order to set out their own ideas for Dalmarnock's immediate future. Along one wall there were thirty-seven packets of cutout shapes, each to scale, and easily recognizable as zebra crossings, adventure playgrounds, rubbish collection areas, community huts, new housing – just about anything that could be useful to the community. To begin with, each group operated on their own, making their own selection from the packets, signing each cutout on the back and placing it where they saw fit, if necessary flagging existing buildings for demolition or conversion. After about an hour, groups began to negotiate with each other where they found themselves competing for the same derelict building or patch of waste ground, or doubling up on the facilities they proposed to provide. Sometimes they literally took scissors and trimmed the cutout areas in order to reach a sensible compromise. Every conflict was settled between the groups concerned without the need for anyone else to step in as arbitrator. At the end of the evening everyone came together and decided, again without fuss, on a list of priorities.

The decisions were realistic. This was the view of a selection of professionals who were in attendance, off duty. There were two senior Regional planners, three District planners, officials from the Social Work department, full-time community workers, the local Councillor, the local Police Inspector. Each of these experts was labelled so that residents knew who did what. The rule was that if you wore a label you couldn't speak until you were spoken to by a resident. This kept the initiative where it belonged – with the residents. They were free to work out their own ideas, check their technical practicability with the specialists, and compare the advice of different experts where they seemed to conflict. The professionals said afterwards that their advice was often sought, though not always taken. They were drawn into down-to-earth discussions in which no one seemed to be striking attitudes. They admitted that sometimes the residents' solutions were a better match for local needs than those they had offered themselves.

A few days later the Action Group got a formal request from the Glasgow Eastern Area Co-ordinating Authority and was able to reply the next day with its list of detailed recommendations, street by street. James Clyde, the chairman of the group, wrote afterwards, in the *East End Forum*:

. . . The night proved fruitful mainly because the authorities and local people worked *together* to discuss how, in an experimental way, to overcome problems in a deprived area. This is a step in the right direction which we, the community and the authorities, must not let go by unnoticed . . . The community realizes the value of these exercises and its potential value in other deprived areas of the City . . .

At first sight the Dalmarnock try-out had an uncanny resemblance to the children's groups working on their 'Living Space' model layouts described in Chapter 1. The room hummed with activity. There were no dominant leaders, no passengers. A mixture of talents and backgrounds had converged to establish a working relationship, based on their common experience of the job in hand. Together, they could literally handle the facts. They showed each other what they meant by manipulating the bits of cardboard which represented houses or shops or refuse sites or play areas – as much as by talking about them. The groups had become self-propelled; the professionals were taken aback, and beginning to revise their own ideas about the capacities of the rank-and-file.

'Beginning.' Experiments like this one show what can be; they don't of themselves convert the hard-core professionals from a lifetime of acting on the principle that they know best. But experience does teach, nevertheless. I told an official from Newry, Northern Ireland, what had happened in Dalmarnock. Oh yes, he said, that's the kind of thing we've been doing – for real. The local planning officers had called a public meeting to discuss their plan for the Markets Redevelopment area. Over 60 per cent of the community turned up. Somehow the officials convinced the meeting that they were open to new ideas, and that the plan could be changed in the light of any suggestions offered. The residents took the plans away and worked on them for several weeks, consulting the officials from time to time. At another well-attended meeting they offered their own plan back. There was hardly anything of the original proposals left. The new plan was built round suggestions drawn from the whole community, which included several people whom the military might call terrorists. The plan itself, spread out on the table, was something that could speak on everyone's behalf. The officials adopted the new plan, not as 'a negotiated settlement of outstanding differences', but as a straightforward improvement on the original. They made modifications to the plans for the surrounding areas to match up roads and pipelines, and began to turn the community's plan into reality. This could happen because they were becoming part of the community, absorbed into it by the job in hand, like the policemen in Gibshill when they volunteered for the beat. They no longer felt they were being 'got at' by the antis. No one needed to strike attitudes or swap accusations in terms of Us and Them.

It is significant that in the early stages in Newry the residents took the plans away to work on, without officials present. This might partly have been to enable some residents to take part who could not show their faces in public. But it also illustrates the distrust which many have for people who seem to like monopolizing the facts.

There is a lurking suspicion that 'experts' might just possibly filter information or slant advice. They might want to soften or to harden people's attitudes to cuts in public services; they might exaggerate the technical obstacles to altering the Council's pet traffic scheme. So it is important to get at the facts direct, where possible. The group members in Dalmarnock made it their business to collect all the information they could at first-hand from their fellow-residents, and from published statistics about the area. They knew exactly what was happening in the neighbourhood: the size of the queues in the doctors' surgeries, the numbers of children 'lifted' by the police, the areas of disused factory space. In describing the problem, and naming the official departments responsible for not solving it, they could not easily be faulted. But when it comes to devising solutions, and putting them through the official machinery, other facts come into play.

An action group which means business has to ration what it does. It can't afford to waste its members' energies on beating about the bush. But before it goes into action it must be able to sort out the practical implications of the choices that are open. This takes some doing. Suppose that premises are needed – to house people, or to provide a social centre, or to serve as a workshop for mums and toddlers or for jobless school-leavers. Each member of the group needs to know what possibilities there are to choose from, on what terms, within what limits. Can we take over short-life property? Or put up a pre-fab hut? Or hire a hall? Or convert a pair of flats? How do the costs compare? What would a contractor charge? Could we save money by doing part of the work ourselves? And what about fire safety, health hazards, food hygiene, third party insurance? What kind of support could we get: grants, loans, allowances, technical services, volunteer local talent, discounts from local firms, gifts of materials? Where do we stand legally on all this: what are our rights and liabilities? Must we have planning permission?

To get this basic information together could fill the Agenda for weeks, even months, while those who can take time off work go scurrying to and fro, contacting officials and getting professional advice. And this is where the group may lose its momentum. It needs the facts on which to base decisions, right there on the table, within everyone's reach. And not more than anyone needs. Too much detail, too soon, gets everybody down. The facts, like the professionals, must be on tap, but not on top.

One line of attack is the NEIGHBOURHOOD FACT BANK: a shortened version follows this chapter. The complete version is on numbered cards so that a group can literally have the facts at its finger tips. The cards give the gist of the relevant legal, technical and financial information. They can be passed around for everyone to see; then spread out on the table, arranged and rearranged as the group works out its order of priority; extended to suggest a critical path; matched up where possibilities conflict or overlap; dealt out for use by working parties set up to check on local possibilities or initiate particular jobs.

The FACT BANK was developed first in England, then in Scotland (the pilot Scottish version was used by the groups in the Dalmarnock try-out). The idea behind it is that any group, anywhere, should be able to size up the possibilities and work out its own strategy without having to depend on anyone else's patronage or influence. It includes reference cards suggesting where else to look for expert advice or what to read for more detail; but it stands or falls on the attempt to put the basic information within everyone's grasp. If everyone has access to the facts it becomes much easier to involve the whole membership in what the group does. Working parties can get down to a range of practical activity which spreads out into the community. They do not have to function as committees to do this, or even include committee members. They can function very well without formal meetings so long as they know what they have been asked to tackle. But they must be able to get at the facts when the need arises. The FACT BANK is for their use, as well as for the Chairperson, the Secretary, the friendly professional adviser, and the other members of the Committee.

Armed with the local information and experience that they accumulate for themselves, reinforced by such things as the FACT BANK, action groups can have an impact. The strength of any group is its reliance on its own resources and its own efforts in its own time; but its effectiveness is limited and local so long as each group stays entirely on its own. The walls of Jericho won't come tumbling down, if they ever do, until a great many people start blowing their horns together. Action groups operating in the same field must be able to pool their experience, publicize their findings, exert maximum pressure where it does most good. But it would be fatal if they tried to do this by forming yet another top-heavy organization, all Head Office and no 'body' worth noticing.

## Networks

A more promising approach is what I shall call the network: a form of organization which exists to exchange information between groups so that they can build up a composite picture of what is actually happening, and what ought to be done about it. They

122

can then use the network to publicize their findings, give examples from their first-hand experience of what can be done; and so challenge those institutions which are falling down on the job.

The pioneers in this approach were the pressure groups which originally formed the Consumer Association and began to publish *Which?* They could mobilize hundreds, even thousands of users, trying out products at home; and they backed this up with laboratory analysis and with research on legislation. They set up their own testing organization, announced results, named names, got new laws passed and old ones enforced more effectively, and made manufacturers pay heed to safety requirements, cost-effectiveness, repair and replacement services.

The Industrial Common Ownership Movement (I C O M) began as an informal network of co-operative minded groups comparing experiences so as to learn from their mistakes and help promising newcomers. When they began to make profits they levied themselves, borrowed additional funds, and set up ICOF (Industrial Common Ownership Finance) which in 1977 became the channel for aid under the Industrial Common Ownership Act which they had promoted.

Tenants' Associations in London formed their own Association of London Housing Estates to collect and compare first-hand observation of the ways in which different Borough housing authorities were doing their jobs. They sorted out information on procedures and legal rights, set up their own insurance service, coaxed or badgered their local authorities into setting up 'tenant participation schemes', and (by using sections 101 and 102 of the 1972 Local Government Act) got tenants' representatives co-opted on to Housing Committees and subcommittees where they could directly influence estate management. A survey in April 1975 showed that 71 per cent of the London authorities had been persuaded to set up one or more types of tenant participation schemes, compared with 28 per cent of the other Metropolitan Authorities, and 4 per cent of the District Councils elsewhere in England and Wales, where until recently there were no comparable networks operating. Since the National Federation of Tenants' Associations (now the National Tenants' Organisation) was set up in 1977 the pressure is likely to build up outside London as well as inside it.

The Pre-school Playgroups Movement is another illustration of the way in which individual groups can reinforce each other.

National Associations in Scotland and England and Wales have persuaded successive Labour and Conservative governments to provide pre-school facilities so far for about a fifth of the three to four age group in Britain.

The *Key Contacts* which follow the NEIGHBOURHOOD FACT BANK includes many more examples (pages 273–5). But bear in mind the difference between an action group which sets up its own network in order to do its own job better, and one which links up with other groups in order to operate a network in which everyone shares. For example: the Child Poverty Action Group has its own legal department and runs the Citizens' Rights Office; its local branches give advice on welfare rights, and feed back information on the way social services are being administered. Similarly, Inter-Action has its own complex of training facilities, media services, and technical information, radiating outwards through the operation of NUBS (Neighbourhood Use of Buildings and Space), the City Farms Land Bank, or the other Inter-Action Advisory Services. Groups such as CPAG and Inter-Action are power-houses, using all the local experience they can acquire in order to generate their own highly professional activity within the group. A network such as Gingerbread, on the other hand, is formed from many local groups, linking up to help each other through clubs and shared housing, and to make the authorities give single-parent families a better deal. The headquarters' staff are simply channels for the pressure that builds up in the groups.

In all three organizations the secret of success has been to keep the centre of gravity low. Many-tiered administrations are a bad bargain. The people at the top tend to build empires and assert territorial rights over the areas in which they specialize: Unions waste their energies in demarcation disputes; welfare organizations make ritual contact with one another each conference season, and go their own sweet ways during the rest of the year. Action groups cannot afford to be so exclusive. Their strength is in their roots, and the roots should be stretching out into the community. They are dealing with a mixture of people and a range of problems which can't easily be confined to separate compartments. Very often the problems were mishandled from the outset because the authorities dealt with them separately and centrally in an institutional way – by the Housing Department, or by Education, or Social Services, or Police, or Employment –

when they are crying out to be dealt with locally, as one whole.

Professional skills are better integrated than they used to be: teachers and social workers are on speaking terms nowadays; and within the social services it has become normal for a family in trouble to be dealing with one social worker, based in the area team office, instead of six, all from different divisions and none daring to venture across his departmental frontier. To this extent the idea of 'integrated services' and 'corporate management' has come to stay. But the division between the institutional insiders and the outsiders remains. What could be done about it, in education and training for instance? Schools run clubs outside school hours which could link up naturally with the rest of the community, but they seldom manage to attract much outside help. Is this because there's such compulsive viewing back home? I think there are two more compelling reasons: (1) teachers are professionally used to being know-alls and telling others what to do; (2) other people discover this, and stay clear. If you doubt this explanation check up on the tiny handful of junior schools which have begun to take parents seriously, and make them welcome collaborators, not interfering strangers to be held at arm's length. These schools have the sense to draw on parents' practical help: dropping in during school hours, to hear reading or multiplication tables, or to thread needles; running clubs; joining in supervising educational visits. No problems with them in 'getting parents involved'.

Suppose that it was possible to develop this idea a little further. A school is threatened with closure because it is 'too small to be adequately staffed'. There have been several successful action campaigns on the issue which have brought parents and staff together as a pressure group, sometimes with the parents taking the lead. (In one case, the Save Our School action group, Redbourn, versus the Hertfordshire Education Authority, this was a triple alliance with the children themselves making the running.) The campaign succeeds and the school stays open. But it is still short-staffed. What else could a combined operation achieve? Could parents and teachers club together to form a 'school co-operative', using what money they can raise to expand the school's teaching services – on their own initiative? Need it stop there? Why not, as Michael Young and Eric Midwinter suggest, do a deal with the local authority whereby it contributes the average cost of the schooling for each child, and operates its normal services of advice and inspection, but the school co-operative is free to use its own resources, skills included, in order to do the job in its own way?

## Shared Resources

While we are still daydreaming, consider what could happen if a conventional secondary school began to extend the use of its premises and technical facilities so that other sections of the community could join in, on level terms, in enterprises that involved everybody. What offers? A town pop opera? A charity sports festival? Teach-ins: on community relations and police behaviour; or local traffic congestion; or job prospects and the need for local industries? Weekend and vacation workshops under the job creation scheme? Field trips to find out how other places solve their problems? A bulk-buy food co-operative in which kids learn the ropes of retail distribution? A skills-exchange? A neighbourhood newspaper, edited in the pub, and put to bed on the school press?

Apply the same approach to industry, and youngsters leaving school: many steer clear of factory work if they possibly can. The pay may be better than in some other jobs but the prospects are dim. The only way to escape from a blind alley job, once inside the firm, is to get trained. The Industrial Training Act requires firms to free youngsters for training, on the job, and/or at a local college. But the training is inadequate. Colleges are insufficiently involved with local work places, and cannot afford the equipment to simulate working conditions; and firms are too busy during working hours to provide access to plant. On the dot of five, in many firms, the place is dead. A combined operation could bring together training instructors, trainees, and a handful of older workmates showing how the job is done. Groups of secondary school children, as well as employees on their basic training, could see how the training relates to real life: and get their bearings from people on the shop floor as well as from class notes and examination texts.

# Going it Alone?

Now consider the reaction of the professional educators and trainers to all this. In most areas the short-term answer is obvious. No professional teacher would allow such interference – or be allowed by the Unions or the local Education Authority to countenance it. But can anyone be sure that this rejection is permanent? Compare a couple of examples. Here's the first: People in one Scottish locality grew tired of negotiating with their local authority about evening classes: the regulations set a minimum enrolment for each class, and the range of subjects did not match the demand. So they advertised for suitably qualified part-time instructors, paid them the full rates, and ran their own adult education service, custom-built, at a profit.

Example number two: In the multi-racial area of Handsworth, Birmingham, a group of teachers in the local junior school were at their wit's end to establish effective communications, with parents as well as children. The children's level of achievement was lower than average, especially in literacy, but the teachers could not get the children to respond. So they decided to bring in the parents. Or rather, to go out to them, and to develop a combined operation, outside the school premises. They built up a network of street representatives, mostly parents, who between them organized play schemes, trips, fund-raising, socials. These activities complemented what the school was doing, but they were not school-centred or school-dominated. After a couple of years the project moved into its own premises, disused buildings of an old school. This became a communal area in which the whole neighbourhood could take a share. Over the years school-linked activities developed side by side with neighbourhood projects: pre-school playgroups with a special emphasis on language development, an old folks' club, a corner shop, club activities for youngsters outside school hours, a clothes co-operative, specialist sessions during school hours for children with difficulties, a photographic centre, a job-finding scheme. Parents are able to help children, as well as to follow their own interests. Disturbed children help with the toddlers' playgroup and the repair work, begin to relate again to books and numberwork, and regain self-confidence. Ten years from the teachers' first move it continues to thrive, with teachers still involved, but as a community enterprise, exerting its own influence on the school and the neighbourhood.

Put another way, there are two arguments that favour a change of attitude among teachers, and other professions. The first, as voiced by the Scottish adult education group is: 'We can do better on our own!' The second, hinted at by the Handsworth teachers is: 'We can't manage without you.' The efforts of all sorts of action groups, in housing and industry and the community generally, go to show that the possibility of independent, 'alternative' action has to be taken seriously. But for professionals who are desperately struggling to do a good job in tough conditions, the second argument carries more weight. The job is becoming too much to tackle alone.

Hospitals still treat their local voluntary support groups rather as teachers have tended to treat parents' associations: 'raise the money for us, organize socials, distribute goodies; but don't dare to help me do my job!' But in children's wards parents are at last being allowed in to help look after and reassure their own children. Yet for half a century the professionalism of doctors and nurses demanded exclusive control and kept everyone else at a distance. Staff shortages have forced them to give way, and as a result the welfare of child patients has benefited; and so has professional morale. How long will it be before equally effective use of outsiders' help can be made in out-patient departments, geriatric units, mental hospitals, rehabilitation centres?

All these possibilities have already been tinkered with, in attempts by voluntary groups to give a helping hand here and there. But I am arguing for something more systematic and thoroughgoing, by action groups prepared to go the distance. This means getting parents and teachers combining to deal with child guidance, community involvement, vandalism, careers, creative leisure; inviting experienced shop-floor workers to help plan and assess induction training schemes; bringing together doctors, nurses, administrators and patients to improve appointment systems, make better use of premises and equipment, give more scope to patients and their families to help themselves.

The principal obstacle is the fear of the men and women already on the job – school helper, hospital porter, training officer, planner, works' manager, ward sister, head teacher – that their territory is being invaded and their status threatened. The invasion is a fact. Any intervention by the community, as users, is the thin end of the wedge, and the job of action groups is to drive it home. But the object is to wedge things firm, not to split them open; to make it easier for the professionals to make the most of their skills. Action groups can share the workload, and in the process of sharing they can get across their own expert knowledge of local needs and capacities, so that the professionals have a better idea of the human context in which the work is done.

At this point I must stop peddling possibilities, for I can feel two critics breathing down my neck. Each wants a realistic answer to the question: 'How far do you go?' *Realist A* argues that action groups can be useful, in a small way, here and there. But it's no good claiming too much for them, or pushing them too hard. Far better to settle for a supportive role, and leave the big issues to established institutions, 'natural leaders', and the good sense of the great majority. *Realist B* asks what is the point of propping up institutions which are already crumbling? The only action group worth a damn is the one that goes all out to mobilize public opinion, smash the bureaucracy, and clear the site for revolutionary change.

I don't see things as a simple choice between propping up and pulling down 'the existing fabric of society'. It goes in stages. First, rehabilitation. Some parts of some institutions have to be rebuilt from the inside, while they are still viable. People need something tangible to catch on to. A rough-and-ready version of what is needed carries conviction because you can see and test it, here and now. A blueprint of the future is anybody's guess. There are obvious dangers, however, that rehabilitation gets into the hands of the con-men, and becomes a cosmetic job: improvements to the façade, a lick of paint, new fixtures in the kitchen and the loo – and nothing much done about the drains, or the dampcourse, or the roof. This is what has usually happened when 'voluntary effort' has tinkered with social institutions. It is why the demolition squad wants to make a clean sweep and start from scratch.

Action groups need not fall for either argument. If they are properly equipped with the facts, and can draw on their own experience and that of the professionals, they can see for themselves what actually works in existing conditions as well as what

129

is said to work but doesn't. They can produce something which is neither a picturesque botch-up nor a tearing-down, but a one-off job, thought up, worked out and fitted in to match local needs and resources. But society is not a placid landscape for action groups to cultivate and build on unmolested. It is a devastated area, in which rival interests have staked out no-go zones. Property developers and industrialists reserve their right to use or to withhold their resources, as best pleases their shareholders. Specialists at all levels protect the scarcity value of their skills. Officials guard their secrets. Police and military insulate their young recruits from 'seditious' reminders that as members of the community they too are answerable for what they do, whoever gives the orders. The effect of these embargoes is to disrupt communication between the different sectors of society, and to make them vulnerable to the con-men. 'Security' and 'law-and-order' are easiest to sell when they are offered with an Us-and-Them-get-out-clause ('It's all Their fault that We're in this mess'), and a Leave-It-to-Us-Guarantee that the people in charge will do what is needed, and no one else need bother.

Action groups are close enough to reality to see past the smart enochs and the bully-boysons to the real choices that have to be made: housing needs, or private purchasing power; worksharing, or cut-throat competition; education to bring out a child's whole capacity, or to mould him to an approved pattern. These are uncomfortable decisions to make, particularly for those who still do quite well out of society, even in its decay. They make it necessary to take sides, and the dividing line does not match the conventional loyalties which the con-men sell.

The real conflict is not about what people *say* they believe in – 'freedom', 'democracy', 'the rights of the individual', 'the public interest', 'social justice', 'the rule of law' – but what they do about it. Actions speak louder than words. Once rid of the loyalty blinkers it is easy to recognize intimidation, whether it is police interrogation in the cells, or a racialist march through an immigrant area, or a shop-floor boycott of a worker who exceeds his quota. It is much harder to step out of line and take action which cuts across party affiliations, or threatens departmental interests. Getting the priorities right may mean letting the side down.

This conflict of loyalties lies behind the unspoken decision of most people 'not to get involved'. In the United States this lack of commitment has meant that, as Lewis Mumford put it 200 years after the American Declaration of Independence:

.. under the surface of our constitution we have created a totalitarian society.

In most countries decision-making has gone, or is going, by default to those whose economic and military power is no longer answerable to the community. Unless our society recovers from this inertia, the only alternative left is the 'universal guerilladom' which Mumford predicts.

Action groups enable the community to get back its nerve; and something more, its self-respect. The group is a crucible in which conflicting temperaments, outlooks, emotions, react with each other – in the process ideas and attitudes are tested, toughened, refined. People discover that life has a new quality and zest. Groups find opportunities to apply the everyday skills and experience which most people possess; and they show that these have worth and relevance. They are a new kind of *manifesto*, not just an abstract declaration of what ought to be done, but a working demonstration. They operate at a level where the whole neighbourhood, the whole work force, has something to offer, and they establish a working relationship with the professional sector. Anyone can commit himself or herself, merely by joining in. Labels are irrelevant: people can see what they are doing, and can test others' sincerity by what they do now, not by what they promise later. There is no excuse for delaying until the oil flows or the revolution comes.

Commitment generates mutual confidence: people find they can work together, manage each other, adapt to new circumstances, weigh up advice and take decisions. They find they can, and they do. So gradually the community gets itself together, flexes its muscles, tests its strength – and begins to move forward from rehab. to *new build*.

Meanwhile, we are living in a short-life property. Whether new build takes place as a green fields alternative to the unwieldy institutions of modern society, or is founded in their ruins, depends on how quickly action groups can acquire the professionalism to make community management work; and then to use it to dismantle the old superstructure, piecemeal, so that new cultures of self-government and mutual aid have room to flourish.

There is a slender chance that action groups can be the means of regenerating society in the nick of time. They are down-to-earth; they deal with reality, at first-hand. They generate their own staying-power through the satisfaction of achieving things together.

They are the grass-roots, whose strength seems negligible – until the blades come bursting through the tarmac.

# Part Two

# Introducing the Neighbourhood Fact Bank

The ideas behind it were outlined in the previous chapter (pp. 121–2).

For a quick glimpse at the subjects it covers, look at the SIGN-POST lists of general headings, beginning on the following page and continuing to page 147.

The information in the Bank is arranged alphabetically from page 151. Most of it applies anywhere in the United Kingdom, but because there are some differences in Scotland, mainly arising from Scottish law, a parallel version of the Fact Bank has been developed. I have drawn on this to make 'The Fact Bank in Scotland' on pages 281–5. Wherever there is a Scottish variation, the corresponding English entry is marked S.

## Follow-up to the Fact Bank

Books, pamphlets, leaflets giving further information are listed on pages 262–72. They are grouped under the same Signpost headings used earlier.

## Key Contacts

Useful addresses in alphabetical order – pages 273–5.
A supplementary Scottish address list – pages 287–8.

You may also find it useful to complete your own local lists, with the help of your nearest public library, using the outlines on pages 277–9.

# Signposts to the Fact Bank

The next few pages list the contents of the Fact Bank under the following *general headings*:

BUILDING AND
  CONVERTING
COMMUNITY USE OF WASTE
  GROUND AND EMPTY
  PREMISES
COSTS AND BUDGETING
FUNDS FOR SELF-HELP
HANDICAPPED AND
  ELDERLY
HEALTH AND CLEANSING
HOUSING
HOUSING CO-OPERATIVES

INFORMATION AND ADVICE
LAWS, LEGAL AID, LEGAL
  PROTECTION
LIABILITIES
OFFICIAL CHANNELS
OFFICIAL PLANS
RIGHTS
SELF-HELP
SOCIAL ACTIVITIES
TENANTS AND OWNER-
  OCCUPIERS
YOUNGSTERS

There is a deliberate overlap: some information items are shown under more than one of the general headings.

# Building and Converting

# Community Use Of Waste Ground and Empty Premises

See also: BUILDING AND CONVERTING; SOCIAL ACTIVITIES

# Costs and Budgeting

See also: FUNDS FOR SELF-HELP; RIGHTS

# Funds for Self-help

See also: RIGHTS

# Handicapped and Elderly

# Health and Cleansing

# Housing

See also: OFFICIAL PLANS; TENANTS AND OWNER-OCCUPIERS

# Housing Co-operatives

See also: BUILDING AND CONVERTING; FUNDS FOR SELF-HELP;
SOCIAL ACTIVITIES

# Information and Advice

# Laws, Legal Aid, Legal Protection

See also: RIGHTS

# Liabilities

# Official Channels

See also: OFFICIAL PLANS

# Official Plans

See also: OFFICIAL CHANNELS

# Rights

See also: HOUSING; TENANTS AND OWNER-OCCUPIERS

# Self-help

# Social Activities

# Tenants and Owner-Occupiers

See also: HOUSING

# Youngsters

See also: FUNDS FOR SELF-HELP

# The Fact Bank

Entries marked [S] have Scottish variations listed on pages 281–8.

# Adapting Housing for Handicapped People

Local Councils can provide grants to handicapped people to adapt their homes.

Grants from Social Services* cover various aids and adaptations (including body hoists, stair lifts, safety handles in bathrooms and the construction of extra wide doorways) to all properties *except* Council housing. Adaptations to Council property are paid for out of the Housing Revenue Account and carried out by the Housing Department.

Handicapped people permanently moved by the Council from homes which have been adapted can claim a disturbance allowance to cover the cost of making fresh adaptations.

Homeowners and landlords can obtain intermediate grants to install amenities for handicapped people, but the applicants have to pay 50% of the 'eligible' expense (maximum £1,200).

* Chronically Sick and Disabled Persons Act 1976.

See: DISTURBANCE ALLOWANCE; ELIGIBLE EXPENSE; IMPROVE-
MENT GRANTS (A); INTERMEDIATE GRANTS (A)

# Adventure Playgrounds

These allow kids to experiment with earth, tools and materials, and to take risks – but under supervision. Usually run by voluntary groups and/or parents with a play-leader paid by local authority who may also pay up to 85% of capital cost. National Playing Fields Association also make grants towards initial costs. Area should be more than ¼ acre, less than 1½ acres (or it's too big to supervise and maintain). It may be waste land awaiting development and held on short lease (five to ten years) – or sometimes for one season only. To get started: produce evidence of the need, find likely areas, get support from parents and councillors, set up a steering group, apply to the Council committee which deals with amenities and recreation. Get insurance cover.

See: COST GUIDELINES (L); HUTS; INSURANCE (C); NATIONAL
PLAYING FIELDS ASSOCIATION; PLAY AREA (A) (B)

# Allotment Gardens [S]

Local Councils should provide allotments from the rates if they know that people want them. Ask for information at the Council's Parks Department. The Council sets the rent and can compensate the occupier if the land is needed for any other purpose.* The Council has to give twelve months' notice to quit if they want the land back. They can also claim compensation from the occupier if the land is not looked after and evict an occupier for rent arrears or any other breach of agreement. An allotment is usually about ¼ acre of land.

* Allotment Acts 1922 and 1950.

See: RENT-A-PLOT

# Alternative Meeting Places

No ready-made clubroom or hall? Need somewhere to meet? Have you tried to get (1) short-life property, e.g. empty pubs, churches or shops, (2) a site hut, a portakabin, demountable building, or (3) an empty flat? Empty underground garages have been successfully converted into meeting places for youngsters.

Ask at the Town Hall about short-life property. Some Councils keep a list of properties empty for two years or more. You have to pay rates and some rent. Ask the Council to do major repairs. If the building needs altering or its use is going to change, the Council's Planning Department will give advice. Find an architect to help you. Plans have to be checked for safety by the Building Inspectors or (in inner London) the District Surveyor.

See: COST GUIDELINES (B) (M); HUTS; SHORT-LIFE PROPERTY

# Bar Licences [S]

For an *occasional licence* to sell alcohol at a special event ask a local publican to apply, on your behalf. Give twenty-four hours' notice to the area Police Chief. The publican appears at the Magistrate's Court. Each licence costs £2.

For a *permanent licence* you need control of a hall and the Council's permission. Get five copies of application forms and club rules for licensed premises from the local Law Society. Keep one form. Send three to the Clerk of the Magistrate's Court with your constitution (altered for licensed premises). Copies are sent to the police, Council and fire department. They all inspect the premises. A hearing is held at the Magistrate's Court. Costs £3 (for one year); £3 (second year); then £3 for ten years. The Secretary and Chairman are named on the Registration Certificate and are responsible.

See: FIRE SAFETY; MUSIC, DANCING AND PLAY LICENCES

# Bingo (A)

*For Socials and Fund-raising*

There are three ways to organize games of bingo. For one of the ways the club will have to get a licence from the local Council. Bingo can be played at social functions without a licence,* but only one payment of not more than £1 may be made by each player (as an entrance fee or stake). The total value of all the prizes must not be more than £100. This is the best way to raise funds, the other two ways are more for just socializing. It is difficult to get a licence to play on premises selling alcohol.

* Gaming Act 1968, section 41.

See: BINGO (B) (C)

# Bingo (B)                                          [S]

A permanent club wanting to charge more than 5p a day for bingo, which is one of their activities, must* register with the local licensing authority (the Council). Only members, and guests who do not pay, can play. No advertising is allowed.

Apply for registration† in January or February of each year. It costs £48 (1979) for one year, and £24 for a renewal which can last for ten years. A charge for playing bingo can be up to £2.00 per person per day. There is no limit on the stakes but these must be distributed in full as winnings (less bingo duty).‡ So this method is no good for fund-raising.

* Gaming Act 1968, section 40, part II.
† The Gaming Board, Berkshire House, High Holborn, London WC1.
‡ Details on bingo duty from H M Customs and Excise, King's Bean House, 39–40 Mark Lane, London EC3R 7HE.

See: BINGO (A) (C)

# Bingo (C)

Bingo can be played at social functions *without* a licence,* if only one payment of £1 or less is made by each player (as an entrance fee or stake or otherwise) for all the games played.

The total value of all the prizes must not be more than £100. Members of the public may take part.

* Gaming Act 1968, section 41.

See: BINGO (A) (B)

# Building Regulations [S]

These are laws; if you build something that breaks then you can be ordered to pull it down. Get advice and information from the Building Inspector of your local Borough or District Council*; in London, from the District Surveyor (phone number under GLC).† Their job is to see that the Regulations (published by HMSO) are followed.

The Regulations apply to (1) all new buildings, (2) alterations and extensions to existing buildings – including putting in solid-fuel fires, toilets, sinks, baths, etc., (3) plans for home improvements.

Their purpose is to ensure that what you build will stay up and that you have taken proper fire precautions.

Remember new buildings and some alterations and extensions also need Planning Permission.

* Public Health Acts 1936–61.
† London Building Acts 1930–39 and 1963.

See: FIRE SAFETY; IMPROVEMENT GRANTS; PLANNING PERMISSION

# Bulky Refuse

Councils must (it's the law)* provide skips, special areas of land or separate covered storage areas, where people can take bulky refuse, i.e. old sofas, mattresses, etc. Separate covered storage areas on estates should be at least 80 sq. ft (or 10 sq. metres) in area for every fifty dwellings, but not more than 30 sq. metres for one storage area.† Councils must also remove abandoned vehicles.

If the Council fails to provide these facilities, first complain *in writing* to the Council's Chief Executive or Town Clerk. If nothing happens after this, get advice about writing to the Secretary of State for the Environment to ask him to hold an inquiry.

* Civic Amenities Act 1967.
† British Standards Code C9306.

See: CITIZENS' ADVICE BUREAU; LAW CENTRES

# Burglary Insurance

There are certain conditions which apply to insurance for theft and burglary.

You have to make sure that:

1. five lever mortice dead locks are fitted to all external doors (with minimum 6″ steel box striking plate);
2. all exterior windows are fitted with suitable Chubb window locks;
3. fire exit doors have a suitable lock for when the building is empty.

See: COST GUIDELINES (G); INSURANCE (B) (C)

# Car Parking (A) [S]

*On Estates*

If an estate has a *private* road the Housing Department is responsible for its maintenance and the management of parking. If Housing has the money it can do a number of things to control parking or traffic through the estate.

1. 'Humps' in the road to slow traffic down.
2. A gate across an entrance to the estate (except there must be access for fire and ambulance).
3. Car stickers authorizing residents' parking, provided by the Town Clerk's Department.
4. Lockable posts to reserve parking spaces for tenants.
5. *No Parking* notices.

Discuss your ideas with the Housing Department and involve local councillors. The control of parking or traffic on public highways involves other authorities.

See: COST GUIDELINES (D); PEDESTRIANS; TRAFFIC HAZARDS

# Car Parking (B)

*Planning Requirements*

Before 1975 there was a Government recommendation that one car-space per dwelling be provided on Council estates. However studies soon showed that parking provision, especially garages, was under-used.

The Government now recommends* that Councils should plan parking provision according to local needs with mainly open parking space, and not garages, except on high-density estates where the garages are part of the buildings.

Some underground car parks and garages have been converted for use by youth groups, craft workshops, etc.

\* Department of the Environment Circular 24/75.

See: CAR PARKING (A)

# Car-sharing Scheme

This is only successful when people know and trust each other before-hand. The scheme should be launched through a local club, college or firm where people are already on good terms. Talk to people, then advertise on the notice boards.

Pass round car-sharing sheets to fill in. Drivers making regular journeys write down their times and directions, names, addresses and phone numbers. The lists are then displayed in a prominent place. Those wanting lifts contact the drivers.

No special licence is needed and no insurance problems arise if no fares are charged. Petrol-sharing arrangements can be made privately.

See: MUTUAL AID CENTRE; SELF-HELP GROUPS; TRANSPORT (C)

# Charitable Status

Tenants' Associations which can prove they are charitable do not have to pay income tax.

To qualify as 'charitable': (1) the association must exist to improve the life of people who use its facilities. If it is concerned only with its own members, it must be of benefit to them because of their youth, age, infirmity, disablement, poverty, or social circumstance; (2) the association must be 'non-political'.

Further advice from the Charity Commission, 14 Ryder Street, London SW1.

See: VALUE ADDED TAX

# Child Poverty Action Group (CPAG*)

CPAG works in two ways: directly helping families living at or below the official poverty line, and putting pressure on Government (e.g. to get increases in Child Benefit and Supplementary Benefit, free school meals).
1. Its local branches help and advise families on their welfare rights and how to claim benefits; and act as 'watch dogs' over local public services.
2. In London CPAG has a legal department and a Citizens' Rights office. It collects facts and figures (e.g. about the way allowances are administered, and how many people claim them) and provides information for politicians and the Unions, and gives evidence to Government Committees.

* CPAG, 1 Macklin Street, London WC2B 5NH. Tel: 242 3225. Citizens' Rights office, Tel: 405 5942.

# Children

*Needing Care and Protection*

If a child has been ill-treated, neglected, is beyond the control of parents, or at risk in some way, *Care Proceedings*\* can be started by the local Council (normally by a social worker), the police, or the local inspector of the National Society for the Prevention of Cruelty to Children (all will accept anonymous messages about children at risk).

If the situation is urgent, the child can be removed from home at once, if a magistrate agrees, by means of a *Place of Safety* order. This lasts for up to 28 days, during which time 'Care Proceedings' may be started. This involves the case being brought before a Juvenile Court and, if proven, parents may be ordered to take better care, the child may be placed under the supervision of a social worker, or may be taken into the care of the Local Authority.

\* Children and Young Persons' Act 1969.

See:  HOME HELPS; LAW CENTRES; SOCIAL WORKERS; TRUANCY;
      *Useful Local Contacts p. 277*

# Citizens' Advice Bureau

CAB are run by people who have expert knowledge and advice they can offer on particular problems. If they don't know the answers themselves they know where to look, or where to find the agency that will give you more specialist help.

Some bureaux give legal advice, but this is mainly to help you decide whether your case comes within the law and is worth proceeding with. From then on they will put you in touch with a Law Centre or a solicitor.

They can also put you on to other sources of help and advice. They are usually good at talking things over informally, and interpreting official language.

See:  LAW CENTRES;  NEIGHBOURHOOD  ADVICE  CENTRES;
      SOLICITORS

# Clubrooms and Social Centres  [S]

Local *Housing* Authorities, with the approval of the Minister for Housing, have powers to provide, equip and furnish clubrooms for tenants, pensioners, etc. They can charge the costs to 'Miscellaneous Management Expenses' or (if you have applied far enough ahead), it can be part of the Council's annual estimates (e.g. for the Leisure Services Committee).

Local *Education* Authorities can provide multi-purpose community centres; they also help with running costs of smaller centres started by voluntary effort. The Greater London Council builds clubrooms (1000–1500 sq. ft) including meeting room, kitchen, toilets and furniture. They charge a normal rent and the tenants' association pays running costs.

See:  COST GUIDELINES (B) (M); FIRE SAFETY

# Coach Trips Insurance

Passengers, while on a coach, are covered by the coach company's insurance. Coach companies have to insure themselves for public liability, i.e. against being sued by an injured passenger.

Organizers of trips, e.g. TAs, may take out public liability insurance cover (it is only a small premium) for a party staying together, after leaving the coach; but do not have to for groups splitting up and going off in smaller groups or alone.

Individuals can always take out personal insurance cover when going on trips, from a local insurance office, in the same way that they can if travelling by British Rail or when going on holiday for a few weeks. The premium is low. Local insurance offices will have information about commercial policies.

See:  INSURANCE (B)

# Collecting Money

Tenants' Associations need money, but to make sure that they are bodies set up for charitable purposes their constitutions should explain that all money raised by and on behalf of the TA will be used to further the objects of the TA; to benefit the people who use its facilities and for no other purpose. The amount of subs should be decided by the Association's Annual General Meeting.

When the TA committee is elected, appoint a treasurer and direct him/her to open a bank account in the TAs name, in which to deposit all money raised. Have three people authorized to sign cheques – two signatures per cheque. Collecting subs by street or block representatives is a good way to keep in touch with members.

Get advice about VAT if the TAs turnover in taxable goods or services (e.g. bar profits) exceeds £5000 p.a.

See:   CHARITABLE STATUS; DEMOCRATIC PROCEDURES (A) (B);
       VALUE ADDED TAX

# Communications

*Opening Up*

*Grapevine:* visit neighbours (outside peak TV hours), telephone friends and acquaintances, and make personal contact with key members of local clubs, shops, pubs, churches, etc. Collect information about problems that need solving, and invite suggestions and offers of interesting, short-term, practical help* (make sure you don't frighten people off by asking too much at first).

*Meetings:* bring contacts home to meet and discuss further over a cuppa or a pint. At bigger meetings arrange the chairs, and the procedure, so that there's no 'platform and audience' feeling, and everyone can talk without speechifying.

*Activities:* involve people in practical schemes† that show results and give scope to those who find meetings boring.

* 'Local Talent' survey sheets and † 'Tryout' kits are available as part of the Neighbourhood Action Packs.

See:   FOOD CO-OPS; FUND-RAISING; NEIGHBOURHOOD ACTION
       PACKS; PUBLICITY

# Community Health Council (CHC)

This is the local 'watchdog' body looking after the interests of everyone in the area who is on the National Health.

It is run by people suggested by the local authority or by representatives of voluntary associations involved in community health work. It has full-time staff who have direct contacts with the area health authorities and with doctors, dentists, chemists, hospitals, clinics, etc.

Its job is to follow up complaints, questions, and suggestions for mprovements to the health service in the community.

See: PATIENTS AND LOCAL DOCTORS; PATIENTS AND HOSPITALS; *Useful Local Contacts* (*for the address*), *p. 277*

# Community Workers

Not all areas have them yet. Some are employed by the Council (attached to the Social Services Department, or Town Clerk's Department). Others may work for independent voluntary organizations such as Advice or Law Centres, or the Association of London Housing Estates.

Their main job is to help groups to put into effect what they decide to do, e.g. form a tenants' association; set up and run clubs for youth or for the elderly; organize play groups, social events and outings; raise funds; obtain grants; run a hall; keep local officials up to the mark; help put wrongs right.

They may not be experts on a particular subject. But they have a broad knowledge of the Council – how it works and which official will deal with your problem. They can tell you how to tap other sources of help and expert advice if needed.

See: CITIZENS' ADVICE BUREAU; NEIGHBOURHOOD ADVICE CENTRES; SOCIAL WORKERS

# Consumer Advice Centres

There may be a Consumer Advice Centre in your area. They advise and help shoppers who think that they haven't received a fair deal from a shopkeeper, trader, contractor, manufacturer or finance company. There are trained staff to help you make a wise choice before buying something.

Cases concerned with faulty goods, poor service, misleading prices, goods or services falsely described should be taken up with the trader first, and if you don't get satisfaction contact the Consumer Advice Officer at your nearest centre; or your local Trading Standards Officer.

See: TRADING STANDARDS OFFICER; *Useful Local Contacts p. 277*

# Cost Guidelines (A)

*Introduction*

Figures given are based on costs in London and in northern England in January 1979, assuming the work is organized on or very near the site. But there will be big variations even within one area. Use the figures as starting-points for three kinds of comparison:

1. *proportion of labour cost to other costs* (materials, equipment, etc.) – to work out whether it's worth cutting costs by organizing volunteer work parties*;
2. *relative costs of different schemes* – e.g. erecting a hut, or clearing a play area – to decide what can be tackled right away within the group's resources, and what must wait until more funds can be obtained;
3. *detailed breakdowns of estimates* by local firms.

*The Neighbourhood Action Packs include 'Local Talent' survey forms which could be used to find out what skills are available.

See: COST GUIDELINES (B) TO (N); NEIGHBOURHOOD ACTION PACKS

# Cost Guidelines (B)

*Alternative Meeting Places*

| | £s (in Jan 1979) | |
|---|---|---|
| *Small Huts* (80–200 sq. ft) | up to | 550·00 |
| *Large Site Hut* (1,080 sq. ft) | | 2,690·00 |
| *Portakabin* (try for a discount) (720 sq. ft) | | 5,260·00 |
| *Mobile Building* (fixtures inc.) (320 sq. ft) | | 1,500·00 |
| *Demountable Building:* | | |
| shell (1600 sq. ft) | | 12,000·00 |
| substructure | | 1,230·00 |
| foundation slab | | 608·00 |
| floor finishes | | 996·00 |
| sanitary fittings | | 743·00 |
| kitchen | | 590·00 |
| heating, hot water services | | 2,420·00 |
| electrical installation | | 2,900·00 |
| decorating | | 850·00 |
| drainage | | 1,090·00 |
| service connection (gas, electricity, phone) | | 330·00 |
| site works (Min. for surfacing immediate surroundings) | | 550·00 |

See: COST GUIDELINES (A) (M); COST PLANNING; HUTS

# Cost Guidelines (C)

*Domestic Repairs*

| | £s (in Jan 1979) | |
|---|---|---|
| | Labour | Other Costs |
| Glazing a window* (2′ 6″ × 4′ 0″) | 8·80 | 6·60 |
| Replacing broken door (internal) | 17·60 | 18·00 |
| Unblocking sink waste pipe | 1·50 | |
| Clear drain | 15·00 | |
| Replacing broken roof tile | 3·30 | 0·60 |
| Replacing W C lavatory pan | 16·50 | 27·50 |
| Replacing W C seat | 1·50 | 2·75 |
| Replacing wash handbasin | 7·20 | 22·00 |
| Replacing broken electrical fitting | 2·75 | 2·20 |

* Bigger windows require heavier glass. Cost increases by 25%.

See: COST GUIDELINES (A) (F); COST PLANNING

# Cost Guidelines (D)

*Estate Improvements*

|  | £s (in Jan 1979) | |
|---|---|---|
|  | Labour | Other Costs |
| Two benches for elderly, on paved area | 132·00 | 264·00 |
| Tree saplings, *each* |  | 5·50 |
| Concrete base for portable building (40 yds × 4 yds) | 440·00 | 350·00 |
| Lockable parking posts, *each* | 11·00 | 16·50 |
| Lockable road barrier | 22·00 | 44·00 |
| Access road (load bearing, for refuse vehicle or skip truck; assuming easy natural drainage), *per sq. yard* | 11·00 | 11·00 |
| Turning bay for refuse vehicle, *per sq. yd* | 2·20 | 2·20 |
| Skip base with minimum roof cover | 220·00 | 330·00 |
| Litter bins, *each* | 2·20 | 22·00 |

See: cost guidelines (a); cost planning

# Cost Guidelines (E)

*Estate Maintenance*

(*Yearly* costs for *100* dwellings)

|  | £s (in Jan 1979) | |
|---|---|---|
|  | Labour | Other Costs |
| Cleaning roof gutters | 600·00 | |
| Servicing rubbish chamber | 530·00 | |
| Servicing heating appliances | 1,100·00 | |
| Landscape maintenance (grass cutting – 11 cuts) | 275·00 | 110·00* |
| Making routine surveys and inspections: | | |
|   1. minimum (responding to complaints, average ½ hour visit); | 275·00 | |
|   2. best (systematic check up, average 2 hours visit) | 1,100·00 | |

*Includes petrol and equipment depreciation.

See: cost guidelines (a); cost planning

# Cost Guidelines (F)

*Frequency of Repairs*

Normal wear and tear, *excluding* deliberate damage, produced this average rate of repair for the houses and flats serviced by two large Housing Associations – *per dwelling:*

Once a year:             unblocking sink waste/replacing broken electrical fixture
Once in 2 years:         cleaning out drains
Once in 3–5 years:       repainting front door and windows (external)
Once in 7 years:         reglazing window/replacing W C seat
Once in 10 years:        replacing broken door/broken roof tiles
Once in 20 years:        replacing wash handbasin/replacing W C pan

See:   COST GUIDELINES (C); COST PLANNING

# Cost Guidelines (G)

*Insurance*

| | Commercial | ALHE–FEIA Ltd* (1977/78 prices) |
|---|---|---|
| Employer's liability (1 person) | £10 | £2 (payroll up to £500 p.a.) |
| Public liability by law per £250,000 | £30 | £10 (200 members) |
| Personal accident (assault) | | £1 |
| Fire and Perils | £25 per £10,000 | £10 per £300 + £2 for each additional £100 |
| Theft, damage | £50 | |
| Insurance of money (up to £100) | £10 | £2 |

In the ALHE–FEIA Ltd scheme (under review), the lowest premium which can be paid is £15, but you can choose the cover that you need (adding up to £15). Local insurance brokers will find out the costs of insurance cover for you. Be sure you know what you need.

*ALHE–FEIA: Association of London Housing Estates–Federated Employers Insurance Association Ltd.

See: INSURANCE (B)

# Cost Guidelines (H)

*Modernization*

|  | £s (*in Jan 1979*) | |
| --- | --- | --- |
|  | Labour | Other Costs |
| Installing new kitchen cooker | 25·00 | 110·00+ |
| Installing new bath and wash handbasins | 138·00 | 138·00 |
| Rewiring throughout | 210·00 | 66·00 |

See: COST GUIDELINES (A); COST PLANNING

# Cost Guidelines (I)

*Office Work*

When routine repair and maintenance work has to be arranged through a central office (in the Council, or the HQ of a large Housing Association), each job may require time to 'process' the work:
1. checking that what's requested is really needed;
2. commissioning the work;
3. certifying that the work has been done properly.

*Admin. Labour Cost*

(a) For a 'day to day' routine work estimate 15% of job cost.
(b) For structural work requiring specialist skills (e.g. dampness, dry rot, infestation) estimate 25% of job cost.

See: COST GUIDELINES (A); COST PLANNING; PLAY AREA (A) (B)

# Cost Guidelines (J)

*Sports and Play Facilities*

| | £s (in Jan 1979) | |
| | Labour | Other Costs |
|---|---|---|
| Fenced toddlers' area (15′ × 15′ × 2′) | 28·00 | 28·00 |
| Concrete base for swings (2 yds × 4 yds) | 33·00 | 22·00 |
| Flexible rubber safety slabs (for toddlers' swings) | — | — |
| Toddlers' swing, *each* | | 83·00 |
| Swing for older children, *each* | | 110·00 |
| Play mound with slide | 110·00 | 165·00 |
| Joy wheel | 110·00 | 330·00 |
| Climbing Frame | 55·00 | 220·00 |
| Long Jump Pit | 22·00 | 33·00 |
| Paddling Pool (10′ × 10′) | 66·00 | 44·00 |
| Swimming Pool (50′ × 25′) | 2,200·00 | 4,400·00 |
| Kick-about area (rubble base plus hard surface), *per sq. metre* | 6·00 | 4·00 |

See: COST GUIDELINES (A); COST PLANNING; PLAY AREA (A) (B)

# Cost Guidelines (K)

*Redecoration*

| | £s (in Jan 1979) | |
| | Labour | Other Costs |
|---|---|---|
| Repainting the front door | 3·50 | 2·10 |
| Repainting the outside of a maisonette* (provided no scaffolding required)† | 77·00 | 33·00 |
| Repainting the inside of a maisonette (all rooms) | 230·00 | 154·00 |

\* Assuming maisonette has 1,000-square-feet floor space.
† Wages rise to time-and-a-half for work at over 12 feet high.

See: COST GUIDELINES (A); COST PLANNING

# Cost Guidelines (L)

*Running Adventure Playgrounds*

| | |
|---|---|
| Salary of each play-leader (inc. NHI) | £3,700 |
| Consumable material (paint, nails, etc.), Maintenance | 1,100 . |
| Insurance | 30 |

See: ADVENTURE PLAYGROUNDS; GRANTS (B); INSURANCE
(C); PLAYGROUNDS ON THE CHEAP; PLAY AREA (A) (B)

# Cost Guidelines (M)

*Running Social Centre*

| | £s (*in Jan 1979*) | |
|---|---|---|
| | Labour | Other Costs |
| Annual rates might be: | | 220·00 |
| Rent to Council (nominal) | | 11·00 |
| Telephone (for information bureau) | | 220·00 |
| Electricity | | 550·00 |
| Part-time cleaner | 330·00 | |
| Maintenance (minimum, for short life property*) | 440·00 | 110·00 |
| Insurance | | 165·00 |
| Warden/Community Worker (salary NHI, superan., at start†) | 3,000·00 | |

*On new property full maintenance might be 1% of capital value of property.

†Allow for increments in later years.

See: COST GUIDELINES (A); COST PLANNING

# Cost Guidelines (N)

*Structural Alterations*

|  | £s (*in Jan 1979*) | |
| --- | --- | --- |
|  | Labour | Other Costs |
| Demolishing a non-loadbearing partition wall *per ft run*\* | 5·50 | 2·20 |
| Erecting a non-loadbearing partition wall *per ft run*\* | 16·50 | 11·00 |
| Inserting *interior* fire door | 70·00 | 41·00 |
| Inserting *exterior* fire door | 88·00 | 50·00 |
| Inserting kitchen serving hatch | 22·00 | 11·00 |

\* Assume height of wall is 9 feet.

See: COST GUIDELINES (A); COST PLANNING

# Cost Planning

Budgeting effectively depends on weighing up alternatives. Some items might be worth tackling earlier than others, e.g. a social centre refreshment counter which could soon pay for itself. Other items might come cheaper if group members decided to do the work themselves, borrowing or hiring the equipment needed.

To work out whether this would pay, consult COST GUIDELINES, which show the proportions of each type of cost that would be saved by doing the work direct instead of paying someone else to do it.

To estimate their man (or woman) power, groups could use the 'Local Talent' survey sheets provided in the Neighbourhood Action Packs.

See: COST GUIDELINES (A) TO (N); NEIGHBOURHOOD ACTION PACKS

# Councillors

Councillors are elected every four years to represent (1) wards on the local District or Borough Council or (2) constituencies on the County or Greater London Councils. The political parties select candidates to be voted for. Councillors are not paid, they have their own jobs, but they can claim some expenses.

Councillors do constituency work (helping people with problems) and policy work (serving on a main Council committee like housing, social services, education, etc.). Dates of Council and committee meetings are published in the Town Hall, local Press or libraries. Go and see what happens.

Councillors have most power when their political party has most members on the Council. Contact your councillor by letter at the Members' Lobby, Town or County Hall, or go to his surgery. Complaints about the Council to the local ombudsman must go first to a councillor.

See: COUNCILS (A) (B); OMBUDSMAN (LOCAL)

# Council Officers

The officers of the Council are the paid employees who carry out the everyday work of running the Council's services. They are the people you meet at the Council's different offices. The various Council committees give authority to the officers to make decisions on their behalf on some things, but others have to be decided by elected councillors. The chief officers or directors of the Council departments, e.g. housing, social services, provide advice and information for Council committees and keep the chairmen informed about progress.

Co-ordinating the work of all the different departments and the chief officers is the Chief Executive in the Town Clerk's Department. When writing letters of complaint to any other Council department send a copy to the Chief Executive.

Some Councils publish a booklet to show the departments, their personnel and addresses.

See: COUNCILLORS

# Councils (A)                                          [S]

*England and Wales*

This shows three ways in which Councils at different levels are organized, depending on whether they are in London, or in counties with big cities in them, or otherwise:

| (1) | (2) | (3) |
|---|---|---|
| Greater London Council | Urban Counties or Metropolitan County Councils | Shire Counties or non-Metropolitan County Councils |
| London Boroughs    City of London | Metropolitan District Councils | non-Metropolitan District Councils |
| | Parishes or Towns | Parish Councils and meetings   Welsh Community Councils and meetings |

See:   COUNCIL (B) (C); COUNCIL OFFICERS; COUNCILLORS

---

# Councils (B)                                          [S]

*Parish or Town*

These local Councils are the smallest unit of local government. They possess no legal duties but have the powers to provide or assist in providing services and facilities for the benefits of the people of the parish. Parish or town councils have to hold an annual parish assembly by law. Parish councils can raise a General Rate for halls, playing fields, burial grounds, car parks, footpaths, entertainment, arts, tourism, shelters and allotments. They can buy land for the community. They can also raise a 2p rate for almost anything thought to be for the good of the local people, e.g. concessionary bus fares for the elderly or unemployed teenagers, tree planting, youth clubs, nature trails, etc.

See:   COUNCILS (A) (C)

# Councils (C)

*Responsibilities*

All Councils have some responsibilities for recreation, roads, transport and planning. In addition:

*Metropolitan County Councils* provide fire, police, consumer protection and refuse disposal services;

*Metropolitan District Councils* provide environmental health, social services, education, housing, library and youth employment services and local plans;

*Non-Metropolitan County Councils* provide police, fire, consumer protection, refuse disposal, social services, education, youth employment services and structure plans;

*Non-Metropolitan District Councils* provide only environmental health, housing services and local plans.

In London the Greater London Council provides fire, refuse disposal, education and housing services while the Borough Councils provide consumer protection, environmental health, social services and housing services. The London Metropolitan police force is responsible to the Home Office.

See: COUNCILS (A) (B)

# Court Appearances

When you take out a summons, you will be consulted before the date for the Court Hearing is fixed, so that you can attend.

Beforehand keep a careful note of phone calls, visits, and conversations, which have anything to do with your case. Note dates, and write your notes while the information is fresh.

Discuss all this information carefully with someone else, preferably with a professional who understands how the law works (e.g. a solicitor, or other worker in a Law Centre).

Try to arrange for a solicitor to speak for you when the case is heard in court.

See: LAW CENTRES; SOLICITORS

# Credit Reference Agencies (CRAs)

A trader may refuse you credit because he has consulted a Credit Reference Agency about you. CRAs are private firms which collect and store information about people's 'credit-worthiness' and sell the information to inquirers.

The law* now gives you the right to find out what information has been stored. Ask the trader in writing for the name and address of any CRA he has approached. He must give you this information within seven working days. You then write to the CRA with a fee of 25p asking for a copy of the file on you. The CRA must, by law, send you a copy, or tell you that it does not have one, within seven working days. If there is anything wrong or misleading you may send a correction. If the CRA refuses to act, or to accept the correction, ask the Director of Fair Trading† to intervene.

* Consumer Credit Act 1974, section 157.
† Field House, Breams Buildings, London EC4 ALPR.

See: CITIZENS' ADVICE BUREAU; CONSUMER ADVICE CENTRES; TRADING STANDARDS OFFICER

# Day Centres for the Elderly

The best ones have paid workers who provide a range of activities for both active or handicapped members. Some have specialists to work with the blind. Others simply provide a place to meet, talk, or play bingo.

Town Halls usually keep a list of the day centres in the area. To start a new one, go to the Social Services department for advice. You might get funds from them too.

Grants for paid workers might be available from educational bodies (Local Authorities; or Workers' Educational Association) or charitable organizations (Help the Aged).

Handicapped or frail elderly may need more help, both at the centre, and in getting to and from it.

See: TRANSPORT (A); VOLUNTARY HELP FOR THE ELDERLY; WORKERS' EDUCATIONAL ASSOCIATION

# Democratic Procedures (A)

*Constitution*

A constitution is a set of rules carefully worked out and agreed by the group to make sure that every member has a chance to know what's going on and to share in deciding what to do at each stage. It should also say what the group's aims are, so that newcomers know what they commit themselves to when they join.

The rules set out how the group can appoint certain members to do jobs or take decisions on its behalf, and how they must account to the group for what they have done, and be replaced if need be. To become legally recognized, and be able to apply for grants and other official support, the group's constitution has to be approved and registered under the Industrial and Provident Societies Act, 1965, or the Companies Act.

See: DEMOCRATIC PROCEDURES (B); SELF-HELP GROUPS

# Democratic Procedures (B)

*Membership*

Membership of a group should be open and voluntary. This doesn't mean that anyone who asks has to be accepted. But the whole group should be able to decide whether someone applying to join is likely to support the group's aims as set down in the constitution (e.g. working together, without discrimination, for the neighbourhood benefit). It could also limit size so that it is easy for everyone to have a say; or the group could decide that only locals and/or those with special needs (e.g. for housing) could join.

If a committee is needed it's up to the members to tell the committee what needs to be done, and not the other way round. The committee can act on other members' behalf, but the best results happen when everyone shares the workload (and the credit!).

See: DEMOCRATIC PROCEDURES (A); SELF-HELP GROUPS

# Discrimination

It is against the law* to discriminate against any person because of his or her race or sex, in matters of:
1. employment, promotion and training;
2. housing, and the disposal and management of other types of premises;
3. provision of goods, facilities or services;
4. advertising.

The law also says† that people doing similar work should get equal pay.

Send complaints to:
(*a*) The Commission for Racial Equality (for racial discrimination);
(*b*) The Equal Opportunities Commission (for sexual discrimination).

* Race Relations Act 1976; Sex Discrimination Act 1975.
† Equal Pay Act 1975.

See: RACE RELATIONS

# District Plans [S]

Your Council might be getting a *District* Plan ready. This explains what the Council wants to get done over the next ten years or so, e.g. in housing, industry, shopping, roads, recreation, school building.

The Plan must* show how general policies (described in a separate *Structure* Plan for the whole County) apply in detail to particular properties on particular areas of land. Check with the Council's Planning Department to find when the District Plan is to be put 'on deposit'. This means the public can see what is proposed, and make objections. It is also worth finding out about the Structure Plan because it may deal with some local matters not covered by the District Plan.

Preliminary comments are useful while plans are being prepared, and before the formal stage of the Public Local Inquiry which considers objections.

* Town and Country Planning Act 1971, section 12.

See: PUBLIC PARTICIPATION (A) (B); STRUCTURE PLAN

# Disturbance Allowance [S]

*Modernization*

Tenants who are moved while their homes are being modernized by the Council or by a Housing Association are entitled to a *disturbance allowance*; and possibly a *home loss payment* if they are not moved back again* (they must have lived there five years or more).

Most Councils offer a fixed amount for a disturbance allowance. It usually covers removal costs, and disconnection/connection of home appliances like cookers, telephones, etc. Some Councils have their own removal contractors, so no charge is made; some Councils pay a certain amount for curtains and carpets.

*All* expenses can be claimed for (so keep receipts, invoices, etc.) and the Council or Housing Association must pay.

* Land Compensation Act 1973.

See: ADAPTING HOUSING FOR HANDICAPPED PEOPLE; HOME LOSS PAYMENTS

# Education (A) [S]

*Rights*

Most legal rights support the Local Education Authority and the teacher.

Parents' wishes on choice of school need only be 'borne in mind' by LEA; but it is worth seeking an appointment with the Education Director, particularly if you can argue on (1) religious grounds, (2) travel convenience, traffic, (3) brother/sister at same school, (4) special facilities offered, (5) medical reason or (6) wish for single-sex or mixed school.

Once in school parents must be 'consulted'* about their children's education, but they can't insist; though as a last resort they can appeal direct to the Secretary of State.†

Corporal punishment: if concerned request *details* of LEA and school regulations. If you disagree, put it in writing (or use STOPP‡ form) so that it's on school file in case of trouble. Parents have one right, to arrange for an alternative education.

* Education Act 1944, section 76.        † Education Act 1944, section 68.
‡ Society of Teachers opposed to Physical Punishment, 12 Lawn Road, London NW3.

See: EDUCATION (C) ALTERNATIVES

# Education (B)

*Welfare*

Most LEAs now have Education Welfare Services, but they vary widely.

The EW Officer links home, school and local Education Office and can (1) help families on low incomes with free dinners, clothing and uniform grants, maintenance grants for children staying on at school, bus/rail passes, etc.; advise on special schools, boarding schools and home tuition where needed; (2) link up with School Psychological Service and Child Guidance Clinic, and advise on trouble at school or home, e.g. bullying, truancy, refusal to go to school, child neglect, and counselling for teenagers.

Parents might start with sympathetic teacher or headmaster or ask at local Education Office, or contact Citizens' Advice Bureau or local branch of Child Poverty Action Group.

See: CHILD POVERTY ACTION GROUP; CITIZENS' ADVICE BUREAU; TRUANCY

# Education (C) — Opportunities [S]

*Alternatives*

You have the legal right* to set up your own 'education for school-age children' if you are willing to let the local Education Authority satisfy itself (usually by sending an inspector) that you are fulfilling the law by providing 'efficient full-time education' suited to each child's 'age, ability and aptitude'.

Doing this on your own means finding the money from local fund-raising by parents and others, and possibly a charitable grant. But you might be able to get your project back under the LEA's umbrella if you can persuade them (1) to use their powers† to provide education different from the usual because the children's circumstances are out of the ordinary, e.g. perhaps serious truancy and vandalism, and (2) to let your group do the job on the LEA's behalf.

* Education Act 1944, section 36.
† Education Act 1944, section 56.

See: EDUCATION (A) (B); FUND-RAISING; GRANTS (A);

# Electricity

The Electricity Board should check *all* wiring for safety before electricity supply is reconnected. A report and a test on wiring can cost anything from £15 to £50 (1979), depending on the size of the premises. After the first visit, which is free, visits cost a minimum of £3 (1979). No charge is made for reconnection where there is an existing service cable suitable for use, provided all previous bills have been paid.

Service cables are often removed from empty buildings for safety reasons. New ones cost from £150 to £200 (Jan 1979) to replace.

A different tariff to that charged for electricity at home is charged for clubrooms and halls.

# Eligible Expense

*Renovations*

The Council has an upper limit to the money it will pay for each type of house renovation grant. When someone applies for a grant the Council work out what should be the cost of the improvements. This is the *Eligible Expense* and it must be within the maximum limits:

| Grants | Maximum Eligible Expense | |
|---|---|---|
| Improvement: | £5,000 | (£5,800 each for *flat* conversions) |
| Intermediate: | 1,200 | – for standard amenities (£1,500 for repairs) |
| Special: | depends on number of amenities | |
| Repair: | 1,500 | |

The amount of each type of grant is worked out as a percentage of the *Eligible Expense*. In a Housing Action Area, the grant may be up to 75% (or in cases of hardship 90% of the Eligible Expense. In General Improvement Areas the rate is 60%; and elsewhere 50%.

See: HOUSING ACTION/GENERAL IMPROVEMENT AREAS;
HOUSING GRANTS

# Eviction

Eviction is the legal, or sometimes illegal, way that tenants or squatters are removed from where they are living. No landlord (private, Council or housing association) can evict a tenant without a Court Order, i.e. the say-so of the Court. Illegal eviction is a criminal offence and so is harassment. Some Councils have a harassment officer to deal with bad landlords.

How the law deals with cases for eviction depends on what kind of tenancy the people have (protected or unprotected) and the reasons for the eviction. The law is very complicated on this so *get legal advice* quickly.

A tenant does not have to leave his home immediately he receives a Notice to Quit, unless he wants to and/or he has somewhere else to go.

See: HARASSMENT; HOUSING AID/ADVISORY CENTRE; LAW CENTRE; PROTECTED TENANTS; UNPROTECTED TENANTS

# Fair Rent Registration

Landlords and tenants separately or jointly may apply to the local Rent Officer (in phone book) to register a Fair Rent, saying what they think the rent ought to be. If either party objects, or the Rent Officer disagrees with the suggested rent, both parties will be invited to a meeting. (Local councils can ask the Rent Officer to set a Fair Rent for a *regulated* tenancy.)

Landlord and tenant can appeal to the Rent Assessment Committee if they disagree with the rent finally set.

Landlords cannot charge more than the Fair Rent nor increase it for three years. The new rent also has to be increased gradually.

Council tenants, tenancies created after 1974 with resident landlords and controlled tenants (in property with a rateable value in 1972 of under £70) cannot have Fair Rents set.

See: HOUSING AID/ADVISORY CENTRES; HOUSING ASSOCIATIONS

# Fêtes Insurance

Get advice about insurance cover for any fête or social event that you may hold. It is advisable always to inform your insurance company that you will be holding such events.

The TA's public liability insurance may cover a fête held outside of, but near to the community centre, but extra cover might be needed.

It is possible for fête organizers to insure against *rain* on the day for a premium costing about £10 (1976 price) from a local insurance office. Eagle Star Insurance, 1 Threadneedle Street, London EC2, offers the 'Pluvius' Weather Insurance.

See: INSURANCE (B)

# Fire Safety

Any building used by the public must be fire-safe and a Fire Certificate must be obtained from the fire authorities (the county council or, in London, the GLC) to show that it has been checked.

The Fire Certificate (keep a copy on the premises) states the use(s) of the building, means of escape and arrangements for their safe use; fire safety equipment, alarms and also instructions about keeping escape routes in repair and free from obstructions. A limit is set for the number of people using the building, and instructions given for training and drill for escape.

If a building is going to be altered plans must be checked by the fire authority. Local authorities sometimes give loans to cover the costs of making buildings fire-safe.*

*Fire Precautions (Loans) Act 1973.

# Food Co-op (Bulk Buy Club) (A) – Opportunities

*Which Kind?*

A food co-op or bulk buy club is a group of people who have got together to buy food in large amounts – from wholesalers, local farmers, markets, cash-and-carry warehouses – so that it is cheaper for individual members.

Clubs can either be 'shop' distribution (at least fifty regular members choosing on the spot), or 'pre-order' (best if you are a solid group of about twenty-five members). Clubs can be run in different ways, to suit different systems of ordering and distributing the food.

Up-to-date advice on setting up a Food Co-op or Bulk Buy Club can be obtained from the Bulk Buy Bureau, National Consumer Council, 18 Queen Anne's Gate, London SW1H 9AA.

See: FOOD CO-OP (B) (C) (D) (E)

# Food Co-op (B)

*Jobs and Volunteers*

If there are no volunteers, there'll be no cheap food! Jobs to be shared between the volunteers:

1. *choosing where to buy* (for price and distance);
2. collecting members' orders or estimating demand, and *making up a shopping list* with amounts needed;
3. *calculating costs and collecting money* before or after buying; keeping the books, organizing 'cash flow';
4. *buying* from market, cash-and-carry warehouse, wholesaler or farmer;
5. *transport* to selling or distribution point;
6. *distribution* – weighing out, packing, sharing out goods.

A 'Local Talent' sheet to help attract volunteers is available in the Neighbourhood Action Packs.

See: NEIGHBOURHOOD ACTION PACKS

# Food Co-op (C)

*Distribution*

For a 'do-it-for-others' co-op '*shop*' *distribution* is best. A large number of members can choose what they want and pay on the spot.

For clubs of fifteen to twenty members (do-it-yourself) *a pre-order system* is better – with exact pre-paid ordering of a wide range of food there is no waste, no storage and no permanent base needed. A pre-order system relies on volunteers and has to be organized carefully.

'Shop' distribution needs a meeting-place which can be used regularly and, unless there is a freezer, food must be non-perishable. You will need about £50 to start the shop (try fund-raising or applying to the Council or a local charity for a grant).

You must be insured and safe and secure. Get advice about food hygiene regulations.

See: FIRE SAFETY; FOOD CO-OP (B) (D) (E); FOOD HYGIENE; PUBLIC HEALTH INSPECTOR; TRADING STANDARDS OFFICER

# Food Co-op (D)

*Getting Organized*

Decide whether the food will be distributed through a 'shop', or according to individuals' orders (a pre-order system). The 'shop' could be a local meeting-place, hired once a week.

Decide what food to deal in, where to get it from, and finally who is going to do what, e.g.:
1. teams take turns to do all the jobs for an agreed period; *or*
2. members specialize according to their experience (e.g. accounting); reserves will be needed; *or*
3. everyone does each job by turns. (Careful planning needed!)

The Neighbourhood Action Packs include materials to help the group work out what it wants to do.

See: FOOD CO-OP (B) (C) (E); FOOD HYGIENE; NEIGHBOURHOOD ACTION PACKS

# Food Co-op (E)

*Insurance*

Make sure that:

1. *premises* are insured (if using a community centre or church hall);
2. *drivers* of cars, vans, etc. are properly insured; no special licence is needed;
3. *contents of a freezer* are insured against loss of food due to power cuts, cleaners pulling out plugs, etc.; it is not too expensive;
4. if a community worker is *employed* (not necessarily by the co-op) he/she should be covered by National Insurance contributions.

See: INSURANCE (C)

# Food Hygiene

Any person handling food, not just shopkeepers or restaurateurs, will be guilty of an offence* if the food sold is in any way a danger to public health or is not the right quality or quantity. This applies to a community group operating a canteen, or a food co-op, unless a food manufacturer was at fault.

Get advice from the local Environmental Health Officer; and also the Trading Standards Officer to check scales, etc.

* Food and Drugs Act 1955.

See: PUBLIC HEALTH INSPECTOR; TRADING STANDARDS
OFFICER

# Fund-raising

*Goods and services* are often easier to raise, at first, than cash. They may be sold in jumble sales, Nearly New shops; or raffled (prizes individually contributed – and publicized – by local shops and pubs); or hired out (car washers, gardeners, wood choppers); or the materials used direct as part of a project (telegraph poles, army assault course nets, oil drums – for adventure playgrounds). Make the most of local talent* – for collecting from door to door/inventing attractive stunts to sponsor/ organizing dances, barbecues and socials that yield profits as well as enjoyment/locating the sources of grants and allowances and making effective applications/wheedling discounts from suppliers and surplus materials from manufacturers.

  * A specimen 'Local Talent' sheet to attract volunteers is available as part of the Neighbourhood Action Packs.

See: BINGO (A); CHARITABLE STATUS; GRANTS (A); MUSIC, DANCING AND PLAY LICENCES; NEIGHBOURHOOD ACTION PACKS; PUBLICITY

# Gas Supply

If it is just a matter of reconnection, because the meter is still on the premises, there is no charge for restoring supply.

A meter will normally be installed without a charge if it has been removed but the gas supply is still live.

When the supply has been cut off at the mains a charge is made, proportional to the amount of work done.

The tariff that gas central heating is charged on is the Commercial Heating Rate. The General Credit Rate is charged for all other uses.

# General Improvement Areas (GIAs)

The Government has given powers to local Councils to improve areas of basically sound, mainly private housing, and the surroundings. After improvement the houses must have a life of at least thirty years.

House owners get grants to carry out improvements, while the Council improves the surroundings, e.g. street schemes, lighting, trees, etc. Councils can make unwilling landlords improve their houses.

To get the Council to 'declare' a GIA* there must first be a report of the area by experts: local residents, Council officers, or consultants. The Council has then to get approval from the Department of the Environment.

* D O E Circular 14/75 (outline report).

See: HOUSING GRANTS; REPAIR GRANTS

# Grants (A)
*How to Apply*

Find out* the kinds of grant available, the different bodies that award grants, and what kinds of project each body likes to support. Write an outline of your scheme, so that it appeals to the interests of the body you are applying to. Explain what the grant will help you to do; who will benefit; who will run it; what you can already contribute (workers? premises? equipment? money?); what the grant money will be spent on; what local support there is (residents, councillors, teachers, police, etc.). Show the *rough draft* to local councillors, members of appropriate Council Committees, or (if you're applying to a charitable Trust) the Trust Secretary, and get their advice on the formal application.

* *Grant-Making Trusts*, published by Shelter (6½p plus s.a.e.).

See: GRANTS (B) (C); HOUSING CO-OP (C); HOUSING GRANTS; PLAYGROUPS (A); SHELTER

# Grants (B)

*Adventure Playgrounds and Play Schemes*

Show that you are organized and are also trying to raise your own funds (apply to local firms and shops for money and/or equipment, apply to local charities, or hold fund-raising events).

Local Councils can meet initial costs (up to 85% of capital costs) for adventure playgrounds and pay for a play leader. Your local councillors can tell you how, and which committee you should approach to present a request, for a site or money.

Ask the Council's Youth Officer for advice about obtaining money, equipment to run a scheme and pay for a leader.

The National Playing Fields Association can give money towards the first year's salary of a play leader and the initial capital costs and equipment.

See: FUND-RAISING; GRANTS (A) (C); NATIONAL PLAYING FIELDS ASSOCIATION; PLAYGROUNDS ON THE CHEAP

# Grants (C)

*Youth Service*

Grants are available (dependent on the financial climate) to youth clubs registered at the local Youth Office. The club should be run by an established group, should fulfil local needs, should not be competing with similar clubs, and should have accounts for inspection.

Grants usually cover part or all of salaries, running costs, equipment and furniture and capital grants for building premises or major structural repairs.

There may also be help for training courses, play-leaders, sports instructors, loans of special equipment, camping, films, sports, and premises; and in making arrangements for holiday projects and foreign exchange visits.

See: GRANTS (A); NATIONAL ASSOCIATION OF YOUTH CLUBS; NATIONAL PLAYING FIELDS ASSOCIATION; YOUTH CLUBS

# Harassment [S]

The law says* it is a criminal offence to harass an occupier. This could include unlawful eviction, landlord cutting off essential services – heating, refusing access or changing locks without notice. Go to the Rent Officer or the Council's Legal Department – their solicitors must prosecute the offending person. Maximum penalty in Magistrates Court £400 and/or six months' imprisonment (1972); if it reaches the Crown Court an unlimited fine and/or two years' imprisonment.

* Rent Act 1965, part III, section 30.

See: EVICTION; FAIR RENT REGISTRATION; HOUSING AID/ADVISORY CENTRES; TENANCY AGREEMENTS

# Health Checks on New Uses for a Building

When a building, new or old, is taken over for community use, it's wise to check first with the Environmental Health Department of the local Council.

The same applies when new activities – such as a luncheon club, or a nursery – are introduced in a well-established centre.

There may be regulations, e.g. on food hygiene, or sanitation, which the new use brings into force.

See: FOOD HYGIENE; INSPECTION REPORT; PUBLIC HEALTH REGULATIONS

# Home Helps

Home helps are available to anyone in need because of ill health, maternity, old age or the welfare of children.

Apply to the area Social Services Office.

A Home Help Organizer calls to see how much help is required and what it will cost. Anyone on supplementary benefit may not have to pay for home help, but others have to pay according to their means.

Help given varies from a few hours per week to full-time assistance; it may include a night attendance service.

A Child Help can come to live in the family's home, as a mother substitute, when the mother is in hospital or temporarily missing, so that children do not have to go into care.

See: SOCIAL SERVICES DEPARTMENT

# Homelessness

The homeless are families, or single people, who have no accommodation, or who have accommodation but cannot use it (e.g. battered wives), or who have been threatened with homelessness and will be homeless within twenty-eight days, or who live in mobile homes and have nowhere to park.

Housing Departments must* now house people who are genuinely homeless or threatened with homelessness. They must give priority to families with children, pregnant women, the elderly or handicapped, emergency fire and flood disaster cases.

Councils make sure first that homelessness was not intentional. If their inquiries take longer than a day, they may provide temporary accommodation.

Other applicants, without priority, are entitled to have the Council's decision in writing, with appropriate help or advice.

The Secretary of State can provide grants or loans to voluntary bodies concerned with the homeless.

* Housing (Homeless Persons) Act 1977, sections 3 and 4.

See: EVICTION; SHELTER

# Home Loss Payments

A person who has to move out permanently from a home he has lived in for five or more years is entitled* to *home loss payment* (= three times the rateable value, min. £150, max. £1,500), provided the claim is made within six months of the move. This also applies to a tenant who can't return because modernization has made the dwelling unsuitable for the tenant's needs.

The Council must pay up within three months. Temporary moves may be covered by Disturbance Allowances.

* Land Compensation Act 1973, section 29.

See: DISTURBANCE ALLOWANCE; LAW CENTRES; NUISANCE FROM PUBLIC WORKS; OMBUDSMAN; RATES

# Home Ownership

Need a mortgage? The main sources of mortgage loans are building societies and local authorities, but you can also get loans from insurance companies. Many building societies are reluctant to lend at all on old property; or they will only lend up to 90% of the property's value (and above 80% they ask for an insurance guarantee). Besides this they usually want you to have saved with them for at least six months already.

If you cannot get a loan from a building society, try the local authority. They will often lend up to 100% of the value of the property, and will also consider older houses and conversions.

Building societies and local authorities will tell you how much they will lend on the security of your, and your spouse's income. You can also get advice about home buying from the CAB.

See: CITIZENS' ADVICE BUREAU; HOUSING GRANTS; IMPROVEMENTS GRANTS (A) (B); MATURITY LOANS; MORTGAGE LOANS

# Housing Action Areas (HAAs)  [S]

Where there is bad housing and poor social conditions, local residents and voluntary groups can get together with Council officers to produce a *report* recommending that the area should be 'declared' a Housing Action Area* by the Council. This means that various improvements can be pushed through without waiting for the whole area to be knocked down and 'redeveloped'.

The Council must give special attention to problems such as racial tension, unemployment, lack of social facilities. It can encourage Fair Rent Housing Associations and housing co-operatives; provide renovation and repair grants of up to 90% of the improvement costs; and make landlords either improve their property, or sell it so that someone else (perhaps a housing co-op) takes over and does the job instead.

  * D O E Circular 14/75 (outline report).

See:  GENERAL IMPROVEMENT AREAS; IMPROVEMENT GRANTS

# Housing Aid/Advisory Centres

Some Councils have set up Housing Aid Centres as part of their Housing Department, to provide advice and assistance to the public (*private and Council tenants, owner occupiers and landlords*) on all problems to do with housing.

Some Centres are run by voluntary bodies, e.g. Shelter.

The Centres try to improve existing housing conditions and to find ways of rehousing people who are homeless, or in danger of becoming homeless.

They give advice on buying a home, improving, modernizing or rehabilitating houses and grants available, and also advice on rents, eviction, housing outside London and repair problems.

See:  IMPROVEMENT GRANTS; SHELTER; *Useful Local Contacts*

# Housing Associations (HAs)

These are non-profit making, voluntary organizations providing homes for renting. If they register with the Registrar of Friendly Societies and the Housing Corporation they can receive funds from the Corporation or local authorities.

HAs build new homes, or modernize or convert old houses into flats. Some provide special housing for the handicapped or the elderly; others collectively own or manage their homes, as housing co-operatives. HAs charge Fair Rents, set by the Rent Officer, which may not be increased for three years and then only with his approval. Tenants can apply for Rent Allowances and Rent Rebates, but they are not protected by the Rent Acts.

Apply direct; or through agencies such as Shelter, CAB, or a Housing Aid Centre; or get nominated by the Housing Department or Social Services.

See: CITIZENS' ADVICE BUREAU; FAIR RENT REGISTRATION; HOUSING AID/ADVISORY CENTRES; HOUSING CO-OP (A); RENT REBATES/ALLOWANCES; SHELTER; UNPROTECTED TENANTS

# Housing Co-op (A)
*Which Kind?*

In a *full-scale housing co-op* people get together to buy (and if necessary convert) houses or flats which then belong to the whole group. They decide how best to suit everyone's housing needs, and how to run things. In an area of bad housing the money could come through grants and loans paid direct to the co-op by the Government. Or it could be raised by getting mortgages, or from among the group themselves.

In a *housing management co-op* a group of tenants make an agreement with the landlord (e.g. Council or Housing Association). In return for a set amount of money they take over some or all of the running and/or the improvement work. They can do this themselves or pay someone else. Whatever they save they use as they choose.

See: DEMOCRATIC PROCEDURES (A) (B); HOUSING CO-OPS (B) TO (G); SELF-HELP GROUPS

# Housing Co-op (B)

*Who Manages?*

The co-op runs itself. It decides how much work to tackle itself, and what to pay outsiders to do. Within limits it can employ whoever it wants to. But when it receives money from the Government, it may be on condition that they approve the co-op's choice of architect, contractor, etc. Usually there is a free choice of other workers (though occasionally the agreement in a management co-op requires it to use Council or Housing Association workers when available).

The co-op is the boss. It works out what it wants and says how its employees, in the office or on the site, are to keep members properly informed so that the quality of the work can be checked.

Not really so difficult! Many home owners do it without anyone being surprised.

See: DEMOCRATIC PROCEDURES (A) (B); HOUSING CO-OPS (A) (G)

# Housing Co-op (C)

*Grants and Loans*

Councils and Housing Associations get money from the Government to provide housing. *Management co-ops* can tap some of this money in exchange for what they do themselves*. *Full-scale co-ops* may be able to get government money direct.†

Management co-ops get a share of the rents and modernization money from the Council. Full-scale co-ops, if they register with the Housing Corporation, can get money to buy and modernize or build new, and to cover lawyers', architects' fees, etc. About 80% is given and the rest has to be paid back gradually by the co-op, from its rents. In addition the co-op gets a yearly allowance to cover running costs.

Other full-scale co-ops may be able to get mortgages (from the Council or a Building Society) and/or Improvement Grants (as owners of the property).

* Housing Rents and Subsidies' Act 1975, section 1, para 9; Department of the Environment Circular 8/76.

† Housing Rents and Subsidies Act 1975, section 6.

See: HOUSING CO-OP (A) (D) (E) (G); IMPROVEMENT GRANTS

# Housing Co-op (D)

*Conditions for Registration and Approval*

A co-op needs to have 'legal status'* so that (1) it can get government money, and (2) if it goes into debt its members only lose the value of their own shares.

To become legally recognized as a co-op, it must show that it is a democratic body, existing for the benefit of its members, with everyone having an equal say. It must have written rules which are approved by the Registrar of Friendly Societies† (this costs up to £85).

A full-scale co-operative wanting government money will have also to get registered with the Housing Corporation.‡ It must show it is thinking ahead, that its plans are realistic and that people living in a poor housing area will benefit.§

* Industrial and Provident Societies Act 1965.
† 17 North Audley St, London W1.
‡ 149 Tottenham Court Rd, London W1.
§ Department of the Environment Circular 170/74.

See: DEMOCRATIC PROCEDURES (A) (B); HOUSING CO-OP (G)

# Housing Co-op (E)

*Rents, Deposits, Shares*

If a *full-scale co-op* is getting government money it is not allowed to charge more than the 'Fair Rent' fixed by the local Rent Officer. If it is *not* getting government money it can charge whatever members decide (but make sure this covers borrowing costs!).

A *management co-op* has to agree with the owner (the Housing Association or the Council) on the amount of rent to be charged (e.g. Council may insist on 'Council rents').

Co-ops can charge their members a *deposit* (e.g. to cover damage to furniture and fittings), but it is wise to check the terms carefully first with a solicitor.

Anyone accepted for membership must buy a share (which can't be resold). Usually this is no more than a 'membership ticket' of £1 or less; though it could be much more.

See: FAIR RENT REGISTRATION; HOUSING CO-OP (A) (G)

# Housing Co-op (F)

*How Does it Grow?*

A co-op grows best by spreading its interests so that everyone is able to feel involved and has something to contribute. This means breaking the work down and sharing it out in an interesting way which makes the most of each person's skills and experience,* e.g. separate 'Working Parties' dealing with: Structure and Repairs; Fund-raising; Social Events; Care (toddlers, youngsters, elderly); Members (selection, welcoming, trouble-shooting); Budgets and Book-keeping; Negotiations; Design and Improvements. Members can share other needs and interests: baby-sitting; bulk-buying (spend co-op's surplus on communal freezer?); Car repairs; concern about a better deal for the area.

So long as the co-op is small it can keep everyone in the know, so that they all have a say in what goes on.

*'Local Talent' survey sheets are included in the Neighbourhood Action Packs.

See: HOUSING CO-OP (B); NEIGHBOURHOOD ACTION PACKS; SELF-HELP GROUPS

# Housing Co-op (G)       [S]

*Who Can Advise?*

Get preliminary information from an experienced group.* Write to other groups in your area† for their literature (send s.a.e.). Choose one and arrange a visit to them and/or invite their members over (offer hospitality). Make sure that non-committee members are also involved. Find out how they started, what rules they adopted, how they located properties, where they got their money, how they involve their members, where they are heading.

Study the literature produced by Co-op housing section of the Housing Corporation† or National Federation of Housing Associations‡ and get expert advice from their field officers.

*For example, Manchester Federation of Housing Co-operatives, c/o 14 Seymour Rd, Manchester M22 (061 740 8658).

† 149 Tottenham Court Rd, London W1 (01 387 9466). It also publishes a directory of housing co-ops.

‡ N F H A, 30 Southampton St, London WC2 (01 240 2771).

See: CITIZENS' ADVICE BUREAU; HOUSING AID/ADVISORY CENTRE

# Housing Grants
*Which to Choose*

*Improvement Grants* are to help improve existing dwellings to a high standard; or to convert older properties into flats. The Council decides whether to give a grant, and what work it must be spent on.

*Intermediate Grants* are for repairs or replacements needed in order to provide amenities that are missing. Once certain basic conditions are met, the Council must pay the grant.

*Special Grants* provide certain standard amenities to benefit people in multi-occupied houses. The Council can decide whether or not to give the grant.

*Repair Grants* are for repairs and replacements to dwellings in Housing Action or General Improvement Areas. The Council only pays in cases of financial hardship.

*Maturity Loans* are also available to house-owners to help them meet their share of the costs of improvements.

See: IMPROVEMENT GRANTS; INTERMEDIATE GRANTS; MATURITY LOANS; MULTIPLE OCCUPATION GRANTS; REPAIR GRANTS

# Huts

Portakabins, demountable buildings, site huts, short-life property, e.g. an empty pub, church or shop or an empty flat on the estate may all be worth considering as an alternative to starting out with a purpose-built new building that may take years to obtain.

Site huts can be made to measure. Sometimes a quite small hut provides enough space to store equipment, hold group meetings, and establish a base from which more ambitious schemes can be organized.

Play schemes might use a second-hand 10′ × 8′ hut (perhaps donated by builders) for use of a play-leader only, or a 20′ × 10′ hut for a play-leader plus some indoor use by children.

See: ALTERNATIVE MEETINGPLACES; COS T GUIDELINES (B); FIRE SAFETY

# Improvement Grants (A) [S]

These are given to help owners to repair old houses to a good standard; or to provide flats by converting large houses. The Council decide whether to give a grant and what work it must be spent on. They may give a block-grant to a group of house owners in a street.

The Council lays down that when the improvement work is done, the dwelling will be in good repair; will have a useful life of thirty years, and will have ten 'standard amenities'. They might agree to ease some of these conditions.

The amount of grant will be fixed by the Council, and kept within a certain percentage of the 'eligible expense' (max. £5,000 per dwelling or £5,800 for converting each flat).

See:  ELIGIBLE EXPENSE; IMPROVEMENT GRANTS (B);
      STANDARD AMENITY; TEN-POINT STANDARD

# Improvement Grants (B) [S]

*Conditions*

Dwellings with rateable values of £300 or more in London, £175 or more elsewhere, get no grants. Dwellings with lower rateable values get a percentage of the cost of the work, within a limit set by the Council. Repairs and replacements must not take up more than half this cost.

If one of the old standard grants, or an intermediate or a repair grant has been given, an improvement grant can be applied for to bring the house up to a better standard. An adjustment will be made to take account of the earlier grant.

For registered disabled people, improvement grants can be used to adapt a dwelling to make it easier for them.

See:  ADAPTING HOUSING FOR HANDICAPPED PEOPLE;
      ELIGIBLE EXPENSE; IMPROVEMENT GRANTS;
      INTERMEDIATE GRANTS; REPAIRS; TENANTS'
      RIGHTS (A) (B)

# Industrial Co-operatives

Have you ideas, expert advice and a good organization? Have you found a product or service which is needed? Get a group together which includes the skills needed (Job Centre might help). Get advice from local businessmen or a management department in a college. Do a market survey, rough costing, and outline development plans. Ideas and basic information, in the form of the WORK FACT BANK (the sequel to the NEIGHBOURHOOD FACT BANK) and the PRODUCTION LINE pack, are available through Inter-Action.

Then approach the Industrial Common Ownership Movement* (or COSIRA† for a rural area) and your local Small Firms Information Centre (in phone book) for help. Find out if local council has 'seed money' to lend co-ops. You need seven people to start a registered co-op. ICOM has model rules to help.

* ICOM, 31 Hare Street, London SE18.
† Council for Small Industries in Rural Areas, Queen's House, Fish Row, Salisbury, Wilts.

See: JOB OPPORTUNITIES; SELF-HELP GROUPS; WORK AGENCY; WORK SHOPS

# Industrial Tribunals

By law* no employer can dismiss a worker 'unfairly'. Anyone employed for twenty-six weeks has the right to complain of unfair dismissal and to ask for a written explanation. If this is unsatisfactory, appeal within three months of dismissal to an Industrial Tribunal. Get booklet *Dismissal – Employee Rights* and application form from Unemployment Benefits Office or Job Centre. Get advice on filling it in from Law Centre or union official.

At the tribunal (a lawyer, a union official and an employee) your boss or firm must justify the dismissal. If your appeal is upheld the tribunal can order either a reinstatement (old job back) or re-engagement (similar type of job). The law cannot force employer to take you back but if he won't he must pay compensation.

* Trade Union and Labour Acts 1974, 1976; Equal Pay Act 1970; Employment Protection Act 1975; Sex Discrimination Act 1975.

See: LAW CENTRES

# Inspection Report [S]

(*Under 'Section 99'*)

This is simply a detailed description of what is wrong with the premises and why it is causing a 'statutory nuisance' to the occupier, and/or to neighbours (e.g. spreading damp). Sometimes a Public Health Inspector will help you write it.

In a block of flats the report should cover all the flats affected by the nuisance, though you need only take out summonses on one or two.

Write a warning letter to the landlord enclosing the inspection report, and saying that you will take out a summons unless the repairs are done within fourteen days. If the Council is the landlord, send additional copies of the letter and the report to the Chief Clerk, the Director of Housing, the Chief Environmental Health Officer and the Building Works Manager. Keep a couple of spare sets on file.

See: PUBLIC HEALTH INSPECTOR; SECTION 99; STATUTORY NUISANCE; SUMMONS

# Insurance (A) [S]

*Who Needs It?*

Running a community centre means taking on responsibility for the building; for its contents; and for the people who use it. Damage or injury will happen and where people suffer it is not the association who will be sued but the individual members, or paid employees, of the association.

*It is important* to insure against legal liability for personal injury and to protect the association against the expenses of putting right damaged or lost property.

Insurance cover is necessary for special equipment, for the association's activities – play groups, sport, trips, a youth club, play schemes. If you employ anyone you are required *by law* to be insured as an employer. Insurance cover can be obtained through a commercial insurance broker or special organizations who have policies covering special activities.

See: COST GUIDELINES (G); INSURANCE (B) (C)

# Insurance (B)

*What Kind?*

*Employer's Liability* – any voluntary group employing people must *by law* have this insurance in case a paid employee sues them.

*Public Liability* – if your club or group is organizing anything for other people protect yourselves from being sued by people.

*Personal Accidents* – to members of the group engaged in club business (e.g. carrying money) or activities (sport).

*Building and Contents* – in case the club centre (if you have one) is damaged by flood, fire, vandalism and needs repairs, or the contents get stolen or damaged.

*Special Cover* – for expensive equipment, dangerous sports, rain and fêtes.

See; BURGLARY INSURANCE; COACH TRIPS INSURANCE; COST GUIDELINES (G); FÊTES INSURANCE

# Insurance (C)

*Where to Get It?*

*For TAs and club activities:* Association of London Housing Estates, 17 Victoria Park Square, Bethnal Green, E2 9PE.

*For Youth Clubs and sponsored events:* National Association of Youth Clubs (NAYC), PO Box 1, Bord Gate, Nuneaton, Warwickshire CV11 4DB.

*For Playgroups:* Pre-School Play Groups Association, Alford House, Aveline Street, London SE11 5DJ.

*For Play Schemes:* NAYC and Commercial Union at Seivwright, Young and Co., 11 Forest Lane, Stratford, London E15.

*For Adventure Playgrounds:* National Playing Fields Association, 25 Ovington Square, London SW3 1LQ.

*For Playgroups, Play Schemes and Adventure Playgrounds:* Morton Michel Insurance Brokers, 131 Anerley Road, London SE20.

*For Food Co-ops:* National Consumer Council, Bulk Buy Bureau, 18 Queen Ann's Gate, London SW1.

# Inter-Action*

Inter-Action is a charitable trust serving neighbourhood groups wanting to involve people in improving their surroundings, providing better services for children, better job opportunities, and better leisure and recreation facilities.

Its *Advisory Service*, drawn from a pool of thirty experts, gives free advice on problems of fund-raising, organization, publicity and publishes practical handbooks.

*NUBS – Neighbourhood Use of Buildings and Space* is a branch of the advisory service offering community groups architectural know-how, ranging from preliminary survey to detailed control of contracts on site. Initial consultation free, subsequent charges based on the group's ability to pay.

*The City Farm Land Bank* helps groups negotiate with local authorities to convert derelict land and buildings so that youngsters and adults can run mini-farms (from $\frac{1}{2}$ acre upwards).

* 15 Wilkin St, London NW5 3NG (Tel: 01 458 0881).

# Intermediate Grants (A)

These are given for basic improvements to provide missing amenities and necessary repair work for which the 'eligible expense' is limited to £1,500. There are five conditions that must be met by the completion of the work. If you fulfil them the Council cannot refuse a grant.

The Council will say how much of the eligible expense is related to standard amenities (max. £1,200), and how much to repairs and replacements (max. £1,500), and will give a certain percentage of this. They may increase the eligible expense for unforeseen needed additional work.

Grants may cover the provision of alternative standard amenities for disabled people.

See: ELIGIBLE EXPENSE; INTERMEDIATE GRANTS (B); STANDARD AMENITY

# Intermediate Grants (B)

*The Five Conditions*

The Council checks that when the repair and improvement work is finished:

1. the standard amenities are provided for the use of the occupants only;
2. the dwelling will be in a good state of repair (not counting internal decoration), considering its age, character, and location;
3. the roof insulation is up to the standards set by the Building Regulations;
4. in all other respects it is fit for people to live in;
5. that it will last for at least fifteen years as a dwelling.

If these conditions are met, and approval was given before the work started, the Council cannot turn down an application for an intermediate grant.

Councils sometimes agree to ease these conditions in special circumstances.

See: BUILDING REGULATIONS; INTERMEDIATE GRANTS; STANDARD AMENITY

# Job Opportunities

Training helps: there are several ways to get it: local Further Education Colleges/Adult Institutes (local library has brochures and addresses); the Government's TOPS (Training Opportunities Scheme) courses for men/women over 18 who have been away from full-time education for over three years. In many practical subject courses lasting up to twelve months you can get tax-free grants and other benefits. YOP (Youth Opportunities Programme for 16–18's) and STEP (Special Temporary Employment Programme for 19's and over) give the young unemployed a chance to learn skills under supervision. Details from local Job Centres, which should have 'help yourself' information cards on jobs available; and someone to offer careers guidance, and arrange (if you want) vocational tests to find out what you're good at. (You can also get advice on training from TOPS.)

Explore on your own by replying to small ads, or making direct approach to personnel officers in local firms and organizations.

A group can set up its own work experience, work agency, or even an industrial co-op with Government support.

See: INDUSTRIAL CO-OPERATIVES; WORK AGENCY; WORK EXPERIENCE PROGRAMME; WORK SHOPS

# Law Centres

They are especially interested in cases in which the good of the community is at stake. They will collect similar complaints from different people and take them up as a whole with the authorities concerned.

They will give you some general advice, usually without charge. They may take your case up for you and perhaps represent you in court, depending on whether they think your case is important to the community as well as to you. If they go this far, you may have to make a contribution to the cost, but they will tell you what this is likely to be beforehand.

Before you consult them, make notes about your problem, and take with you any letters or documents that have anything to do with the case.

See: CITIZENS' ADVICE BUREAU; COMMUNITY WORKERS; NEIGHBOURHOOD ADVICE RIGHTS CENTRES; SOCIAL WORKERS; SOLICITORS

# Legal Aid*

The Legal Aid Scheme helps anyone of limited means to get a solicitor. Sometimes this is free; usually the client pays part of the cost, according to his income.

Legal aid includes legal advice and assistance, e.g. writing letters, drafting wills, obtaining opinions from a barrister and visiting a police station (up to £25 solicitor's costs); legal aid for *civil* court proceedings; and legal aid in *criminal* court proceedings for people facing prosecution.

* *Guide to New Legal Aid* is free at most Advice Centres.

See: CITIZENS' ADVICE BUREAU; LAW CENTRES; NEIGHBOUR-HOOD ADVICE/RIGHTS CENTRES; SOLICITORS

# Lotteries [S]

*The Three Types*

1. *Small lotteries* which must be run *during* a dance, fête, etc.

2. *Private lotteries* run by a club, society or association to sell tickets to members only. Neither of these need legal cover.

3. Lotteries run by a club to sell tickets to *the public outside*. These must be *registered*,* on a form obtained from the Town Clerk's department at the Town Hall. It costs £10 to register, renewable on 1st January each year (£5). The club has to name and authorize a promoter to make a return after the lottery has been held. Return forms, also from the Town Hall, must be correctly filled in, certified by two adults (over 21) appointed by the club in writing, within three months of the winner's draw – or else there is a fine of up to £400.

* Lotteries and Amusements Act 1976.

See: REGISTERED LOTTERIES; UNREGISTERED LOTTERIES

# Lunch Clubs

*For the Elderly*

Groups thinking of starting a luncheon club should collect information showing the need, and make sure their premises are suitable. Get advice from the Environmental Health Inspector. The Council Social Services Department and/or local charities might help with money and equipment.

Charges for meals should cover costs of the food, rent, lighting and heating, with no profit. The work is done by volunteers.

Make sure that you have adequate insurance cover. Age Concern* have a low-rate scheme.

* 60 Pitcairn Road, Mitcham, Surrey.

See: FOOD HYGIENE REGULATIONS; HEALTH CHECKS ON NEW USES FOR A BUILDING; PUBLIC HEALTH INSPECTOR

# Magazines and Newsletters

To get started: you need a group of five to six people meeting regularly to rough-out the nature, style, frequency, circulation and costs. Then contact other groups and hold a public meeting to get ideas, money and practical help. Raise advertising from local shops. Obtain short articles, interview people, find artists, poets, *and* typists with access to high quality typewriters, preferably with 'golf-ball' selection of different type styles and carbon ribbons (which give crisper reproduction). Decide on how you will print it. Litho or duplicated? Commercially, with a friendly press, or d-i-y? Do the lay-out and paste-up. Print. Throw a party to get all the collating done. Distribute it by street selling, in shops, through clubs, at meetings, in schools, colleges and canteens. Advertise. Hold one open meeting per issue. Persuade each local group to send one person to report response and pass on offers of help and suggestions for improvements.

See: COMMUNICATIONS; MEDIA; PUBLICITY

# Maturity Loans

House owners can obtain maturity loans from the Council to help them meet their share of the costs of improvement. The Council have details. Usually only the interest is paid back, unless the house is sold. When this happens the owner pays back to the Council the amount originally borrowed.

Pensioners may be able to get the interest paid by the Department of Health and Social Security.

See: HOUSING GRANTS; IMPROVEMENT GRANTS; REPAIR GRANTS; SOCIAL SERVICES DEPARTMENT

# Meals-on-Wheels

Councils sometimes provide a meals-on-wheels service. They do not legally have to. It is an expensive scheme to run (because of petrol costs) and often it is not a daily service.

Any person who is unable to cook a meal for him/herself can apply to Social Services for meals-on-wheels if there is a service operating; they do not have to be elderly.

Some Councils have tried schemes where neighbours or home helps cook a meal for an elderly person. The Council then refunds most of the costs and the elderly person pays the rest.

See:   HOME HELPS; LUNCH CLUBS; 'POP-INS'; WOMEN'S ROYAL
       VOLUNTARY SERVICE

# Media

*How to Use*

Spark off controversy through letters to local Press, phone-ins on local radio or regional TV. Try to pick on reporters, editors and producers whose work you respect. Contact them individually, offering *hard news*:

1. *short letters* to spark off a correspondence;
2. *pictures* with two-line explanations;
3. *'filler' items*, 100–200 words ready-made for columnists;
4. *handouts* providing facts and quotes for use in a hurry;
5. *a Press conference* to reveal a new situation or launch a subject that makes news. Check that you schedule it to suit the routines of the Press people you invite, and it leaves them time to meet their respective deadlines.

See:   COMMUNICATIONS; PUBLICITY; VIDEO (A) (B)

# Members of Parliament (MPs)

Your rightful link with Parliament whether you voted for him or not is your local MP. Go to him or her on any matter concerning government – *not* council policy, e.g. overall educational policy, discrimination, individual rights. It can then be passed to the Ministry concerned. It is the MP's job to see that someone acts, or explains why no action is taken. Many MPs are helpful at grass-roots level – sorting out individual cases of hardship. Write to your MP at the House of Commons, London SW1.

Your MP usually holds a surgery in the constituency. The time and place will be given in the local paper.

Complaints to the Ombudsman about any central government department *must* go first to your MP.

See: COUNCILLORS; OMBUDSMAN

---

# Minibus

*For Community Use*

Minibuses will not succeed where there are other competing forms of transport. But in rural areas when there are no buses, local people can run their own. A local committee arranges the time-table, and a rota of voluntary drivers. Cooperation is needed with: the County Council, to secure clearance with the Traffic Commissioners; local and Community Councils, to support you; and the bus company, to give Public Service Vehicle training to the drivers, and perhaps to donate a minibus.

Special legislation is not needed. To get going – contact local groups and councillors for an initial meeting. Make a survey of the needs, and of potential driver support, before approaching the County Council.

See: TRANSPORT (C)

# Mortgage Loans

Choose which type to fit your income and your future circumstances.

*Ordinary mortgage:* with tax relief on the mortgage interest at the basic rate.

*Option mortgage:* the mortgagor pays a subsidized mortgage interest rate and does not receive tax relief. Annual net payments start off at a high level, but decrease over the years.

*Endowment mortgage:* only interest has to be paid each year. The capital is paid off when a linked life insurance policy matures.

*Low start mortgage:* useful for first-time buyers, and for people choosing an option mortgage. You start low, but gradually rise to higher than normal payments in later years.

*Equity sharing:* a purchaser buys a lease on a house for half its market value, and then pays rent equivalent to normal renting on the other half.

See: HOME OWNERSHIP

# Multiple Occupation Grants

These grants are for basic improvements to houses in multiple occupation, and are made towards the costs of putting in standard amenities which will be shared by all the occupiers (who may be several households).

Each item to be installed must be within a limit set by the Council. The Council limits the total cost of the improvement to what is called the 'eligible expense'; and they give only a percentage of this (about 50–60%). They might help to install the amenity, and also to increase the eligible expense if unforeseen additional work is needed.

See: ELIGIBLE EXPENSE; STANDARD AMENITY

# Music, Dancing and Play Licences

Getting a licence, and the cost, both depend on the number of people you plan to admit. You must obey the fire, health, and safety regulations; and so must anyone who hires the premises from you.

Apply to the Council (in London, the GLC*). Before deciding whether to grant a licence they must check that:

1. the regulations are being applied;
2. no one living near has a reasonable objection.

| London costs 1979* | Music; music and dancing for 100 people | plays for 100 seated people |
| --- | --- | --- |
| Full licence | £35 a year Rises to £55 for 200 | £15 a year |
| Occasional licence | £10 a day plus £1 per additional days for up to 28 days | £1.25 a week |

\* GLC: Room 212, County Hall, London SE1 7PB.

See:  BAR LICENCES; FIRE SAFETY; PUBLIC HEALTH REGULATIONS

# Mutual Aid Centre*

The Centre aims (1) to encourage existing self-help groups to take on new activities, e.g. tenants' group or pre-school group adding on a bulk buy group; (2) to support new mutual aid projects, e.g. domestic appliance repair co-operative, or a parent–teacher cooperative to save school that the local authority wants to close; (3) to act as national grapevine and network so that small local groups can pool ideas and draw on each other's experience, and to be a power house to back up any group needing to campaign or lobby; (4) to give advice to individual groups with special problems; and also to produce general-interest publications, e.g. keeping accounts, legal status, fund-raising, publicity, links with LEAs.

\* 18 Victoria Park Square, London E2 9PF (01 980 6262).

# National Association of Youth Clubs [S] (NAYC)*

NAYC aims to help youth, through leisure activities, to develop as individuals and members of society. It has three national divisions and fifty-two local associations and has a membership of over 300,000 young people in nearly 4,000 clubs. Affiliation costs about £10 (1977).

NAYC organizes training courses for youth leaders and young people, including courses for clubs for Physically Handicapped and Able Bodied (PHAB) Youth.

It helps with club programmes, exhibition material, visual aids, and literature for clubs, including an insurance scheme. Two residential centres provide facilities for training courses for leaders and members, as well as holidays.

*NAYC, PIO Box 1, Bord Gate, Nuneaton, Warwickshire CV11 4DB.

See: *Useful Local Contacts (for nearest branch)*

# National Playing Fields Association*

This body encourages the provision of recreational facilities for all age groups. It provides technical advice for indoor and outdoor sports and has specialist information on recreation for children and young people, and in particular promotes training in play leadership. It works with councils and other bodies to buy land to protect existing recreational and sporting facilities.

*25 Ovington Square, London SW3 1LQ.

See: *Useful Local Contacts (for nearest branch)*

# Neighbourhood Action Packs (A) — Opportunities

*What They Contain*

This FACT BANK is part of a bigger scheme developed with the help of tenants' associations, local action groups, voluntary agencies, the Department of the Environment and Nottingham University. It presents basic facts and real-life situations in a form which any group can use at once to work out for themselves what needs doing first, how best to do it, what obstacles have to be overcome, where to look for support.

The packs include 'Case Histories' outlining how different groups overcame setbacks and got results; various 'Tryouts', using table-top models, charts, and cards, which a group can move around to explore practical possibilities and foresee conflicts of interest and personality that could arise; and a 'Planning For Real' participation scheme, adaptable to each local situation, enabling residents to deal with professionals on level terms.

See: NEIGHBOURHOOD ACTION PACKS (B) How to Follow Up

# Neighbourhood Action Packs (B) — Opportunities

*How to Follow Up*

During 1978 the packs were tried out by many groups and agencies. The idea is that grass-roots participation should be locked into the operation and development of the whole scheme. This involves two kinds of feedback, (1) your suggestions for improvement, (2) arrangement by local groups to link up together in order to feed in their own experience and develop the packs to meet the special needs of their own areas, including the use of the 'Planning for Real' techniques as a tool for participation in local development plans.

Eventually it should be possible to organize the exchange of updating information and development ideas between such groups.

Meanwhile, send inquiries about the packs (which include format blanks for users' own materials), and suggestions for improvement, to the publishers: 'Education for Neighbourhood Change', School of Education, Nottingham University, University Park, Nottingham, NG7 2RD.

# Neighbourhood Advice/Rights Centres

These, like the CABs, are run by people with expert knowledge to offer in particular fields. They tend to take on fewer cases than a CAB does, but to work more intensively with you. Some will concentrate on a particular problem area, e.g. the Child Poverty Action Group, which employs its own lawyer, and has contacts with other solicitors and barristers.

Like the Law Centres they are especially interested in cases in which the welfare of the community is at stake. They will collect similar complaints from other people and give them publicity, and take them up as a whole with the authorities concerned.

Before you consult them, make notes about your problem; and take with you any letters or documents that have anything to do with the case.

See: CITIZENS' ADVICE BUREAU; SOLICITORS; SOCIAL WORKER/
COMMUNITY WORKER

# Nil Valuation

No rates are payable on a building which is out of use because of conversion.

As soon as conversion work begins the Rating Department of the Council should be told, and they will send a Referancer to check that the building is not being used.

The valuer then places a nil valuation on the building. The valuation office, in the Rating Department, should be informed when the work is completed. The Referancer then makes a survey on which the valuer reassesses the *Rateable Value*.

See: RATEABLE VALUE

# Noise [S]

Noise from burglar alarms, ice-cream vans and other vehicles is covered by local by-laws. Report it to the police. Councils have a duty to inspect their areas for 'statutory nuisance'.*

To deal with excessive and persistent noise from public works, industrial and commercial premises, ask the Council to serve a notice to make them reduce their measured noise level within a certain time.

Councils also have the power to declare noise-free areas.† It is a legal offence for householders to cause annoyance by noise to neighbours. Under the new law† you do not need three witnesses to complain to the Magistrate's Court for an order to stop the noise.

Get advice from your Council's Environmental Health Department.

* Public Health Act 1936, section 91.
† Control of Pollution Act 1974, part III.

See: NUISANCE FROM PUBLIC WORKS; PUBLIC HEALTH
INSPECTORS; PUBLIC HEALTH REGULATIONS

# Nuisance From Public Works

If a house is affected by public works (such as new roads, roundabouts, road-widening, altered airport runways) the *owner* can claim *compensation for pollution*, e.g. from noise, fumes, dust, smoke, vibration, artificial lighting, or the discharge of solid or liquid waste.* The compensation is worked out a year after the pollution started, and the owner (not the tenant) must claim within three years of the start. If the claim succeeds, legal and valuation expenses will be repaid. But get advice at the very beginning, before incurring expense.

If your home is affected by noise from new or improved roads you can claim an *insulation grant*† for double windows, double doors, ventilation, etc., even if you are not the owner, from the Highway Authority. But you must apply within the year.

* Land Compensation Act 1973, section 3.
† Land Compensation Act 1973, section 20.

See: DISTURBANCE ALLOWANCE; HOME LOSS PAYMENTS;
HOUSING AID CENTRES; LAW CENTRES; STATUTORY
NUISANCE

# Ombudsman (Local)

Gross inefficiency, neglect, or prejudice by a public body, e.g. a Council, the police or water authority, are examples of 'maladministration' which the Ombudsman can investigate.

After you have complained to the body concerned and given them reasonable time for a reply, get the help of your local councillor and send a complaint *in writing* to the Commissioner for Local Administration (the Ombudsman), 21 Queen Anne's Gate, London W1 9BU.

The Commissioner investigates the problem and writes a report which must be made available to the Press and the public. The public body being complained about then has to tell the Commissioner what it will do about the complaint. For other types of complaint –

See: COUNCILLORS, COUNCIL OFFICERS; MPS;
DISCRIMINATION; HARASSMENT; INDUSTRIAL
TRIBUNALS; LAW CENTRES; POLICE BEHAVIOUR

# Patients (A)

*Local Doctors*

Everyone has a right to a NHS doctor – if you can't find one, write to local Family Practitioner Committee. (Look under 'Executive Council' on your NHS card or ask at Post Office.) Patients should by law be treated with reasonable skill and care. 'Reasonable' means what other doctors, dentists, radiographers, etc. would reasonably have done under the circumstances.

If professional negligence is proved, the patient (NHS or private) has a legal right to compensation and damages. First get legal advice from Law Centre or CAB.

An NHS patient also has the right to make a complaint concerning a doctor, dentist, optician or pharmacist to his local Family Practitioner Committee. A patient has the right to change his doctor without giving a reason (NHS card explains how to do this).

See: CITIZENS' ADVICE BUREAU; LAW CENTRES; PATIENTS (B)
Local Hospitals

# Patients (B)
*Local Hospitals*

A patient has a legal right (1) to be treated with reasonable skill and care, (2) to refuse any treatment or procedure, e.g. induction of labour in childbirth. If a patient is examined or treated against his will* it is an assault. Even when you sign the consent form before an operation the surgeon is responsible under (1) above. (3) To refuse to be used for teaching.

Patients have no right to insist on particular kinds of treatment, or to see a consultant, or to have information, results of tests, etc. But don't let that stop you asking.

Take complaints about possible professional negligence to Hospital Secretary or Area Health Authority; finally to the Health Service Commissioner.

*Except for compulsorily-detained mental patients. In this case refer to MIND (National Association for Mental Health), 22 Harley St, London W1.

See: PATIENTS (A) Local Doctors

# Pedestrians
*Safety*

Get help from a councillor on the Highways Committee in order to press for:

*Traffic Wardens*, appointed by the police authority, duties include school crossing patrols and to control traffic.

'*Lollypop' Persons*, appointed by the highway authority (county council or borough, or in the Metropolitan Police District by the Commissioner of Police).

*Pedestrian Crossings*, the responsibility of county councils, or in London, the GLC (after consulting the boroughs) for all roads *except* trunk roads (controlled by the Secretary of State for the Environment).

Local planning authorities, in consultation with highway authorities, can submit plans to the Secretary of State *to close roads*. Plans have to be publicized so that people can object.

See: CAR PARKING (A); TRAFFIC HAZARDS

# Pets [S]

Dogs can be a nuisance to people on estates. Councils usually only allow dogs to be kept in homes with a garden; but it is such a controversial subject that councils often try to get tenants themselves to decide the policy on pets for their own estates.

In law, dogs over six months must have an up-to-date licence and dog owners are held responsible for any nuisance their dogs may cause. Neighbours should contact the local branch of the Royal Society for the Prevention of Cruelty to Animals (if they suspect cruelty); or the police or the Council's Environmental Health Department if there is a noise or health problem.

See: PUBLIC HEALTH INSPECTORS; *Useful Local Contacts p. 277*

# Planning Action Areas [S]

The Government has given power to local Councils* to say which places ought to be redeveloped, or improved, or both. These localities are to be called Planning Action Areas and must be listed in the county Structure Plan. An Action Area Plan must give details of the changes it is proposing to make in such matters as homes, shops, factories, roads, bus routes, play space, open land, school sites and playing fields.

Before the Council decides to 'designate' an area for Planning Action it must take account of residents' views. It is valuable to get comments and suggestions in early, before plans have been formalized. Once the plan has been placed 'on deposit' it can only be dealt with by formal 'objections'.

* Town and Country Planning Act 1971, section 11.

See: PUBLIC PARTICIPATION (A) (B); STRUCTURE PLAN

# Planning Blight

A Planning Blight arises* when you cannot sell your home at its full value because of the likelihood that the Local Authority will purchase it compulsorily at a later date.

The owner-occupier has to serve a *Blight Notice* on the Council, requiring them to buy the property at the value it would have had if it had not been for the Blight.

To qualify for this, the rateable value of the property must be at least £1,500.

If the Council refuses to buy they must serve a counter-notice within two months, giving their reasons. If you are not satisfied with the reasons they give, apply to the Lands Tribunal for the UK, 5 Chancery Lane, London WC2. (Tel: 01 831 6611).

Get legal advice at each stage, particularly in wording the Blight Notice.

*Town and Country Planning Act 1971, section 192.

See: DISTURBANCE ALLOWANCE; HOME LOSS PAYMENTS; SHORT-LIFE PROPERTY (A)

# Planning Permission

If the *use* of a building is going to be changed, or its *structure* is going to be altered, *two* kinds of agreement have to be obtained: Building Approval and Planning Permission. Begin by getting architectural advice.* Then consult the Council's Planning Department. Plans will need checking with the Building Inspector (or in Inner London, the District Surveyor), the Environmental Health Officer, and probably the Council's drainage inspector, and the Gas and Electricity Boards. When the plans are shown to be workable, and satisfy fire and health regulations, the Council has to advertise them in the local Press so that the public has an opportunity to object.

*The Architectural Association, 34 Bedford Square, London WC1, can sometimes arrange for community groups to get volunteer help.

See: BUILDING REGULATIONS; FIRE SAFETY; HEALTH CHECKS ON NEW USES FOR A BUILDING; PUBLIC HEALTH INSPECTORS

# Play Area (A)
*Size*

The size of a play area for children depends on the number of child bed spaces in all the dwellings on the estate (i.e. total *all* bed spaces *minus* total *adult* bed spaces).

Government recommendations (1972) are:

| Number of child bed spaces | 10–19 | 20–49 | 50–99 | 100+ |
|---|---|---|---|---|
| Minimum play space in sq. metres | 30 | 50 | 100 | 150 |

Play areas should be sheltered from extreme weather conditions and have hard wearing surfaces with some greenery. They should be sited close to family dwellings but away from elderly people's homes. All play equipment should be checked frequently, cleaned and maintained and should satisfy British Standards for design and safety. No pools or sandpits should be provided if they cannot be cleaned daily.

See: ADVENTURE PLAYGROUNDS; PLAY AREA (B); PLAY
EQUIPMENT; PLAYGROUNDS ON THE CHEAP

# Play Area (B)
*Design*

Make sure the area gets some shelter from the worst of the weather, and that it's not too far from family dwellings, and not too close to elderly people's homes. Make the most of any trees, bushes, and natural dips and slopes in the ground level.

If you're using commercial playground equipment, check first that it is up to British Standard for safety, and that there are reliable arrangements for regular inspection and maintenance (e.g. by the manufacturers). But it is often better to get the children themselves to help build equipment from locally-donated materials – wood, tyres, ropes, nets, sewage pipes. Getting them involved from the start makes the play area *theirs*, and they're less likely to vandalize it.

Get advice on layout, safety, and maintenance from the manufacturers and/or from London Adventure Playground Association, 57B Catherine Place, SW1.

See: NATIONAL PLAYING FIELDS ASSOCIATION; PLAY AREA (A);
PLAY EQUIPMENT; PLAYGROUNDS ON THE CHEAP

# Play Equipment

*Safety*

Make sure there's a first-aid box within reach, agreed access to a private telephone, and if possible a parent or play-leader on site.

If fixed equipment is provided, the Government recommends equipment from the list below, and at least one bench for adults in all play areas:
(1) swing, (2) slide, (3) climbing frame, (4) seesaw, (5) joy wheel, (6) rocking horse*, (7) pendulum seesaw*, (8) sandpit, (9) paddling pool. (8) or (9) must be provided with something from (1) to (5); both need regular cleaning arrangements.

| Size of play area in sq. metres | 30 | 50 | 100 | 150 |
|---|---|---|---|---|
| Minimum provision of equipment | 1 piece | 1 piece | 2 pieces | 3 pieces |

* But these two items have proved more dangerous than the others and it may be wise to do without them.

See: PLAY AREA (A) (B); PLAYGROUNDS ON THE CHEAP

# Playgrounds on the Cheap

Safe, stimulating playgrounds that provide pleasure and excitement, don't have to depend on expensive manufactured equipment. Some of the best playgrounds have been created with cheap or free materials.

Parents may have work contacts with a construction plant, or be able to provide transport and materials. Local contractors with earth-moving equipment can be persuaded to create mounds of rubble and then top-dress and grass them. Unwanted materials on factory sites, railway sidings, army dumps, or garages can be coaxed from managements, particularly if somebody is willing to loan transport for an hour or two, and volunteer loaders can be provided. Tyres, ropes, telegraph poles, netting (including discarded 'assault' nets) and railway sleepers can be used to make climbing structures, swings, tree houses, forts, etc.

With adult help children will work enthusiastically clearing sites, deciding the layout, helping build equipment, and decorating huts.

See: ADVENTURE PLAYGROUNDS; GRANTS (B); HUTS; PLAY AREA (B); PLAY SCHEMES; YOUNG VOLUNTEERS

# Playgroups (A)

*Getting Started*

Social Services Departments are responsible for playgroups and can give advice and possibly grants or help with equipment. The Pre-School Playgroup Association* has information leaflets and runs courses for leaders. Ask them about insurance. You need a group of interested people and premises which are clean and in good repair, with space, heating, storage, lighting, ventilation and sanitation. Get advice about fire and health safety from the Environmental Health Officer. If changing the use of the building or altering the structure ask the Council's Planning Department for advice. Start with a small number of children (2½–5-year-olds) and two trained leaders (perhaps Mums already in your group who have gone on courses).

* Alford House, Aveline Street, London SE11 5DJ.

See: FIRE SAFETY; INSURANCE (A); PLAYGROUPS (B); PUBLIC HEALTH INSPECTORS

# Playgroups (B)

Social Services Departments are responsible for voluntary playgroups in their areas. Social Services or Education Departments might pay for equipment, running costs and possibly second-hand furniture for a playgroup. You may be able to use the local authority's furniture catalogue which has discount prices.

They may also pay for the leaders to go on a course run by the Pre-School Playgroup Association* or by a local college. The Department of Health and Social Security will provide free milk by reimbursing you quarterly. You have to pay the bills first. Charge a small fee per child attending.

* Alford House, Aveline Street, London SE11 5DJ.

See: INSURANCE; PLANNING PERMISSION; PLAYGROUPS (A)

# Play Schemes

*Permanent or Temporary*

Get together a small organizing group. If you don't have your own premises ask the Youth Office or Community Education Department for help. Premises, such as church halls, should be central, with separate rooms for different activities, a kitchen, toilets, some furniture and an outdoor play area. Obtain play equipment through the Council – ask around for other play materials.

Enrol volunteers, including Mums and local 5th and 6th formers who like helping smaller kids (some Councils run short volunteer training courses); but try to get an experienced play-leader, to have overall responsibility and to work with the committee. Involve local councillors. Get insurance cover for the scheme. You may have to pay for hiring, heating and lighting of the hall.

See: FUND-RAISING; GRANTS (C); INSURANCE (A);
      NEIGHBOURHOOD ACTION PACKS; PLAYGROUPS (A) (B);
      YOUNG VOLUNTEERS

# Police Behaviour

Good relations between the police and the community are worth taking trouble to support and develop. Bad relations need investigating, and the roots of the problem exposed.

In either case collect evidence from as many different people as possible, and put it forward on behalf of a group, such as a tenants' association. Publicize anything that is good, and any constructive suggestions (e.g. more foot patrols, more police involvement in community activities).

Make sure that individual rights are well understood* and that police powers (e.g. Prevention of Terrorism Act) are not misused. If local police exceed their powers, report them at once to their senior officer. Take up general complaints with the local officer in charge of community relations; or go direct to the Chief Constable. If no action results, publicize that too.

*NCCL, 186 King's Cross Road, London WC1X 9DE, publishes pocket-sized Fact Sheets *Know Your Rights*.

See: LAW CENTRES; NEIGHBOURHOOD RIGHTS CENTRES

# Pollution
*Of the Air*

Councils have a duty to inspect their areas for statutory nuisances, e.g. discharge from factory chimneys.*

They have the power to control atmospheric pollution† and can take measurements of what factories discharge into the air, or get a factory to supply its own measurements. The Council can order a factory to stop polluting the air, within a time limit. If a factory does nothing it can be fined.‡

Some chemical factories are registered with the Alkali and Clean Air Inspectorate which monitors their discharges.

For advice or information about a local problem contact your Council's Environmental Health Department. Councils have the power to declare pollution-free areas.†

\* Public Health Act 1936, section 91.
† Control of Pollution Act 1974, part IV.
‡ Clean Air Act 1968.

See:   PUBLIC HEALTH INSPECTORS; STATUTORY NUISANCE

# Pop-Ins'

'Pop-Ins' are similar to old-fashioned tea shops and really are a good idea for groups interested in helping the elderly. A 'Pop-In' does not require much equipment nor room, but needs to be on a route well used by the elderly (e.g. between local shops and home).

It only has to provide tea, cakes and/or biscuits, and the opportunity for a natter. Once the premises are obtained, the elderly could well run the 'Pop-In' themselves, and this might expand to provide facilities for a weekly bulk-buy food co-op.

The Neighbourhood Action Packs include 'Local Talent' forms to help in attracting volunteers.

See:   FOOD CO-OP (BULK BUY CLUB); FOOD HYGIENE; HEALTH CHECKS ON NEW USES FOR A BUILDING; NEIGHBOUR-HOOD ACTION PACKS

# Priority Neighbourhoods (PNs)

If a Council decides that the physical and social conditions in an area are bad, but they are unable to deal with them immediately, they can 'declare' a Priority Neighbourhood (PN). The Council's decision is based on a report made by Council officers, local residents or consultants.*

The area must be next door to a General Improvement Area (GIA) or Housing Action Area (HAA).

Once an area is a PN it means that the Council must get something done eventually. The Council has to bring under control the housing situation in the area, improve conditions and give special help to residents. The first step may be to declare it HAA or GIA.

*DOE Circular 14/75 (outline report).

See: GENERAL IMPROVEMENT AREAS; HOUSING ACTION AREAS

# Protected Tenants
*Grounds For Eviction*

Tenants are *protected* if:

1. the tenancy is *un*furnished and *began before 14 August 1974* and living accommodation, e.g. kitchen, bathroom, etc. is *not* shared with a resident landlord; *or*
2. the tenancy which *began before 14 August 1974* with a resident landlord can be proved to be *un*furnished; *or*
3. there is a fixed term tenancy agreement (e.g. a six-month lease) and no resident landlord.

If there is a resident landlord and a fixed term agreement (lease) a tenant is still protected unless the lease *began after 14 August 1974* and he had no previous tenancy in the house; or unless there was a lease on furnished premises which *began before 14 August 1974* and expired afterwards.

See: LAW CENTRES; SHELTER; UNPROTECTED TENANTS

# Public Health Inspectors

(*Environmental Health Inspectors*)

Health Inspectors are employed by the Local Authority and deal with health and safety inside buildings in the area, and with anything outside that could endanger health and safety. They cover sanitary facilities, food hygiene in shops and restaurants, working conditions in factories and offices, heating and ventilation, noise and air or water pollution, and facilities for the handicapped.

Get their *help* if you think someone (a landlord, a factory owner, a neighbour) is endangering health or safety. The Inspectors can take offenders to court.

Get their *approval* for any changes in your premises or the services you offer which could affect health or safety.

See: PUBLIC HEALTH REGULATIONS; SECTION 99

# Public Health Regulations

The law protects the health of the public in four main areas.

*Water* – supply, drainage and sanitation.

*Air* – cleanliness and pollution.

*Food* – hygiene, food storage, preparation, cooking and disposal.

*Environment* – conditions of housing, working conditions of paid employees, safety in public buildings – vermin, refuse disposal, noise, etc.

See: BULKY REFUSE; COMMUNITY HEALTH COUNCIL; HEALTH CHECKS ON NEW USES FOR A BUILDING; INSPECTION REPORT; POLLUTION; SECTION 99; STATUTORY NUISANCE

# Publicity

*Home Made*

Use *posters*, *circulars* and wall or stall *displays* to make a visual impact (colour of paper; layout of words, pictures, outlines, silhouettes). Get help from staff in Art Schools, Colleges, Area Resource Centres, Teachers' Centres, and use of silk-screening, photo-litho and other duplicating facilities for, e.g. extracts from documents, plans, specially-taken snapshots.

Give the gist of the message in few words. Mention easy ways to help,* and how to make contact.

Make the most of any wall-space or window-space on offer in shops, homes, schools, libraries, churches, pubs, clinics, doctors' and dentists' waiting rooms, advice centres, bingo halls, launderettes, and stall space in markets.

*'Local Talent' survey sheets are available as part of the Neighbourhood Action Packs.

See: COMMUNICATIONS; MEDIA; NEIGHBOURHOOD ACTION PACKS; VIDEO (A) (B)

# Public Participation (A)

*Kind of Plan*

Plans are meant to be adaptable, and the public are meant to have a say in altering them to suit local needs and preferences.

There are two main types of plan, both concerned with the way the land is used:

1. a *Structure Plan* is a bird's-eye view of what might happen over the next fifteen years in a particular county, taken as a whole;
2. a *Local Plan* (District Plan, Action Area Plan, or Subject Plan) goes into detail about the ways general policies would affect individual property – factories, shops, homes, play areas, etc. (A *Subject* Plan deals with one topic that is particularly important for the whole area, but can be considered largely on its own, e.g. green belt, caravan sites, recreational space, exploitation of minerals.)

See: DISTRICT PLANS; PLANNING ACTION AREAS; PUBLIC PARTICIPATION (B); STRUCTURE PLAN

# Public Participation (B)        [S]

*Getting Through*

Planners usually tell the public in advance when plans are being prepared. They must* say what background information has been collected (e.g. by surveys), and must make the plans available for people to see (e.g. in a public library) so that they can say what they think of them. Most Councils display plans and then ask for questions and comments on them, through residents' associations and/or public meetings. If this is not happening, contact the regional office of the Department of the Environment.

One way to bring local preferences and experience to bear is to contact planners early, before plans have been drafted, and arrange informal discussions involving residents, on the spot as well as in the planners' offices. Once plans are drafted, let everyone know in time to look at them, clear up misunderstandings, and think out implications, well before public meetings take place.

*Town and Country Planning Act 1971, sections 8 and 12.

See:   DISTRICT PLANS; PLANNING ACTION AREAS; PUBLIC PARTICIPATION (A); STRUCTURE PLAN

---

# Race Relations

There may be a *Community Relations Council* in your area. These are voluntary agencies generally financed by the local Council and by the Commission for Racial Equality.* They bring together representatives of a wide range of local groups who work together to promote equal opportunity and to eliminate racial discrimination. They have voluntary helpers and paid workers (Community Relations Officers) who can give advice on racial matters and help in local programmes to build up positive multi-racial relationships.

*Elliot House, 10/12 Allington St, London SW1.

See:   DISCRIMINATION; *Useful Local Contacts p. 277*

# Rateable Value

Rates are calculated for every building in an authority by the Valuation Officer. He works out the possible yearly rent for each property (called the *Gross Value*) and subtracts from this upkeep expenses. The figure left is called the building's *Rateable Value*. This figure is multiplied by the '*Rate in the £*' fixed by the Council each year after it has worked out what it is going to spend and receive in Government Grants. The *Rateable Value* multiplied by the Council's '*Rate in the £*' figure gives the amount which has to be paid in rates.

*Example:*
Rateable value £100
Rate in the £ is 80p
to calculate rates due:
100 × 80p = £80

See: RATES; VALUATION OFFICER

# Rate Rebates

Owner-occupiers, Council tenants and private (furnished or unfurnished) tenants can all apply for a rate rebate. The Council works out a rebate by comparing the weekly rates with the combined weekly income of everyone in the household.

Get application forms from the Council Treasurer's Department. Tenants who pay rent can apply for a *Rate* rebate when they apply for a *Rent* rebate.

A rate rebate does not cover water rates or sewerage charge, nor for that part of rent which covers furniture in a furnished flat. The Council works it out.

If the Council refuses a rebate, it is possible to appeal within one month. If the appeal fails and you want to go further – get legal advice.

See: LAW CENTRES; RENT REBATES; SOLICITORS

# Rates

Tenants' Associations usually have to pay rates, and water rates, for a community hall, twice a year to the Council.

Rates are charged from the first day that a building is used and are based on the *rateable value* of the premises and the '*Rate in the £*' calculated by the Council.

The amount to be charged in rates is worked out by the *Valuation Officer*.

Rates do not have to be paid on a building if it is out of use for a period, e.g. being converted. The building is then given a *nil valuation* by the Council Rating Department, which checks that the building is not being used and has to be informed when the building is ready for use.

See:  NIL VALUATION; RATEABLE VALUE; VALUATION OFFICER; WATER RATES

# Rats, Mice and other Vermin

Councils must* keep their districts, as far as possible, free of vermin. They must carry out regular inspections† of the district; and deal with any land or property infested with vermin.

Rats and mice cause disease/damage. Councils provide a free rat control service, but householders usually have to get rid of mice themselves.

If you find any signs of pests, report it *in writing* to the Chief Environmental Health Officer.

If the Council is slow to take action, get legal advice about asking the Minister of Agriculture, Fisheries and Food to investigate the Council or hold a public local inquiry.

* Pests Act 1949, section 12.
† Public Health Act 1936, section 91.

See:  CITIZENS' ADVICE BUREAU; LAW CENTRES; PUBLIC HEALTH INSPECTORS; SECTION 99; STATUTORY NUISANCE

# Refuse Chambers and Containers

Moveable refuse containers (e.g. Paladins) hold 1 cubic metre (= about 9 dustbin loads) and serve five to six flats each, allowing for a change over every two or three days.

They should be kept in a ventilated rubbish chamber with a tap near it, and a floor gulley for sluicing out. At least 6″ handling space is needed round each container (dia. 3 ft).

Beside the rubbish chamber there should be a separate storage area, covered, for bulky refuse.

If container wheels are so noisy that they create a 'statutory nuisance' ask the owner (sometimes Council, sometimes a private landlord) to refit them with rubber castors.

See:   BULKY REFUSE; REFUSE COLLECTION; REFUSE DISPOSAL IN FLATS; NOISE; STATUTORY NUISANCE

# Refuse Collection

No householder should have to carry rubbish further than 30 metres (100 ft) to the nearest chute or container, and this should be on the same floor, or a half-landing.

Refuse collectors should not be expected to carry dustbins further than 25 metres, nor to push a Paladin further than 9 or 10 metres to the nearest access road (unless an electric trailer is provided).

Collection vehicles need reinforced access roads, minimum width 5 metres, with turning bay to avoid having to reverse the vehicle and endanger children.

The noise made by the vehicle, and its bin-lifting machinery must not exceed the maximum legal limit for Heavy Goods Vehicles (92 decibels).

See:   BULKY REFUSE; COST GUIDELINES (D); REFUSE CHAMBERS AND CONTAINERS; REFUSE DISPOSAL IN FLATS

# Refuse Disposal in Flats

An average household (= 2·8 persons) produces *at least* 13½ kilos (about 30 lbs) of rubbish each week – enough to fill one dustbin (capacity 0·11 cubic metre: or 4 cu. ft).

In flats, disposal is complicated because dustbins in passages block the way and are a fire risk; bulky refuse won't go down the chutes; the chutes may be noisy, and if the refuse jams, they smell; if materials catch fire the chutes may act as chimneys.

Possibilities for improvement? Ask local Fire Station and Environmental Health Officer for inspection on grounds of fire risks and health dangers. Apply to Council for covered Bulk Refuse area. Organize voluntary help for elderly to shift their dustbins or refuse bags to convenient collection points.

See:   BULKY REFUSE; FIRE SAFETY; PUBLIC HEALTH INSPECTOR; REFUSE CHAMBERS AND CONTAINERS; REFUSE COLLECTION

# Registered Lotteries

*Running Conditions*

*Tickets:* (limited to 25p) can be sent by post to members only, but must not be sold or bought by people under the age of sixteen. They can be sold to the general public.

*Prizes:* cash or in kind, but of not more than £1,000 in value and limited in total value to half the whole proceeds.

*Sales:* limited to £5,000 max. If sales exceed £5,000, the lottery also has to be registered with the Gaming Board.

*Registration:* costs £10. Renewable every year (1 January) £5.

*Proceeds:* lottery expenses or 25% of whole proceeds (whichever is less) can be deducted and cost of prizes up to half the proceeds.

*Profit:* for club purposes only.

The lottery's accounts must be detailed on a Council form and returned to the Council.

See:   LOTTERIES The three Types; UNREGISTERED LOTTERIES

# Rent-a-Plot

Allotments can be applied for at the Council's Parks Department. There may be a waiting list. Meanwhile, look for unused sites belonging to the railway, church, etc.; or write to the Parks Department, or to the local Press, to find out whether any locals would be interested in Garden Sharing.

Garden Sharing is an idea promoted by Friends of the Earth (FOE, 9 Poland Street, London W1) whereby people let part of their land to be cultivated by others (*Crops and Shares*, 20p plus s.a.e.).

Gardening tips for beginners are given by the London Association of Recreational Gardeners, T. A. Harrison, 17 Chigwell Road, South Woodford, London E1 1LR, (fee £1.50 p.a., 1976).
Information is not just London-based.

See: ALLOTMENT GARDENS

# Rent Arrears

Not paying rent is a breach of the conditions of a tenancy. Some Councils begin by sending a home visitor, or they advise tenants in arrears to see their Estates Officer. In each case this is to make sure that the tenant is claiming rent rebates, supplementary benefits and other entitlements such as Exceptional Needs Payments, from the Social Services Department.

Other Councils go straight to the next stage, sending a Notice to Quit giving twenty-eight days' warning, and stating the tenants' rights.

A tenant does not have to leave his home, but if he does not offer to pay off the arrears, the Council will summons him to court. If the tenant fails to attend, the Court may give the Council an Order for Possession. If the tenant does attend court and admits the arrears this order will be suspended for fourteen days so that arrangements can be made to pay off the arrears.

See: EVICTION; RATE REBATES; RENT REBATES/RENT ALLOWANCES; SUPPLEMENTARY BENEFITS

# Rent Rebates/Rent Allowances

Anyone who pays rent can apply for a *rebate* (for *Council* tenants, forms from the Housing Department) or an *allowance* (for *private* tenants, forms from the Treasurer's Department). How much (if anything) the tenant gets depends on the weekly gross income (before tax deductions), the rent level and size of family. The Council works out whether anything can be allowed, and either reduces the rent for Council tenants, or pays an allowance (through Giro without the landlord knowing) to private tenants.

A private tenant whose rent has not been registered may have the allowance worked out on the basis of an estimated registered rent – lower than it actually is. Get advice about taking the landlord to a Rent Tribunal.

All tenants and owner-occupiers can also apply for a *Rate* rebate.

See: CITIZENS' ADVICE BUREAU; FAIR RENT REGISTRATION; HOUSING AID/ADVISORY CENTRES; RATE REBATES

# Repair Grants
*For Owner-Occupiers*

The Council only gives these grants to owner-occupiers who cannot afford the necessary repairs and who have houses in Housing Action and General Improvement Areas. They are given for repair work or replacement which has nothing to do with improvement or conversion work. The Council has to make sure that when the work is done the dwelling will be in good repair (considering its age, character and locality).

The Council works out the cost of repair work to the dwelling (the 'eligible expense', which must not be more than £1,500). The percentage of the estimated costs of the work varies from area to area. If further, unforeseen, work is needed, the Council may increase the grant.

See: ELIGIBLE EXPENSE; HOUSING ACTION AREAS; GENERAL IMPROVEMENT AREAS; REPAIRS

# Repairs [S]

Tenants are entitled to get necessary repairs done within a reasonable time by a landlord (Council or private). Landlords must* repair all structural and external parts and maintain services (no matter what the agreement says). If they don't, private tenants should go to the Council's Environmental Health Department, who can take action, e.g. do the necessary repairs and claim costs from the landlord.†

If Council tenants have repair defects which are prejudicial to health they should get advice about taking the Council to court under Section 99 of the Public Health Act 1976. First send an inspection report on the building to the Director of Housing (copy to the Chief Executive). Council tenants can also complain to the local ombudsman.

Owner-occupiers in HAAs or GLHs can apply to the Council for repair grants.

\* Housing Act 1961, section 32.
† Housing Act 1961, section 26.

See: LAW CENTRES; REPAIR GRANTS; STATUTORY
NUISANCE; SECTION 99

# Savings Banks

*Community*

A group wanting to form a 'money co-op' could join a local Credit Union,* or set up their own.

Credit Unions are non-profit-making, owned and run by the members, electing their own unpaid directors on the basis of one person, one vote. Members agree to save regularly and borrow at fixed interest rate of 1% per month, i.e. £100 loan costs £106·50 over twelve months.

Membership conditions are that each group should have a common bond, e.g. living in the same area or working in the same firm. So there are community CUs for towns, housing estates, tenants' associations, etc.; industrial CUs for factories; parish CUs for village and church groups; professional CUs for local government employees, hospital doctors, teachers, police, postmen, ambulance and firemen, etc.

\* Advice from Credit Union League, Ecumenical Centre, Firbeck, Town Centre, Skelmersdale, Lancs.

See: MUTUAL AID CENTRE

# Section 99 [S]

*Public Health Act 1936*

Councils use this Act to take those responsible for causing public health nuisance(s) to Court, but do not use it against themselves. But Section 99 of this Act enables council tenants to take their councils to Court for not doing repairs. A 'statutory nuisance' has to be proved to exist, i.e. a defect must be harmful (not just uncomfortable) to the tenants' mental or physical health.

To use Section 99, do an Inspection Report – detailing the faults in the building. Send it to the Director of Housing (copy to Chief Executive) with a letter warning Court action. If nothing is done within fourteen days take out a summons (it's free) under the Act at the Magistrate's Court. A date for the Court hearing will be arranged then. Meanwhile, find a solicitor to put your case.

See: COURT APPEARANCES; INSPECTION REPORT; REPAIRS; SOLICITORS; STATUTORY NUISANCE; SUMMONS; TENANTS' RIGHTS (B)

# Self-help Groups

Groups (such as residents' associations, local action groups, sports clubs, bulk-buy clubs, community workshops) stand more chance than individuals of getting the authorities to take notice and give support. They can focus local ideas and experience, tap expert knowledge, keep people informed and help them to get to know one another.

This can mean that the place becomes more of a neighbourhood and that people are more determined to get things done in spite of obstacles and setbacks. But don't expect everyone to join in right away. In the early stages do small things which get quick results and involve practical activities as well as meetings. Make sure that there's scope for many different talents,* not only talkers and organizers. Even serious business can be done enjoyably, without formality.

* Neighbourhood Action Packs include 'Local Talent' survey sheets.

# Shelter* [S]

Shelter raises funds for the homeless, and campaigns as a powerful pressure group, on both central and local government, to get homeless families housed, and to explain and protect tenants' rights, and to investigate and report on housing problems.

It supports charitable housing associations; independent Housing Advice Centres; projects to make use of empty short-life property, and Neighbourhood Action Projects in housing stress-areas (helping people to help themselves). It funds the Family Squatting Advisory Service and a Youth Education Programme.

\* 157 Waterloo Road, London, SE1 8UU. Tel: 01 633 9371.

See: HOUSING ASSOCIATIONS; *Useful Local Contacts* (*for nearest branch*)

# Sheltered Housing

Sheltered housing is provided by the Council or by a Housing Association for the elderly. The residents pay rent for a flat which they look after themselves. There is a warden in the block to call on in an emergency.

Sheltered tenants can also receive such services as Home Helps, Meals-on-Wheels, District Nurses – just as other elderly people do. Sheltered housing is difficult to obtain because there is so little of it. Fill in a housing application form at the local Housing Department office, or Social Services office. Ask about Housing Associations working in your area.

There are other possibilities open to the elderly: *almshouses* (similar to sheltered housing); *residential homes*; or having their present homes *modified*.

See: HOUSING ASSOCIATIONS; SOCIAL SERVICES DEPARTMENT

# Short-Life Property (A)                    [S]
*Compulsory Purchase Orders*

Councils can use Compulsory Purchase Orders (CPOs) to buy private houses if they are unfit, *or* if they have been empty for over six months, *or* if the land is needed for roads, parks, or new housing.* The Council has to announce its intentions beforehand, and if anyone objects an Inspector from the Department of the Environment may be asked to hold a Public Inquiry. CPOs take up to eighteen months to put through. Once the CPO is confirmed the Council can start buying houses, and rehousing the occupants.

Any houses bought can be temporarily improved so that they can be used by the homeless† until the time comes to demolish them. The improvements must come up to the standards set by the Public Health Acts.

* Housing Act 1957.
† Housing Act 1957, sections 29 (1) and (3).

See:   DISTURBANCE ALLOWANCE; PUBLIC HEALTH REGULA-
       TIONS; SHORT-LIFE PROPERTY (B); SQUATTERS

# Short-Life Property (B)
*For Community Use*

Some Councils publish a list of properties (houses, halls, shops) which have been acquired for demolition but which will have at least two years of life before that happens.

Apply to the Council giving details of your organization and what you would like to do with the property (e.g. turn it into a social centre). The Council may then agree to grant you a licence or short lease, and will tell you what rent and rates will cost. If the building needs altering, or if its use is going to change, get advice from the Planning Department. Find an architect to help with plans and get them checked by Environmental Health Officer, and Building Inspector (or in Inner London, the District Surveyor).

See:   ALTERNATIVE MEETING PLACES; BUILDING REGULA-
       TIONS; PLANNING PERMISSION; PUBLIC HEALTH INSPEC-
       TORS; SHORT-LIFE PROPERTY (A)

# Skills Exchange

This is a very simple system to help people pick up skills from each other.

Publicize your plans by word of mouth, contacting local groups, leaflets, posters, a letter in the local newspaper.

Put up a noticeboard in a sheltered public place – post office, shop, canteen, club, etc.

Put blank cards on the board, each with a marked space for (1) each subject, (2) the names and addresses of people wanting to learn, (3) for people offering to teach. When you want to learn a new skill, you write the subject at the top, and fill your name in. People are left to contact each other. The co-ordinator just keeps the board tidy, and helps solve problems.

See: COMMUNICATIONS; SELF-HELP GROUPS

# Social Services Department [S]

This is the local Council department which employs social workers. It is responsible for dealing with the elderly, the handicapped, children in need of care, and families under stress. It must also by law see that people get the welfare rights due to them. It can make grants for welfare activities run by community groups (luncheon clubs, playgroups, etc.). It also employs residential Social Workers providing special residential care for children, adults with mental, physical or social handicaps, or the elderly.

Find out who to contact by ringing the Council, asking for Social Services Department, and then mentioning your particular problem (e.g. children in trouble, old people needing better heating, supplementary benefits) so that they can put you on to the right person. In emergency, at night or at weekends, contact through police.

See: COMMUNITY WORKERS; SOCIAL WORKERS; VOLUNTARY SERVICE

# Social Workers

Most are employed by your local Social Services Department, and work in teams from Area Offices. Ring direct asking for the duty social worker. Obtain the phone number from SS Department (listed under name of your Council).

Social workers deal with the elderly, the handicapped, children in need of care and families under stress. They have the power to remove children in need of care from their parents and to take people to a mental hospital for admission. Social workers are also employed by the Probation and After-care services, and by voluntary organizations (e.g. Help the Aged).

They must also see that those in need get the welfare rights due to them by law.

See:   SOCIAL SERVICES DEPARTMENT; COMMUNITY WORKERS; *Useful Local Contacts*

# Solicitors

You can employ a solicitor to advise you, and to put a case through the correct legal channels; but it is important to choose a solicitor who is used to working with community groups. C A B will advise.

Many solicitors will do Legally-Aided work, which means that you may not have to pay the full cost yourself. Ask at the beginning for advice under Legal Aid (there are various schemes for different types of cases).

Before you consult the solicitor, make notes about your problems and take with you any letters or documents that might be relevant.

See:   CITIZENS' ADVICE BUREAU; LAW CENTRES; LEGAL AID

# Squatters

Squatters are trespassers if they occupy property without the permission of the owner. But family squatting groups or associations sometimes have arrangements with Councils and are given a licence (not a proper tenancy) to squat in Council short-life property (doing their own repairs and renovations).

Squatters commit a criminal offence* if:

1. they use violence to enter the premises;
2. they are carrying an offensive weapon;
3. they are trespassing in an embassy or foreign mission;
4. they obstruct the bailiff recovering the premises, if he has a court order.

Shelter operates an advisory service for squatters.

* Criminal Law (Amendment) Act 1977.

See: SHELTER; SHORT-LIFE PROPERTY (A)

# Standard Amenity

Standard amenities, and the 'eligible expense' limits, are (1977):

| Amenity | Maximum Eligible Expense |
|---|---|
| Fixed bath or shower normally in a bathroom | £180 |
| Wash handbasin | 70 |
| Sink | 180 |
| Hot and cold water supply at a: | |
| 1. fixed bath or shower | 230 |
| 2. wash handbasin | 120 |
| 3. sink | 150 |
| Water closet (WC) | 270 |
| Total | £1,200 |

See: ELIGIBLE EXPENSE; INTERMEDIATE GRANTS (A) (B)

# Statutory Nuisance [S]

By law,'* a Statutory Nuisance is any defect which affects people's mental health. (Anything that merely interferes with personal comfort cannot be put right through these procedures.)

It is not the actual defect which is the Statutory Nuisance but the effects of the defect. You have to be able to show that it is doing harm to people. A Statutory Nuisance has to be proved to exist, so you need to contact an Environmental Health Officer.

Defects which might result in a Statutory Nuisance include: leaking roofs; rising or penetrating damp; blocked lavatories; accumulations of rubbish near buildings; rotting or infected materials; chemicals dumped or not stored properly; materials attracting vermin.

* Public Health Act 1936, section 92.

See: NOISE; POLLUTION; PUBLIC HEALTH INSPECTORS; REFUSE COLLECTION; SECTION 99; NUISANCE FROM PUBLIC WORKS

# Structure Plan

The Government has asked each County Council to get ready a structure plan in book form, with a 'key diagram', describing changes that might happen in the next fifteen years or so. This could affect how many houses will be built or rehabilitated, and where they should be; which shopping centres will be built or run down; where factories will be sited; which new roads are planned and what car parking and bus services there will be; and how much land will be kept as open space. While the plan is still in draft, and before the County Council decides on it, the public must* be given the opportunity to see it and comment. There's another opportunity to 'make representations' before the Secretary of State (DOE) finally approves it.

Get advice from Royal Town Planning Institute, 26 Portland Place, London W1, for nearest 'Planning Aid Centre'; or Town and Country Planning Association, 17 Carlton House Terrace, London SW1 75AS.

* Town and Country Planning Act 1971, section 8.

See: PUBLIC PARTICIPATION (A) (B)

# Summons [S]

To take out a summons is now free and takes about thirty minutes. Tell the Clerk of the Court which part of which Act is being used (e.g. Section 99 of 1936 Public Health Act to make your landlord do repairs).

Bring with you two copies of each letter or report mentioned in that section of the Act.

You will be called in to the courtroom for a short meeting and you might be asked to explain any points in the documents that are not clear. The Court will then fix a date for the case to be heard and the landlord to attend.

See: COURT APPEARANCES

# Suspicion of a 'Fiddle' (A)

*Within the Tenants' Association*

Suspicion is not enough. There must be evidence.

Prevention is better than cure. Make sure there is a regular routine for all payments, and that everybody understands it. When spending funds make two committee members jointly responsible. Get brief routine statement by the Treasurer at each committee meeting. Have Accounts audited before the AGM.

If suspicion is aroused arrange for two members to check through the books and vouchers. If the problem cannot be sorted out within the group, get legal advice about prosecution.

See: COLLECTING MONEY; LAW CENTRES; SUSPICION OF A 'FIDDLE' (B)

# Suspicion of a 'Fiddle' (B)

*Within the Council*

Suspicion is not enough, there must be evidence.

If you suspect a Council employee get a councillor to ask questions in Council. If an elected representative is suspected look up decisions made in Council minutes. Ask the Council department involved for information.

Community Action's *Investigator's Handbook* (30p), a guide for investigating public figures, companies and organizations, might be useful. (Obtainable from Community Action, PO Box 665, London SW1X 8DZ.)

If there is evidence of 'maladministration' – refer to local ombudsman or contact the Press.

See: LAW CENTRES; OMBUDSMAN; SUSPICION OF A 'FIDDLE' (A)

# Telephone

*Installation Costs (1978/9)*

You can rent a coin box phone or have a new phone installed or reconnected. Quarterly rental has to be paid for both, but the money in the coin box can be used towards the bill. You have a key.

Installation costs:

1. coin box, with new line £45 + coin box charge of up to £10. Quarterly rental £5;
2. new exchange line/new phone costs about £45 + VAT + £60 deposit*;
3. existing number/new phone in different building costs about £30;
4. existing phone/new number costs about £5–£10 + £15 deposit*;
5. existing phone (temporarily disconnected) reconnected costs about £3. Deposit of £15*.

 * Deposits are usually credited to the first bill.

See: COST GUIDELINES (M)

# Tenancy Agreements

The law says that every landlord (private or Council or Housing Association) must provide an agreement stating the duties of the landlord and the tenant to each other. This is a contract, legally binding on both sides. It should include all the following information; names and addresses of landlord and tenant; date the tenancy starts and notice required for ending it; rent and rates payable, and when due; landlord's duties to repair; tenant's duties; tenant's right to possession/security of tenure (at present this applies only to private landlords).

Tenants can not be evicted without a court order for possession. If there's a dispute, get advice from the local authority harassment officer or go to a local advice centre.

See: EVICTION; HARASSMENT;

# Tenants' Associations

*Setting Up*

Any resident can take the first step. Contact a wide cross-section of local residents (not just personal friends and neighbours) and get them to share in promoting the idea and collecting comments and offers of help. Tap experienced outsiders – representatives of other TAs, community workers, etc. – for expert advice over a cuppa; but don't feel obliged to swallow their advice whole.

Have a whip-round to cover hire of nearby school room or church hall. Publicize through launderettes, pubs, local shops, etc. and by house-to-house visiting. For meetings arrange seating to avoid feelings of Us and Them formality. Start with a free-for-all on what needs to be done first. Get a *temporary* committee elected to organize street or block representation, follow up offers of help, involve other members. Contact the National Tenants' Organization, 189a Old Brompton Road, London SW5  OAR (Tel. 01 373 3923).

See: COMMUNICATIONS; FUND-RAISING; PUBLICITY; SELF-HELP GROUPS; TENANTS' RIGHTS (A) (B)

# Tenants' Rights (A)

*To Housing Improvements*

Various grants are available to landlords (freeholders or leaseholders of five years or more) to do improvement work on buildings that are still sound.

Tenants can ask Councils to use their powers to make landlords do such improvements.

Grants are paid after the work is done, and provided it is covered by planning permission and meets building regulations (Councils can lend money to cover the costs while the work is going on). The landlord has to undertake to use or live in the dwelling for up to five years after the improvement is completed.

See: HOUSING GRANTS; PLANNING PERMISSION

# Tenants' Rights (B)

*Repairs*

Councils do not take themselves to court, but they will take action against private landlords. If Councils fail to do necessary repairs the tenants can:
1. get an order from the County Court* to make the landlord do any repairs that are its responsibility;
2. apply for a summons at the Magistrate's Court† to make the landlord put right any defects that are a statutory nuisance;
3. claim to a Justice of the Peace‡ that their house is unfit for living in, i.e. their home is defective in one or more of the ten-point standard;
4. claim compensation from the local authority if repairs (which are the landlord's responsibility) have not been carried out within a reasonable period without reasons for delay. Tenants should get legal advice. Tenants can apply to the local ombudsman.

* Housing Act 1974, section 125.
† Public Health Act 1936, section 99.
‡ Housing Act 1957, section 157.

See: OMBUDSMAN: PUBLIC HEALTH INSPECTORS: REPAIRS; SECTION 99; STATUTORY NUISANCE; TEN-POINT STANDARD

# Tenders, Contracts and Consultants

Shop around. Before choosing a builder, get bank and trade references and an architect's report. If the job requires a consultant (architect or quantity surveyor), begin by shortlisting firms which are used to working for groups like yours. Then check on work each has previously done. Find out what fee would be charged, and which member of the firm would be given the work.

Work out (with architect if you have one) what you want, standards of quality, the order of jobs, and the deadline. Your loan or grant may require you to send out these detailed specifications to several builders for written estimates.

These 'tenders' must be opened together, in front of witnesses (e.g. your Committee).

If you have to sign a legally-binding Building Contract – get the architect's advice first.

See: BUILDING REGULATIONS; COST GUIDELINES (N)

# Ten-point Standard

Improvement Grants are given to improve dwellings to 'a high standard'. This means that the house must last for thirty years; have all 'standard amenities' and meet the following requirements:

1. be free of damp;
2. have adequate natural lighting and ventilation in living-rooms;
3. have adequate and safe electrical provision;
4. be in a stable structural condition;
5, 6. have satisfactory internal arrangements and facilities for preparing and cooking food;
7, 8. have adequate facilities for heating and drainage;
9. have proper fuel and refuse storage facilities;
10. have roof insulation that conforms with Building Regulations.

See: BUILDING REGULATIONS; IMPROVEMENT GRANTS;
STANDARD AMENITY

## Toy Libraries (A)

*Who Runs?*

The idea of a toy library is that children can borrow toys for a while and when fed up with them take them back to exchange for a new toy. It is a meeting-place for Mums too.

Some Councils run toy libraries for child minders, some voluntary organizations run them for handicapped children but others are run by Mums for Mums.

The Hackney Toy Library Association, 145 Roding Road, London E5, made up mainly of Mums, have had experience of setting up and running their own toy libraries and can give advice. They raised their own money to buy the toys. Additional advice from Toy Libraries Association, Sunley House, Gunthorpe Street, London E1.

See: PLAYGROUPS (A) (B); TOY LIBRARIES (B)

## Toy Libraries (B)

*Setting Up*

Find some space in a local hall or health clinic with lockable storing cupboards.

Raise money to buy toys, about £100 to start. Social Services or a charity might give money.

Find out which age group is most likely to use the toy library. Ask round the neighbourhood.

Get advice on what toys to buy – especially toys for handicapped children. Don't try to include toys which are difficult to get, or too expensive for families to buy.

Work out a system for loaning the toys. Find volunteers. (There's a 'Local Talent' sheet in the Neighbourhood Action Packs to help in attracting volunteers.)

Work out a rota for running the place and making tea. Get publicity (local Press? local schools? leaflets?).

See: GRANTS (A); NEIGHBOURHOOD ACTION PACKS; PLAYGROUPS (A) (B); PUBLICITY

# Trading Standards Officer

Inquiries or complaints about the sale of articles of food, domestic goods (e.g. coal by weight measure or number) should be made to the local Trading Standards Officer. He/she will also deal with complaints about misleading prices of goods or misleading descriptions of goods, services, accommodation or facilities.

See: CONSUMER ADVICE CENTRES; *Useful Local Contacts p. 277*

# Traffic Hazards

Estate road or highway? Find out which authority is responsible. (Some estate roads are private and are the responsibility of the Council's Housing Department.)

Usually the large authorities (GLC, Non-metropolitan counties and Metropolitan counties) are responsible for transport planning, highways traffic, parking, passenger transport and road safety. The small authorities (London boroughs, Non-metropolitan districts and Metropolitan districts) maintain roads and control local parking.

Collect evidence and investigate possibilities (pedestrian crossings; traffic wardens; 'lollypop' patrols; limiting road access to residents; play streets; road humps). Contact councillors, MPs, officials and the media. Photograph or video-tape danger areas.

See: COUNCILLORS, COUNCIL OFFICERS, MPS; MEDIA; PUBLICITY; VIDEO

# Transfers

Most Councils make transfers according to their estimate of each applicant's special needs and the shortage of suitable dwellings. Applicants fill in a form at the local housing office and go on a waiting list.

Discuss any special cases with the Housing manager; and with Social Services. In medical cases a hospital specialist could be asked to advise the Council about a tenant's housing need to get a quicker transfer. Special accommodation for handicapped people is very hard to get, but Social Services can advise on aids and adaptations to dwellings.

Schemes for transfers within an estate, and to allow relatives to transfer near to each other, are being tried by some Councils. Transfers to other authorities' estates are complicated even when it's an agreed swap, so get advice first.

See: ADAPTING HOUSING FOR HANDICAPPED PEOPLE; CITIZENS' ADVICE BUREAU; HOUSING AID/ADVISORY CENTRE

# Transport (A)

## *For the Elderly*

Find out from Social Services about transport for the elderly or handicapped because they and/or voluntary bodies sometimes have a small bus/buses to transport elderly folk to nearby clubs or entertainments. These buses are much used.

Family doctors will arrange ambulance transport to hospital but journeys can be too long for the elderly. Car transport – organized voluntarily perhaps as a good-neighbour scheme – is better for the elderly. *But* any person using his/her car for regular voluntary transport must tell the car insurance company. It is unlikely that an extra charge for insurance will be made as long as the passengers don't pay.

See: TRANSPORT (B); TRAVEL CONCESSIONS

# Transport (B)

*For Outings and Activities*

Try the local youth authority which may lend buses. Find out whether there is a community transport scheme in your area, or approach other community groups, schools, colleges and youth organizations, and organize one between you.

Make an application to the youth authority or local/national charities for a grant to buy some form of transport. You could try to raise money to buy your own transport.

When hiring a coach from a commercial firm, shop around for competitive rates and in summer book well in advance. Even if the coach is not filled the full cost will have to be paid. Some Social Services Departments pay the cost of coach-hirings for some outings.

See: FUND-RAISING; GRANTS (A); MINIBUS

# Transport (C)

*Rural*

*Post-bus* – depends on careful link-up between County Council (Transport Department), bus company and Head Post Office. Drivers must have Public Service Vehicle (PSV) Licence, and there must be a reserve bus available.

*School bus* – County Council arranges a survey of the need. The bus company applies for a permit* to carry fare-paying passengers.

*Car schemes* – the WRVS operate schemes in many counties, with volunteer organizers in villages and a pool of drivers. People in need apply for transport. County Councils often pay.

*Concessionary Fares* – Councils can† allow reductions in fares to the elderly, to unemployed teenagers looking for work, to single parents, and others; but may need persuading.

* Transport Act 1968, section 30.
† Travel Concessions Act 1964.

See: COUNCILS; MINIBUS; TRANSPORT (A) (B); TRAVEL CONCESSIONS; WOMEN'S ROYAL VOLUNTARY SERVICE

# Travel Concessions

Councils have powers* to operate reduced-fares schemes for men over 64, women over 59, schoolchildren, 15–18-year-olds going to and from educational establishments, the blind, crippled people, local authority workers on duty, and others. But it is up to the Council to decide whether to use these powers. A convincing survey of needs by a local group might help.

British Rail provide cheap(er) travel for the elderly. Details from local ticket office. Inquire also about Rail Cards for regular Tues./Wed./Thurs. travel; and Awayday, weekend returns, 17 day returns, Book Ahead Economy tickets, and free carriage of bicycles.

* Travel Concessions Act 1964.

See: COUNCILS (A); TRANSPORT (A) (B) (C)

# Truancy                                                    [S]

The law* insists on 'full-time' education and makes the parents responsible for regular attendance. Old 'truancy man' is now called the Education Welfare Officer; the link between home and school, drawing on special help, e.g. Child Guidance Clinic. Truancy is often rooted in home problems, or in rejection of school by the child as irrelevant, indifferent or hostile.

If the EWO is not already on your doorstep, contact him for help and advice via school or local Education Office. Larger scale truancy has been tackled successfully by concerned parents, teachers and other residents working together as a group. As a last resort LEAs can by law† prosecute parents in a Magistrate's court, but will more likely use the law‡ to bring care proceedings in a juvenile court.

* Education Act 1944.
† Education Act 1944, section 39.
‡ Child and Young Persons Act 1969.

See: EDUCATION (B) (C);

# Unprotected Tenants

*Grounds for Eviction*

Tenants are *not* protected if:
The landlord is resident and the tenancy (furnished or unfurnished) began *after* 14 August 1974; *or* the landlord is resident and the *furnished* tenancy began *before* 14 August 1974; *or* meals, snacks or services are provided by the landlord; *or* the tenants are students with a college or university landlord; *or* the accommodation is a holiday or out-of-season letting; *or* the accommodation is wanted by the landlord for retirement (the landlord must give the tenant a notice stating this); *or* the tenancy is rent-free or at a low rent; *or* the accommodation goes with a job; *or* the landlord is the local authority or a housing association or a trust.

Get expert advice.

See:   EVICTION; LAW CENTRES; PROTECTED TENANTS; SHELTER

# Unregistered Lotteries

*Running Conditions*

*Small Lotteries:* no cash prizes; tickets any price to be sold only at social event; no age restriction on buyers or sellers of tickets; money raised to be used to cover the costs of entertainment, but not the promotion of the lottery, costs of printing the tickets and costs of prizes up to £50. The money raised can be used for any purpose, except private gain.

  *Private Lotteries:* prizes in cash or kind; tickets to be sold to members only but at any price; no age restriction on buyers or sellers of tickets; the lottery can only be advertised on club premises; money raised can be used to cover the expenses of the lottery, cost of prizes and for the benefit of the club.

See:   LOTTERIES The Three Types; REGISTERED LOTTERIES

# Valuation Officer

The Valuation Officer or District Valuer is a skilled valuer of property who has the job of making a list of property values in his area (the list is kept in the Council offices) and of altering this list as changes in the properties happen or new properties are built.

Although his offices will sometimes be found in the Council buildings, he is not working for the Council. He works for the Commission of Inland Revenue.

Local authorities have their own Valuation Officers for when they are buying properties (e.g. for use as community halls) or giving Council finance for other people to buy property (e.g. loans to housing associations, or mortgages for co-operatives).

See: HOUSING ASSOCIATIONS; RATES; RATEABLE VALUE

# Value Added Tax (VAT)

If the club's turnover is going to be more than £10,000 per year on taxable goods or services, get advice from Customs and Excise about registration for VAT. Charities may have to pay VAT as well!.

The club pays *Input Tax* on supplies it receives, and users of the club pay *Output Tax* on supplies provided, e.g. hiring out a hall. The general rate is 8% (but $12\frac{1}{2}$% on some items).

Every three months *Input Tax* paid is added up and the amount of *Output Tax* made is worked out. When *Input Tax* is bigger than *Output Tax*, Customs and Excise pays the difference between the two. If it is the other way round the club pays the difference to Customs and Excise.

# Video (A) [S]

*For Community Use*

From Primary children to Senior Citizens, anyone can soon learn to handle portable TV-cameras-and-recording-equipment (portapacks). Video tape recorders slung from the shoulder can be battery-driven or linked to the mains. Hand-held cameras will give passable results even on a dull day in the open; or using normal room lighting indoors (though an adjustable desk lamp usefully brightens things up). So you can get on-the-spot results without fuss; and afterwards replay, on a suitable screen, wherever and whenever you please.

Video costs almost nothing to run (the tape is reusable); but the equipment is costly. So *borrow* it (with perhaps a student helper) from your nearest Area Arts Centre, polytechnic, School of Architecture, or College of Education.

See:   *Useful Local Contacts p. 277;* VIDEO (B)

# Video (B)

*Home Made*

Video recording is easy and cheap, provided you cut out the frills and pick reasonable working conditions (daylight out-of-doors; or good room lighting indoors).

Record *problem situations* (juggernaut traffic, inadequate play space, botched housing, isolated old people); *projects worth supporting* (adventure playgrounds, play schemes, pre-school playgroups, pensioners' food co-ops, work parties converting premises, local demonstrations and surveys); *interviews* with people too shy to make speeches; *fun art* – improvised drama to show up the absurdity of an everyday situation that no longer makes sense.

Replay, on a suitable screen, in a shop window or the back of a van; at a meeting with officials; at a Press conference; after a religious service or social get-together. Choose beforehand a few short sequences that pack a punch, check the footage indicator, and spool on from one extract to the next.

See:   MEDIA; VIDEO (A)

# Voluntary Help for the Elderly [S]

*Age Concern* – Gives advice and information to people working with the elderly and is consulted by the Government. Has about 1,000 local offices.

*Help the Aged* – Supports day centres and runs local second-hand shops.

*WRVS* – Provides meals-on-wheels services, clubs, second-hand clothing and other help to the elderly.

*Red Cross* and *St John's* – Each provides nursing at home, medical aids and volunteers to run clubs, meals-on-wheels, second-hand clothing, ambulance services, visiting. The Red Cross has some homes for the elderly.

See: *Useful Local Contacts p. 277*

# Voluntary Service

Your local *Council for Voluntary Service* (sometimes called *Council for Social Service*) is a useful clearing house for both offers and requests for spare-time help. It can also put you in touch with the nearest *Volunteer Bureau* (which can arrange training and give advice).

It is also worth contacting the HQs* of bodies which recruit keen volunteers and send them, in teams or individually, to help local workers in neighbourhood projects, day centres, hospitals, residential homes and on play schemes and outings.

\* *Community Service Volunteers* (CSV), 237 Pentonville Rd, London N19NJ. *Young Christian Workers*, Snow's Fields, London SE1. *Task Force*, Clifford House, Edith Villas, London W14.

See: *Useful Local Contacts p. 277*; YOUNG VOLUNTEERS

# Voluntary Work Projects

Some of the best start up, almost unnoticed, when someone spots something worth doing and gets a few others to help get it done, e.g. helping elderly with bulk-buy shopping service; involving youngsters in an adventure playground, or a city farm; rescuing threatened countryside; salvaging a derelict building.

Practical work speaks for itself; other helpers can join in casually at first. Work parties are more fun when people bring their own food and eat together on the job. Arrange a telephone contact for new offers of help.

As the project takes shape, talk it over with residents' groups, youth clubs, schools and colleges. Contact councillors and council officials. Get outside advice from bodies such as Inter-Action, and Community Projects Foundation*; both offer advice on youth and community work to various agencies, groups and local government bodies.

*7, Leonard Street, London EC2A 4AQ (Tel: 01 251 0033/36).

See: INTER-ACTION; VOLUNTARY SERVICE; YOUNG VOLUNTEERS

# Water Rates [S]

A charge is made for water supplied to any premises. This is levied each year either as a proportion (3·7%) of the annual *Rateable Value* of the property or as a *Rate in the £*.

$$\text{Water Rates} = \frac{3 \cdot 7}{100} \times \text{Annual Rateable Value}$$

$$\text{or} \frac{\text{'Rate in the £'}}{100} \times \text{Annual Rateable Value}$$

Water rates are normally paid twice a year or quarterly in statements in advance.

The Water Boards will arrange for a meter to be placed in the property so that the amount of water used can be measured and charged.

See: RATEABLE VALUE

# Water Reconnection

If the water has been cut off but the supply is intact, Water Board engineers reconnect the supply free-of-charge within about twenty-four hours.

If pipes have been ripped out of a building but the outside pipes from the main stopcock are intact you will have to get a plumber to refit the pipes. The Water Board will inspect the work and turn on the supply.

Outside, underground piping work is done by the Water Board who will give an estimate of the cost of the work. This can take several weeks. It involves the local Council, as well.

The Water Board also advises on structural alterations which may change the water supply.

See:  WATER RATES

# Women's Royal Voluntary Service

The WRVS offer help to the elderly and housebound by organizing the meals-on-wheels service as well as many luncheon clubs. They keep stocks of clothes for anyone in need operate voluntary transport schemes for shopping and visiting and often a 'books-on-wheels' service.

In a community emergency or disaster, e.g. floods, they organize meals, supply clothing and bedding and run information centres.

See:  LUNCH CLUBS; MEALS-ON-WHEELS; TRANSPORT (C);
     *Useful Local Contacts p. 227*

# Work Agency

*How to Set Up*

A Do-it-Yourself Job Centre putting people wanting work in touch with others needing short-term, specialized or casual 'odd jobs' done, usually local, e.g. painting, building, repairs, gardening, housework, typing. You can do it (1) as a service to other people (you rate as 'self-employed' for tax and NI) or (2) co-operatively for yourselves. You need a telephone, telephone rota and good local advertising. You may have to start by financing it yourself or by fund-raising. Later charge 5% of pay, or £5 membership, or £1 a month for signing on. Workers arrange their own rates privately.

As a co-operative you can discuss range of skills needed, kinds of jobs to go for first, and collective payment of costs. Decide how others should join, e.g. trial, associate or full membership to make sure of reliability.

See: FUND-RAISING; WORK SHOPS

# Workers' Educational Association (WEA)*

WEA has twenty-one districts covering the UK. It is a democratic voluntary body made up of students, individual subscribers and affiliated organizations. It is a registered charity and is non-political and non-sectarian.

The purpose of WEA is to interest men and women in their continued education. Courses are worked out *by tutors and students* and cover anything from sociology to science or any subject you want a course on. WEA districts appoint and pay tutors.

WEA is financed by grant aid from central government and it receives contributions from local education authorities and from student fees, subscriptions and donations.

*WEA National Office, Temple House, 9 Upper Berkeley Street, London W1.

See: *Useful Local Contacts p. 277 (for nearest branch)*

# Work Experience Programme

This is run by the Manpower Services Commission (MSC).* It enables jobless 16–19-year-olds to get basic experience on an employer's premises. They are paid £19.50 per week by the MSC, and work for six months in different areas of activity. The programme aims to increase their confidence, skills and experience. WEP schemes are arranged by MSC district offices and county Careers Services. The MSC helps an employer to draw up a suitable scheme, and covers liabilities.

Jobless youngsters with bright ideas, or interested groups can arrange their own schemes by finding a willing employer and putting him or her in touch with the Careers Service. You must have an experienced volunteer to supervise and manage your scheme.

* MSC: Hanway House, Red Lion Sq., London WC1. Tel: 01 405 8454.

See:  JOB OPPORTUNITIES; WORK AGENCY; WORK SHOPS

# Work Shops

Any local authority or voluntary body can sponsor a training work shop to provide introductory training or work experience for jobless 16–19-year-olds, and get a basic allowance of £20.55 per week for the group workers, plus wages for supervisors (who must also have been unemployed) in line with local rates, plus contributions of up to 90% of initial capital expenditure and a substantial part of the running costs.

Disused factory space or warehouses can often be used, perhaps at a nominal rent by arrangement with the Council.

Activities might be furniture renovation, simple woodwork, renovation and alteration of clothes, land cultivation (e.g. Inter-Action's City Farms scheme). Begin by getting local Union support and advice (so you don't choose work which competes with local jobs and employment).

If the group intends to trade, check first on the most suitable legal structure.

See:  INTER-ACTION; JOB OPPORTUNITIES; LAW CENTRES; WORK AGENCY; WORK EXPERIENCE PROGRAMME

# Young Volunteers

If in need of a helping hand, or able to offer one, try local bodies (Scouts, Guides, Red Cross, St John's, the probation service, rural Community Council). Also try national and international organizations that bring keen and lively youngsters together, for the specific purpose of tackling schemes, in groups or individually, that will help handicapped people, or be of general benefit to the community. An outside team (during a holiday period) or a single volunteer (paid a subsistence allowance by the organization for several months at a time) may give your own voluntary efforts a useful shot in the arm, and a breath of fresh air. Sometimes a local group can offer dormitory space and/or individual hospitality, and be reimbursed.

See: VOLUNTARY SERVICE

# Youth Clubs

To get going, set up a lively committee with young people involved, to plan activities, decide club rules, recruit helpers, and raise funds. The Council's Youth Officer may be able to find premises. A local hall could be hired. Some groups have converted derelict buildings, or built their own huts. Check with the Environmental Health Officer on safety, fire, and food regulations. Get insured for club activities.

Once the Youth Officer agrees that the club is reasonably stable and meets a local need, it can be *registered* and becomes eligible for grants and other help.

See: FIRE SAFETY; FUND-RAISING; GRANTS (A); INSURANCE (A) (B) (C); NATIONAL ASSOCIATION OF YOUTH CLUBS; PUBLIC HEALTH INSPECTORS

# Follow-up to the Fact Bank

# Building and Converting

*Do Your Own Home Wiring*, G. Burdett, Foulsham, 1975 (£2.50)

*Home Worker's Guide to Plumbing*, J. M. Haig, Stanley Paul, 1974 (£1.95).

*Guides to Good Building*, Advisory leaflets by the Department of the Environment. All published by H M S O (5p each).
e.g. 10 *Dry Rot and Wet Rot*
     13 *Site Costing for Builders*
     25 *Painting Woodwork*
     26 *Making Concrete on Site*
     30 and 31 *Installing Solid Fuel Appliances*
     47 *Dampness in Buildings*
     58 *Inserting a Damp Proof Course*
     61 *Condensation*
     69 *Reducing Noise in Buildings*
     81 *Electric Ring and Radial Circuits*

*Whole House Omnibus*, R. Bell, Architectural Press, 1978 (£5.95).

# Community Use of Waste Ground and Empty Premises

*Crops and Shares*, Friends of the Earth, 9 Poland St, London W1 (20p plus s.a.e.).

*Handbook of Environmental Powers*, C. Whittaker, Architectural Press (£9.00).

*Law of Allotments*, J. F. Garner, Shaw & Sons, 1977 (£3.50).

# Costs and Budgeting

*Basic Book Keeping for Community Groups*, J. Smith, Community Work Service (65p).
*Controlled Rents to Fair Rents: a Guide for Private Landlords and Tenants*, DOE, 1972.
*How To Pay Less Rates*, DOE, 1976 (free).
*Fuel Debts Handbook*, 75 Elmhurst Mansions, Edgeley Road, London SW4 (35p).
*Money*, NCC, 18 Queen Anne's Gate, London SW1 (25p).
*Review of Payment and Collection Methods For Gas and Electricity Bills*, Department of Energy, Millbank, London SW1P 4QJ (free).
*Keeping Accounts: a Handbook for Voluntary Organisations*, NCSS, 26 Bedford Square, London, WC1, 1974 (40p).

# Funds for Self-help

*Charities Digest*, Family Welfare Association, MacDonald & Evans Ltd, Plymouth (£3.50 plus 50p p.p.).
*Directory of Grant-making Trusts 1977*, Charities Aid Foundation.
*Fundraising*, Scout Association, Baden Powell House, London (£1.50).
*Fund Raising Annual 1976*, Fairlight Pubs Ltd (£1.50).
*Fund Raising by Charities*, NCSS, 26 Bedford Sq., WC1 (75p).
*Fund Raising Handbook*, H. Blume, Directory of Social Change (£2.25).
*Fundraising for Small Charities and Organisations*, H. R. Humphries, David & Charles, 1974 (£1.75)
*Getting a Grant*, Fact sheet No. 2, Fair Play for Children (free).
*Money Raising A–Z*, NAYC, Victoria Chambers, 16/20 Strutton Ground, London SW1 P2H (20p).
*Raising Money from Government*, Directory of Social Change, 14 Saltram Cres., W.9 (£1.50 plus 25p postage).
*Raising Money from Industry*, Directory of Social Change (£1.50 plus 25p postage).
*Raising Money through Special Events*, Directory of Social Change (£1.50 plus 25p postage).
*Raising Money from Trusts*, Directory of Social Change (£1.50 plus 25p postage).
*Where Does the Money Come From?*, Pre-School Playgroups Association, London (30p).

# Health and Cleansing

*Bothered by Noise*, DOE, Building 3, Victoria Rd, S. Ruislip HA4 0AX (free).

*Community Services, the Health Worker's A–Z*, P. Barefoot and P. J. Cunningham, Faber, 1977 (£2.95).

*A Guide to Food Regulations in the U.K.*, D. Amor, British Food Manufacturing Industries Research Association, 1974.

*Law Relating to Air Pollution*, F. Reynolds, National Society for Clean Air (15p).

*Mounting the Guard: Handbook for Community Health Council Members*, J. Hallas and B. Fallon, Nuffield Prov. Hospital Trust, 1974 (90p).

*Noise and Noise Abatement*, Publications Distribution Co-op, 27 Clerkenwell Close, London EC1 (40p plus s.a.e.).

*Refuse and Accumulations*, Publications Distribution Co-operative, 27 Clerkenwell Close, EC1 (35p plus s.a.e.).

# Housing

*Disrepair and Unfitness*, Publications Distribution Co-operative, 27 Clerkenwell Close, London EC1 (40p plus s.a.e.).

*Housing Improvement Handbook*, ed. J. Bloor, 1976, 9 Queenston Rd, Manchester 20 (£2.00).

*Improve Your Home On a Grant*, R. Tattersall, Stanley Paul, 1973 (75p).

*Overcrowding*, Publications Distribution Co-operative, 27 Clerkenwell Close, London EC1 (35p plus s.a.e.).

*Rights Guide for Home Owners*, J. Tunnard and C. Whately, 1977, CPAG, 1 Macklin St, London WC2 (60p).

# Housing Co-operatives

*A Better Place: The Story of the Holloway Co-op.*, Shelter, 1974 (35p).

*Co-operative Housing Handbook*, D. Page, NFHA\*, 1975.

*Co-ownership Housing Association*, NFHA\*, London, May 1975 (25p).

*CHA Directory of Housing Co-ops.*, Housing Corporation, 1977 (£1.00).

*Directory of Housing Co-ops.*, Comm. Work Service of LCSS (25p plus 15p s.a.e.).

*Final Report of the Working Party on Housing Co-operatives*, HMSO, 1975 (£2.00).

*A Guide to Housing Associations*, NFHA\*, March 1975 (35p).

*Housing Co-operatives*, M. Hook, Architects Journal, 29.vi.77.

*Housing Co-operatives*, J. Hands, SCD, London, 1975 (£1.50).

*Housing Co-operatives*, 1976 HMSO, 1976 (30p).

*Housing Management Practice in Housing Associations*, NFHA\*, 1975.

*How to set up a Housing Co-operative*, Manchester Federation of Housing Co-ops (20p).

*Street by Street Improved: Tenants Control in Islington*, North Islington Housing Rights Project, 129 St John's Way, London N19.

\* 86 Strand WC2.

# Information and Advice

*Advice and Contacts in the Community*, R. Willes, NPFA, 25 Ovington Sq., London SW3.

*Alternative England and Wales 1975*, Nicholas Saunders (£2.50).

*Consumer Information Bulletin*, Department of Prices and Consumer Protection, 1 Victoria St, London SW1 (free).

*Fourth Right of Citizenship: a Review of Local Advice Services*, NCC, 18 Queen Anne's Gate, London SW1 (75p).

*Inter-action Community Handbooks*, Inter-action Inprint, 15 Wilkin St, London NW5 3NG:

> *Basic Video* (75p)
> *Bring books to people* (50p)     (OR £2.00 the set)
> *Community Newspaper* (75p)
> *Print: How you can do it yourself* (£1)

*Voluntary Social Services: Directory and Handbook 1973*, NCSS, 26 Bedford Sq., London WC1 (£1.50).

Work FACT BANK, Inprint, 15 Wilkin St, London NW5 3NG.

# Laws, Legal Aid and Legal Protection

*Appearing in Court: Practical Notes*, PHAS* (20p).

*Battered Women and the New Law*, A. Coote and T. Gill, NCCL†, 1977 (60p).

*The Courts and You*, M. J. Cook, Law Society and Oyez, 1976 (£2.00).

*Guide to Public Health and Housing Law*, D. Ormany, PHAS*, 1977 (60p).

*How to Sue in the County Court*, E. Rudinger, CA, 1975 (£1.75).

*Know your rights: a Guide to everyday law*, R. Irving and C. Anthony, David & Charles, 1976 (£2.95).

*Landlords and the Law*, DOE, 1975.

*Legal Aid Solicitor's List*, Law Society, 113 Chancery Lane, London WC2 A1PL (free).

*Plain Guide to Licensing Law*, Brewing Pubs. (40p).

*Police*, NCC, 18 Queen Anne's Gate, London SW1 (25p).

*Rights for Women*, P. Hewitt, NCCL†, 1975 (75p).

*Social Workers, their Clients and the Law*, M. Zander, Sweet & Maxwell, 1974 (£2.70).

*Voluntary Organisations and the Law relating to Lotteries and Gaming*, NCSS‡, 1972 (35p).

*Within the Law: A Practical Guide to the Layman*, F. Bressler, Barker, 1976 (£2.75).

* 27 Clerkenwell Close, London EC1.
† 186 Kings Cross Rd, London WC1.
‡ 26 Bedford Sq., London WC1.

# Liabilities

*Penguin Guide to Insurance*, G. Willman, Penguin, 1973 (40p).

*Insurance Protection for Voluntary Organisations and Voluntary Workers*, 1977 (30p, 10 or more copies 20p each).

*Lotteries and Gaming*, NCSS, 1972 (35p plus 5p postage).

*Vat General Information Pack*, Customs and Excise.

*Vat Notice No 700: A general guide to VAT*, Customs and Excise.

*Vat Notice No 701: Scope and Coverage of VAT*, Customs and Excise.

# Official Channels

*Introduction to the Social Services*, W. E. Baugh, 2nd edition, Macmillan, 1975 (£1.95).

*Investigators Handbook*, 1975, Community Action, PO Box 665, London SW1 (30p).

*The Work of the Office of Fair Trading*, Office of Fair Trading, March 1976 (free).

# Official Plans

*Clearance and Redevelopment*, Publications Distribution Co-op, 27 Clerkenwell Close, London EC1 (25p plus s.a.e.).

*Development Plans*, HMSO (£4.50).

*Local Plans: Public and Local Enquiries*, DOE*.

*Memorandum on Structure and Local Plans*, HMSO, Circular 55/77 (£1.25).

*Planning 1977*, NCC, 18 Queen Anne's Gate, London SW1 (25p).

*Planning Permission: a Guide for Householders*, DOE*, 1976 (free).

*Public Inquiries Action Guide*, Shelter Community Action team, 31 Clerkenwell Close, London EC1R 0AT (15p to action groups, 40p to others).

*Publicity for the Work of Local Authorities*, DOE Circ 45/75 HMSO (12p).

*Your Right to Attend Planning Committee Meetings*, Town and Country Planning Association, 17 Carlton House Terrace, London SW1 (10p).

*Building 3, Victoria Rd, S. Ruislip HA4 0NX.

# Rights

*Battered Women and the New Law*, A. Coote and T. Gill, NCCL\*, 1977 (60p).

*Civil Liberty: The NCCL Guide to Your Rights*, Penguin, 1978 (£1.75).

*Community Action*, PO Box 665, London SW1X 8DZ (6 issues per year £1.50).

*Dismissal, Redundancy and Job Hunting*, 1976, CA, PO Box 665, London SW1 XDZ.

*Guide to Public Health and Housing Law*, D. Ormandy, 1977, PHAS, 27 Clerkenwell Close, London EC1, 1977 (60p).

*Guide to Supplementary Benefits*, T. Lynes, Penguin (75p).

*Guide to the Social Services*, Family Welfare Association, Macdonald & Evans, published annually.

*Housing Legislation: a Guide to Tenants Rights*, H. Hodge, IPC Press.

*Housing Rights Handbook*, M. Cutting, Shelter, 1974 (60p).

*Know Your Rights*, Dr M. Winstanley and R. Dukley, Independent TV Books, 1975 (99p).

*National Welfare Benefits Handbook*, R. Lister, CPAG†, 1976 (65p).

*On the Dole: Your Guide to Unemployment Benefit*, P. Laurie, Kogan Page, 1976 (75p).

*Rights: a Handbook for People Under-age*, N. Berger, Penguin, 1974 (60p).

*Rights Guide for Home Owners*, J. Tunnard and C. Whately, CPAG† and SHAC, 1977 (60p).

*Rights Guide No 3 Contribution and Benefits*, CPAG† (75p).

*Small Repairs Kit: How to Get the Council to Pay for Repairs to Your Home*, Lambeth Community Law Centre, 506 Brixton Rd, London SW9 8EN.

*Supplementary Benefits*, 1977, NCC, 18 Queen Anne's Gate, London SW1 (25p).

*Supplementary Benefits Handbook*, HMSO (65p).

*Welfare Rights Handbook*, CPAG†.

*What Right Have You Got?*, Parts I and II, 1976, BBC Pubs. (£1.35).

*Women's Rights*, A. Coote and T. Gill, Penguin, revised edition 1977 (£1.25).

*Workers' Rights*, P. O'Higgins, Arrow (85p).

\*186 Kings Cross Road, London WC1.

†1 Macklin Street, London WC2.

# Self-Help

*Alternative England and Wales 1975*, Nicholas Saunders, London (£2.50).

*The Bulk Buy Book*, NCC, 18 Queen Anne's Gate, London SW1 (£1.00).

*Closed Circuit Television Single-handed*, T. Gibson, Pitmans, 1972 (£2.00).

*Community Action*, PO Box 665, London SW1 (£1.50 – 6 issues per year).

*Food Co-ops 1976*, Friends of the Earth, 9 Poland St, W1 (60p).

*Getting Across*, C. Sladen, NCSS*, 1974 (75p).

*How to Change to Common Ownership*, R. Sawtell, 1975, ICOM, 31 Hare St, Woolwich, London SE18 6JN (15p).

*In the Making*, ITM, Wolverton, Bucks. (1978).

*A Kind of Challenge*, Home Link, 54 Brittarge Brow, Liverpool 27.

*Making Your Voice Heard*, NCSS* (65p).

*Notes on Workers' Co-ops*, Education Dept, Co-operative Union Ltd, Stanford Hall, Loughborough.

*Rural Transport*, Rural Dept., NCSS*.

*Simple Guide to Exhibition Design*, R. Crawley, NCSS*, 1971 (30p).

*Videotape Book*, M. Murray, Bantam, 1975 (60p).

*26 Bedford Square, London WC1.

# Social Activities

*The Bulk Buy Book*, NCC, 18 Queen Anne's Gate, London, SW1, 1977 (£1.00).

*Lunch Clubs for the Elderly*, Age Concern, Bernard Sunley House, 60 Pitcairn Road, Mitcham, Surrey.

*Community*, B. Dinham and M. Norton, Wildwood House (£3.95).

# Tenants and Owner-Occupiers

*Council Tenants*, NCC\*, 1977 (25p).

*Fair Rents*, J. Prophet, Shaw & Sons, 1976 (£5.25).

*How to Run a Tenants Association*, Association of London Housing Estates†, 1977 (60p to members, 65p to non-members).

*Rent Tribunal – Notes For Tenants*, R. W. Griffin, Shelter Housing Action Committee.

*Tenancy Agreement*, NCC\*, 1976 (35p).

*Tenancy Agreements*, HSAG, 1977.

*Tenants Take Over*, C. Ward, Architectural Press, 1974 (£3.95).

*What Makes a Tenants' Association Work*, Association of London Housing Estates† (10p inc. p. and p.).

\* 18 Queen Anne's Gate, London SW1.
† 17 Victoria Park Square, E2.

# Youngsters

*A B C of toys*, 6th edition, Toy Libraries Association, 1977 (£1.50).

*Adventure Playgrounds*, J. Lambert and J. Pearson, Penguin, 1974 (60p).

*Adventure Playgrounds*, A. Bengtsson, Crosby Lockwood, 1972 (£4.50).

*At Work Together*, D. Knight, Pre-School Playgroups Association, 1976 (£1.25).

*Best of Where on Pre-schooling*, ACE, 18 Victoria Park Sq., London E2 (£1.50).

*Business Side of Playgroups: Or How to Run a Happy Playgroup*, rev. ed., Pre-School Playgroups Association, 1976 (40p).

*Children's Rights*, ed. Julian Hall, Panther.

*Company Day Nurseries*, C. Day, Institute of Personnel Management, 1975 (£1.00).

*Do It Yourself Playgrounds*, M. P. Friedberg, Architectural Press, 1976 (£2.95).

*Grants and How to Apply for Them*, Pre-School Playgroups Association.

*Grounds for Play*, J. Benjamin, NCSS*, 1974 (£1.25).

*Guide to Play Equipment for Young Children*, C. Peterson, Design Council, 1975 (50p).

*Holiday Playschemes*, NCSS*, 1973 (20p).

*Parents School Book*, J. Stone and Felicity Taylor, Penguin, 1976.

*Parent Power*, N. Bagnall, Routledge & Kegan Paul, 1974.

*Penguin Book of Playgroups*, V. McKennell and J. Lucas, Penguin, 1974 (80p).

*Play Fact Sheets* (e.g. Budgeting, Grants, Fund-raising), FPFC, 248 Kentish Town Rd, London NW5 (20p each).

*Play: Its Role in Development and Evolution*, Bruner, Jolly and Sylva, Penguin Education, 1976 (£2.75).

*Play with a purpose for the under 7s*, E. M. Matterson, Penguin, 1970 (75p).

*Playgroups for Free*, P. Hogan, MIT Press, 1975 (£7.50).

NPFA† Leaflets:

    *Comprehensive Children's Playground: Suggested Layout For 1½ Acre Site* (19p).

    *Knock Up Practice Walls for Children's Playgrounds* (17p).

    *Mounds for Playgrounds* (23p).

    *Playgrounds*, 1968 (30p).

    *Playgrounds for Blocks of Flats* (13p).

    *Suggested Layout for ¼ Acre Children's Playground* (19p).

*Playgroup Activities: Why? What? How?*, 1969, PPA‡ (30p).

*Playgroup Book: how to plan, organise and run group activities for pre-school children*, M. Winn and M. A. Porcher, Fontana, 1971 (70p).

*The Playgroup Movement*, B. Crowe, Allen & Unwin, 1973 (£2.75).

*Play Huts*, NPFA† (45p).

*So You Want to Help in a Youth Club*, S. J. Bunt, NAYC, 1972 (17p).

*Toy Libraries: An Introduction*, Toy Libraries Association, 1975, NPFA 25 Ovington Sq., London SW3 (10p).

*Workyards: Playgrounds for Planned Adventure*, N. Rudolf, Teachers Coll. Press, 1975 (£4.50).

*Youth Club Leadership: a Guide to Principles and Practice*, K. R. Matthews, Elek, 1975 (£3.25).

*Workout: Community Action for Kids*, S. Parsons, L. Haddock, and S. Harrison, Prism Press, 1978 (£1.25).

\* 26 Bedford Square, London WC1.
† 25 Ovington Square, London SW3.
‡ Alford House, Aveline Street, London SE11.

# Key Contacts

ADVISORY SERVICE FOR SQUATTERS, 2 St Paul's Rd, London N1. Tel. 01.359.8814.

AGE CONCERN, Bernard Sunley House, 60 Pitcairn Rd, Mitcham, Surrey. Tel. 01.640.5431.

ASSOCIATION OF COMMUNITY WORKERS, 170 New Cross Rd, London SE14. Tel. 01.732.9990 (Thurs. a.m. only).

ASSOCIATION OF LONDON HOUSING ESTATES, 17 Victoria Park Square, London E2. Tel. 981.1221.

ASSOCIATION FOR NEIGHBOURHOOD COUNCILS, PO Box 1, Halstead, Essex. Tel. Halstead (078.74.) 2108.

BIT INFORMATION SERVICE, 97 Talbot Rd, London W11. Tel. 01.229.8219.

CATHOLIC HOUSING AID SOCIETY, 189a Old Brompton Rd, London SW5. Tel. 01.373.4961.

THE CHARITY COMMISSIONERS, The Charity Commission, 14 Ryder Street, London SW1. Tel. 01.214.6000.

CHILD POVERTY ACTION GROUP, 1 Macklin St, London WC2. Tel. 01.242.3225.

COMMISSION FOR RACIAL EQUALITY, Elliott House, 10 Allington St, London W1. Tel. 01.828.7022.

COMMUNITY ACTION, PO Box 665, London SW1 XDZ. Tel. 01.251.3008.

COMMUNITY SERVICE VOLUNTEERS, 237 Pentonville Rd, London N1. Tel. 01.278.6601.

DISABILITY ALLIANCE, 5 Netherhall Gdns, London NW3 5RJ. Tel. 01.794.1536.

EQUAL OPPORTUNITIES COMMISSION, Commission House, Grosvenor Hill, London W1. Tel. 01.629.8233.

FAIR PLAY FOR CHILDREN, 248 Kentish Town Rd, London NW5. Tel. 01.485.0809.

FAMILY SERVICE UNITS, 207 Old Marylebone Rd, London NW1. Tel. 01.402.5175.

FRIENDS OF THE EARTH, 9 Poland Street, London W1. Tel. 01.434.1684.

GINGERBREAD, 35 Wellington St, London WC2. Tel. 01.240.0953.

HOUSING CORPORATION (Co-op advisory section), 149 Tottenham Court Road, London W1 Tel. 01.387.9466.

INDUSTRIAL COMMON OWNERSHIP FINANCE LIMITED, 1 Gold Street, Northampton NN1 1SA. Tel. Northampton (0604) 37563.

INDUSTRIAL COMMON OWNERSHIP MOVEMENT, 31 Hare Street, Woolwich, London SE18 6JN. Tel. 01.855.4099.

INTER-ACTION ADVISORY SERVICE, 15 Wilkin St, London NW5 3NG. Tel. 01.485.0881.

JOINT COUNCIL FOR THE WELFARE OF IMMIGRANTS, 44 Theobald's Road, London WC1X 8SP. Tel. 01.405.5527.

LEGAL ACTION GROUP, 28a Highgate Rd, London NW5. Tel. 01.485.1189.

MIND: NATIONAL ASSOCIATION FOR MENTAL HEALTH, 22 Harley St, London W1.

NATIONAL ASSOCIATION OF CITIZEN'S ADVICE BUREAUX, 26 Bedford Square, London W1. Tel. 01.636.4066.

NATIONAL ASSOCIATION OF YOUTH CLUBS, Victoria Chambers, 16/20 Strutton Ground, London SW1 2PH. Tel. 01.222.1412.

NATIONAL CONSUMER COUNCIL, 18 Queen Anne's Gate, London SW1. Tel. 01.930.5752.

NATIONAL COUNCIL FOR CIVIL LIBERTIES, 186 King's Cross Rd, London W1. Tel. 01.278.4575.

NATIONAL COUNCIL FOR ONE PARENT FAMILIES, 255 Kentish Town Rd, London NW5 2LX. Tel. 01.267.1361.

NATIONAL COUNCIL OF SOCIAL SERVICE, 26 Bedford Square, London WC1. Tel. 01.636.4066.

NATIONAL FEDERATION OF HOUSING ASSOCIATIONS, 30 Southampton St, Strand, London WC2. Tel. 01.240.2771.

NATIONAL FEDERATION OF OLD AGE PENSIONS ASSOCIATION, Melling House, 91 Preston New Rd, Blackburn, Lancs. Tel. Blackburn (0254) 52606.

NATIONAL PLAYING FIELDS ASSOCIATION, 25 Ovington Square, London SW3. Tel. 01.584.6445.

NATIONAL TENANT'S ORGANISATION, 189a Old Brompton Road, London SW5 OAR. Tel. 01.373.3923.

NATIONAL WOMEN'S AID FEDERATION, 51 Chalcot Rd, London NW1. Tel. 01.586.0104.

PRE-SCHOOL PLAYGROUPS ASSOCIATION, Alford House, Aveline St, London SE11 5DH. Tel. 01.582.8871.

PUBLICATIONS DISTRIBUTION CO-OPERATIVE, 27 Clerkenwell Close, London EC1R 0AT. Tel. 01.251.4976 (not Fri. a.m.).

RELEASE, 1 Elgin Avenue, London W9 3PR. Tel. 01.289.1123.

RIGHTS OF WOMEN, 374 Grays Inn Road, London WC1. Tel. 01.278.6349 (Advice Service Wed. 7–9 p.m.).

ROYAL ASSOCIATION FOR DISABILITY AND REHABILITATION (formerly Central Council for Disabled), 23/25 Mortimer St, London WIN 8AB. Tel. 01.637.5400.

SELF-HELP CLEARING HOUSE, 170 Kingston Rd, London SW19 3NX. Tel. 01.540.8775.

SERVICES TO COMMUNITY ACTION AND TENANTS, 31 Clerkenwell Close, London EC1R 0AT. Tel. 01.253.3627.

SHARE COMMUNITY LTD, 170 Kingston Rd, London SW19 3NX. Tel. 01.540.8775.

SHELTER NATIONAL CAMPAIGN FOR THE HOMELESS, 157 Waterloo Rd, London SE1 8UU. Tel. 01.633.9371.

SMALL FIRMS INFORMATION SERVICES, 68 Buckingham Palace Rd, London SW1. Tel. 01.828.2384.

TOWN AND COUNTRY PLANNING ASSOCIATION, 17 Carlton House Terrace, London SW1. Tel. 01.930.8903.

WORKERS' EDUCATIONAL ASSOCIATION, 9 Upper Berkeley St, London W1. Tel. 01.402.5608.

# Useful Local Contacts

*(Get help from your local library and telephone directory in filling in addresses and phone numbers.)*

AGE CONCERN

CAB

COLLEGE OF EDUCATION*

COLLEGE OF FURTHER EDUCATION*

COMMUNITY HEALTH COUNCIL

COMMUNITY RELATIONS COUNCIL

CONSUMER ADVICE CENTRE

COUNCIL FOR VOLUNTARY SERVICE

CUSTOMS AND EXCISE OFFICE (RE VAT)

DEPARTMENT OF THE ENVIRONMENT
 (REGIONAL OFFICE)

FAMILY SQUATTING ADVISORY SERVICE
 (SEE SHELTER)

GINGERBREAD

HELP THE AGED

LAW CENTRE

LAW SOCIETY – LOCAL BRANCH
 (FOR BAR LICENCES)

MAGISTRATES COURT

NATIONAL PLAYING FIELDS ASSOCIATION
 (REGIONAL OFFICE)

* For help from, e.g. video resources centre.

NAYC (LOCAL BRANCH)

NSPCC (LOCAL INSPECTOR)

POLYTECHNIC*

RED CROSS AND ST JOHN

RSPCA

SCHOOL OF ARCHITECTURE*

SOCIAL SERVICES DEPARTMENT
  (YOUR AREA TEAM OFFICE)

TRADING STANDARDS OFFICER

WRVS

*For help from, e.g. video resources centre.

# Emergency Help

*Find out telephone numbers and fill them in on this page (give extension numbers where possible).*

| | |
|---|---|
| Accidents, fires, crime  999 | FIRE, POLICE, AMBULANCE |
| Battered children | NSPCC<br>LOCAL POLICE STATION |
| Home nursing – sick<br> – elderly | COMMUNITY HEALTH CENTRE<br>SOCIAL SERVICES |
| Housing, tenancy<br> homelessness | HOUSING ADVISORY CENTRE<br>SHELTER (local branch) |
| Legal, tenancy or<br>financial problems | CAB<br>LAW CENTRE |
| Racial problems | COUNCIL FOR COMMUNITY<br>RELATIONS (local branch) |
| Suicide or despair | SAMARITANS |
| Trouble with Police | LAW CENTRE<br>RELEASE |
| Urgent family problems | SOCIAL SERVICES DEPARTMENT |
| Urgent repairs<br>Vandalism, etc. | CARETAKER<br>HOUSING DEPARTMENT |
| Vermin, bad housing | ENVIRONMENTAL HEALTH<br>DEPARTMENT |
| Violence against<br> women | BATTERED WOMEN'S CENTRE<br>NATIONAL WOMEN'S AID<br>FEDERATION |

# The Fact Bank in Scotland

*The legislation and many of the organizations mentioned so far apply south of the Border, but need revision for Scottish use. So a Scottish Fact Bank Steering Committee was set up\* to consider the problem, and a Job Creation team was employed to produce a Scottish Fact Bank (details care of SCSS, 342 Argyle Street, Glasgow). Here is an outline of the main Scottish variations under the Fact Bank headings.*

ALLOTMENT GARDENS – Allotment (Scotland) Acts 1922 and 1950.

BAR LICENCES – Licensing (Scotland) Act 1976, parts ii and iv.

BINGO B – Register with the *licensing board* of the District Council.

BUILDING REGULATIONS – Building (Scotland) Acts 1959 and 1970.

CAR PARKING A – Contact the Regional Council's *Roads Department.*

CLUBROOMS AND SOCIAL CENTRES – Regional and District Councils have powers under various Acts of Parliament to make grants to voluntary and community organizations. There are various ways of applying for use of premises. In Strathclyde, school premises may be available; the Community Education Department will give details. The Education Authorities can also provide multi-purpose Community Centres. For other premises such as community flats, or halls, the Housing Management Department and District Estates Department of local District Councils are usually responsible. The Regional Council will consider for urban aid, funding applications for new and innovatory projects – particularly when they respond to direct local initiatives or contain a substantial contribution for local residents.

COUNCILS A – There are no parish or town councils in Scotland. Local government is divided into regional and district responsibilities. In the case of a problem concerning the region, approach would be made to the sub-region offices.

*Regional Services:* Rating and Valuation, Consumer Protection, Education, Fire, Police, Public Transport, Roads and Streets,

* With representatives from the Scottish Council for Social Service, the Scottish Consumer Council, the Glasgow Council of Social Service, the Scottish Association of Citizens' Advice Bureaux, Renfrew District Libraries, the Scottish Housing Corporation, the Scottish Community Education Centre, the Scottish Council of Tenants' Associations, the Social Work Services Group, the Scottish Education Department, the Scottish Development Department, and the author.

281

Sewerage, Social Work, Strategic Physical Planning, Street Lighting, Water.

*District Services:* Building Warrants, Cleansing and Refuse, Leisure and Recreation, Environmental Health, Housing, Licensing, Libraries, Local Planning.

COUNCILS B – Local government in Scotland has been reorganized into Regional, District and Island authorities. Community Councils are officially recognized independent local councils which are designed to bridge the gap between the new authorities and the public.

Each District and Island's authority should advertise its intention to draw up a draft scheme for a community council which the public should be invited to comment upon. You can find out more about community councils by contacting the district council and by attending any meetings in your area.

DISTRICT PLANS – Town and Country Planning (Scotland) Act 1972.

DISTURBANCE ALLOWANCE – Land Compensation (Scotland) Act 1973, part III.

EDUCATION A – In Scotland, particularly Strathclyde, pupils are allocated to schools according to the particular catchment area in which they reside. If the parents object to the school, their objections can be heard by the LEA. Normally, if the LEA believe the objections to be valid, a transfer can be arranged, and very few applications for transfer are rejected (about 2%). So far as is compatible with the provision of suitable instruction and training and the avoidance of unreasonable public expenditure, pupils are educated in accordance with the wishes of their parents.* But, if the pupils shows no reasonable promise of profiting by the parents' choice of secondary education, the parent is not entitled to select a course.

*Corporal Punishment:* If concerned, request details of LEA and school regulations. Corporal Punishment is still widely used in Scotland.

EDUCATION C – The law† states that a pupil may receive education without an educational establishment if the Education Authority decides that there are extraordinary circumstances. They would make provisions, but would also require the approval of the Secretary of State. Independent schools can be set up‡ given that they are registered with the Registrar of Independent Schools in Scotland, and conform to the requirements and regulations laid down by the Secretary of State. 'Efficient and suitable instruction' would have to be provided and staff and premises would have to meet the requirements.

---

*Education (Scotland) Act 1962, part II, section 29.
† Education (Scotland) Act 1962, section 14.
‡ Education (Scotland) Act 1962, part V.

282

FOOD HYGIENE – Food and Drugs (Scotland) Act 1956, section 14.

HARASSMENT – The tenant must go to the police with his complaint. If the police do not seem willing to report to the Procurator Fiscal, contact a lawyer, Shelter or a legal aid centre, and they may be able to help.

HOME LOSS PAYMENTS – Land Compensation (Scotland) Act 1973, part III.

HOUSING ACTION AREAS – Housing (Scotland) Act 1974, sections 15–17.

HOUSING CO-OPS G – Get local advice from Summerston Housing Management Co-op, 3 Torgyle Street, Summerston, Glasgow G26 (Tel. 041.946.3962) and from Lister Housing Co-op, 8 Lauriston Place, Edinburgh, EH3 9EX.

HOUSING GRANTS – For Intermediate Grants read *Standard Amenity Grants*.

IMPROVEMENT GRANTS B – Housing (Limits of Rateable Value for Improvement Grants) (Scotland) No. 2 Order, 1977.

INSPECTION REPORT – When writing to the Environment Health Department about statutory nuisance*, include the following information in the letter – address of property, brief details of complaint, names and address of owner or factor, name and address of persons complaining, times and dates when property is available for inspection. Send one copy to the Chief Environmental Health Officer and keep copies on file. Environmental Health Officers make visits after 10.00 a.m. Do not ask for opinions before an inspection has been made. The opinion must be made on a visual examination of property. Have your rent book on hand to verify name and address of landlord or factor.

INSURANCE A – For addresses of the appropriate Scottish bodies – see Contact List below.

LOTTERIES – Apply for registration forms, and make returns to your District Council's *Director of Administration*.

NATIONAL ASSOCIATION OF YOUTH CLUBS – Scottish Association of Youth Clubs: 13 Eglinton Crescent, Edinburgh. Tel. 031.337.1242.

NOISE
PETS } – Burgh Police (Scotland) Act 1892.

PLANNING ACTION AREAS – Town and Country Planning (Scotland) Act 1972.

PUBLIC PARTICIPATION – Town and Country Planning (Scotland) Act 1972, and contact the *Secretary of State* (*Scotland*), not the Department of the Environment.

REPAIRS – In Scotland it might be theoretically possible to take the Council to Court, but in practice this could be difficult. Landlords' obligations to repair structural and external parts and to maintain

* Public Health (Scotland) Act 1897.

services must be listed under the tenancy agreements. These are usually included in the rent book, which every weekly tenant must be given by the landlord, whether private or council. If the Council is negligent, tenants can use section 146 (Public Health (Scotland) Act, 1897) whereby ten ratepayers living within the district *or* the Procurator Fiscal of local Sheriff Court *or* Secretary of State can give written notice to the Council of the nuisance which exists. If after fourteen days no action is taken, the party concerned can apply to the Sheriff by 'Summary Petition'.

SECTION 99 – The nearest equivalent in Scotland is section 17 of the Public Health (Scotland) Act, 1897. Under this it is the duty of the local authority to ensure that action is taken which will abate a statutory nuisance. It must also make sure that inspections are carried out from time to time to check that no such nuisances exist. If they do, they must use the powers granted them under the Act to remove them.

SHELTER – Scottish headquarters: 6 Castle Street, Edinburgh, EH2 3AT, Tel. 031.226.6347, which also produces Scottish information bulletins. It has Housing Advice Centres in Aberdeen, Edinburgh and Glasgow.

SHORT LIFE PROPERTY A – Unfitness is defined as below *the tolerable standard*. Objectors can refer to the *Scottish Development Department* (not the Department of the Environment). – Housing (Scotland) Act 1966, section 20.

SOCIAL SERVICES DEPARTMENT – Scottish equivalent is *Social Work Department*.

STATUTORY NUISANCE – Public Health (Scotland) Act 1897, section 16.

SUMMONS – To take out a summons in Scotland (e.g. regarding tenancy problems, or the repayment of a debt of less than £500) – get a form of the summons and copy summons from the Sheriff Clerk's Office in the Sheriff Court. (You can ask for them by post.) Specify details of case when completing forms and post summons to Sheriff Court with appropriate fee. On their return you must have the Sheriff Officer serve the copy summons on the defendant. The Sheriff Clerk will tell you where to contact a Sheriff Officer.

TRUANCY – For Education Welfare Officer – read *Attendance Officer* and for juvenile court read *Children's Panel*.
– Education (Scotland) Act 1962; Social Work (Scotland) Acts 1968 and 1972.

VIDEO A – *Video in Scotland* is a survey of video facilities in Scotland, conducted by the Scottish Film Council for Education Technology, 16/17 Woodside Terrace, Glasgow G3 7XN. For advice and information on video at amateur and recreational levels, contact the Scottish Film Council (the SFC is a division of the SCET).

**VOLUNTARY HELP FOR THE ELDERLY** – Age Concern has 200 local groups in Scotland. *The Beild Housing Association*, 55 Albany Street, Edinburgh, builds and manages sheltered housing in different parts of Scotland. For 'Red Cross and St John's' read 'Red Cross and *St Andrew's*'.

**WATER RATES** – for Water Board, read *Water Department* (regional authority).

# Key Contacts in Scotland

AGE CONCERN, 33 Castle Street, Edinburgh. Tel. 031.225.5000.

BEILD HOUSING ASSOCIATION, 55 Albany Street, Edinburgh.

CHILD POVERTY ACTION GROUP (CPAG), 70 Nicolson Street, Edinburgh.

COMMISSIONER FOR LOCAL ADMINISTRATION (the Ombudsman), 125 Princes Street, Edinburgh EH2 4AD.

EAGLE STAR INSURANCE (Glasgow Branch), 17 Blythswood Square, Glasgow G2.

FAIR PLAY FOR CHILDREN IN SCOTLAND CAMPAIGN, 212 Bath Street, Glasgow G2 4HW.

FRIENDS OF THE EARTH, 69 Cumberland Street, Edinburgh EH4 4BL.

HOUSING CORPORATION, (Regional Office), Newton House, Sauchiehall Street, Glasgow G2.

THE LISTER HOUSING CO-OP, 8 Lauriston Place, Edinburgh EH3 9EX.

MANPOWER SERVICES COMMISSION (MSC), Meldrum House, Drumsheugh Gardens, Edinburgh EH3 7QC. Tel. 031.225.1313.

NATIONAL PLAYING FIELDS ASSOCIATION, 12 Manor Place, Edinburgh EH3. Tel. 031.225.4307.

PLANNING AID, c/o Planning Exchange, 186 Bath Street, Glasgow.

PRE-SCHOOL PLAY GROUPS ASSOCIATION, 7 Royal Terrace, Glasgow. Tel. 041.331.1430.

SCOTTISH ASSOCIATION OF YOUTH CLUBS (SAYC), 13 Eglinton Crescent, Edinburgh. Tel. 031.332.1242.

SCOTTISH CONSUMER COUNCIL, 4 Somerset Place, Glasgow.

SCOTTISH COUNCIL FOR CIVIL LIBERTIES (SCCL), 146 Holland Street, Glasgow G3. Tel.041.332.5960.

SCOTTISH FACT BANK STEERING COMMITTEE, c/o SCSS, 342 Argyle Street, Glasgow.

SCOTTISH FILM COUNCIL FOR EDUCATIONAL TECHNOLOGY, 16/17 Woodside Terrace, Glasgow G3 7XN.

SCOTTISH COUNCIL FOR SOCIAL SERVICE, 18/19 Claremont Crescent, Edinburgh, EH7 4QD. Tel. 031.556.3882.

SCOTTISH HOME AND HEALTH DEPARTMENT, St Andrews House, Edinburgh EH1 3DE.

SHELTER, 6 Castle Street, Edinburgh. Tel. 031.226.6347.

SUMMERSTON HOUSING MANAGEMENT CO-OP, 3 Torgyle Street, Summerston, Glasgow G26. Tel. 9041.946.3962.

WORKERS' EDUCATIONAL ASSOCIATION (WEA), Riddle's Court, 322 Lawnmarket, Edinburgh. Tel. 9031.226.3456.